THE POLITICS OF REFORM IN PERU

THE POLITICS OF REFORM IN PERU

THE APRISTA AND OTHER MASS PARTIES OF LATIN AMERICA

GRANT HILLIKER

THE JOHNS HOPKINS PRESS BALTIMORE AND LONDON

Manufactured in the United States of America

The Johns Hopkins Press, Baltimore, Maryland 21218
The Johns Hopkins Press Ltd., London

Library of Congress Catalog Card Number 76-128763

ISBN-0-8018-1168-6

To Miriam, Janet, and Laurie,
for love and concern
when the midnight oil was burning

PREFACE

FOR A FOREIGN SERVICE OFFICER, even while relieved of all official duties and responsibilities, to undertake a personal research project is reminiscent of the dog that walked on its hind legs. One hopes that readers of the result will be charitable enough to marvel at the fact as much as at the quality of performance.

The simile is not inappropriate. Certainly the image of the Foreign Service in the academic community is one of a group unaccustomed to, if not incapable of, imaginative analysis. The fact that there may be a small measure of truth, along with considerable misinformation, in the stereotype makes it all the more important to attempt border-crossing in both directions between the bureaucratic and academic worlds. It was my opportunity to do so as a Federal Executive Fellow at The Brookings Institution from September, 1965, to June, 1966. Following further residence in Latin America, I revised and extended the study in 1969–70.

My pleasure at the prospect of this fellowship arose from past frustrations in trying to keep abreast of the fast-growing literatures of development and of comparative politics while performing more or less related tasks at home or abroad. I saw this venture into research as a chance to renew and advance my own understanding of fields of study that are indispensable to the competent diplomat.

In this study of the ways in which a reform party of a particular type tries to initiate reform, I have tried to take the advice of Latin Americanists and others as to the kinds of problems that are most in need of attention. In particular, I sought to steer a course between the mere collection or ordering of data and the assertion of bold theory. As a result, the study may prove inadequate on either count. If so, I hope that others will carry it forward and develop it in a more comprehensive theoretical framework, using more original data.

Others would expect that anyone taking the Aprista party of Peru as a subject for research must necessarily become either disciple or adversary. Some expand the field to admire or dislike the entire democratic Left of Latin America. I hope that I have avoided either tendency. The problems of development, even in this hemisphere, are too enormous and diverse, too persistent yet transitory in emphasis, to give way to any single solution at a given time or place.

In this last point lies the sole lesson, of a general nature, that I have gleaned from the study. Despite our ideological attachment to the "democratic system," we are inclined—North, South, and Middle Americans—to look mainly to persons and particular organizations or institutions for the solutions to problems. We would do better to think more in terms of a system; and to define and describe the kinds of political systems that seem suitable to the particular conditions of different countries is a task in policy oriented research worthy of the best effort.

Because this is a case study of a political party, I have not been concerned to recount completely the events in Peru since the 1968 coup, or those in Bolivia and Venezuela after about 1964. For the Apristas, the period 1956–68 is a kind of entity; thereafter, a new condition came into existence, in which the place of political parties was not readily apparent. What it will become will be determined only after further observation of the conduct of the Velasco regime, the acts of which I have noted in passing only where they seemed to have special relevance to the previous period.

I cannot hope to acknowledge the advice and assistance that have made this study possible. Except as their names appear in the notes, I have not tried to identify foreign sources of oral information. In some cases I have concealed them to avoid possible embarrassment.

Although I did not rely upon official sources, I have profited greatly from the informal counsel and general advice of numerous officers, both in Washington and in the countries visited (Peru, Venezuela, Bolivia, and Mexico) during 1966 field work. Neither they nor others, however, should bear any of the blame for my mistakes. More than any individual, I am indebted to John N. Plank, for his advice and encouragement in the years before and after I went to Brookings, as much as while I was there.

The correspondence and interviews held with private scholars during this study were the source of my greatest gratification. The names appear in the notes, but particularly helpful were David Chaplin, Alvin Cohen, William P. Glade, Rosendo Gomez, Harry Kantor, William Mangin, James O. Morris, Richard W. Patch, Frederick B. Pike, Lucian W. Pye,

Kalman H. Silvert, and William F. Whyte. In a special group are several doctoral candidates whose work in the countries studied was most helpful: James M. Malloy, Terry L. McCoy, Neale J. Pearson, Alan Sloan, and Richard Weinert. Washingtonians who gave of their resources included Philip Blair, John A. Mackay, F. Webster McBryde, Susan Lennhoff, Alfredo Saco, and Ben Stephansky.

I ask the pardon of all these for impositions on their time, and for names inadvertently omitted, and I particularly thank those who received me so graciously during visits to other countries. Special gratitude goes to Mrs. Elizabeth Blystone, who typed the final manuscript with great accuracy and unusual care.

GRANT HILLIKER

CONTENTS

PREFACE vii

NOTE ON SOURCES xiii

I. THE APRISTA PARTY AND DEVELOPMENT 1

II. SOCIETY AND POLITICS IN PERU 24

III. APRA'S STRATEGIC CHOICES 53

IV. APRISTA ORGANIZATION 74

V. THE METHODS OF APRA 103

VI. PROGRAM APPLICATION AND TACTICS 114

VII. THE AGRARIAN REFORM ISSUE 138

VIII. OTHER REFORM PARTIES OF LATIN AMERICA 157

IX. THE POLITICS OF REFORM 186

APPENDICES

A. APRA's Historical Choices and Decisions 193

B. Dispersion of Presidential Voting by Department, Elections of 1956, 1962, and 1963 194

INDEX 197

FIGURES

II-1. Language Profiles 31

III-1. Strategic Choices in APRA's Search for Power 56

III-2. Alternation of Strategies by APRA, 1956–68 73
IV-1. Regional Concentrations of APRA and AP Strength, 1962 and 1963 Elections 78
IV-2. Regionalism in the 1963 Presidential Election 80
VII-1. Expropriation Levels of Agrarian Reform Bills 151

TABLES

I-1. Mass Reform Parties of Latin America 13
II-1. Language Areas of Peru 30
III-1. Changes of Government in Peru, 1938–68 58
IV-1. Regionalism in the 1963 Presidential Election 79
IV-2. FENCAP Member Organizations 98
VIII-1. Chronology of Attempts to Gain Power 178
VIII-2. Party Characteristics and Attitudes 185

NOTE ON SOURCES

DOCUMENTARY INFORMATION ON Latin American political parties, especially that which was published decades ago, is elusive. No one source is adequate, and I would not claim to have exhausted the possibilities. Aprista party documents might have been examined at the party headquarters, but I preferred to use my time there to seek interviews. Before and after visiting Peru, I used the Library of Congress (Hispanic Foundation), the Library of the Department of State, and that of The Brookings Institution. They were useful for Aprista documents in about that order, with information from the earlier periods being more complete than that for the years since World War II. More recent publications were acquired by combing the bookstores in Lima, accepting gifts, and borrowing from friends who had used similar methods. Except for a few documents from Venezuela and Bolivia, sources for these countries and Mexico were mainly secondary. Translations, including interviews, are my own unless otherwise attributed.

Abbreviations used more than once or twice in the text or notes are explained here for convenience. The name APRA requires special attention. I have adopted the common practice of using it to mean the party in Peru, even though it does not exist under this name, *Alianza Popular Revolucionaria Americana* (American Popular Revolutionary Alliance), which was intended to be an international party. The derivatives of APRA (Aprista and *Aprismo*) are used in this book to refer to the domestic activities of the party which bears the formal name *Partido Aprista Peruano* (Peruvian Aprista party). It is also known in party circles as *Partido del Pueblo* (Party of the People). Party publications are cited by the abbreviation of the formal name (PAP).

Abbreviations

AD Acción Democrática (Democratic Action), Venezuela

Adecos Adherents of AD

Annals, The *The Annals of the American Academy of Political and Social Science*

AP Acción Popular (Popular Action)

APRA Alianza Popular Revolucionaria Americana (American Popular Revolutionary Alliance)

AUFS *American Universities Field Service Report*

CAEM Centro de Altos Estudios Militares (Center for Higher Military Studies)

CIDA Comité Interamericano de Desarrollo Agrícola (Inter-American Agricultural Development Committee)

COB Central Obrero Boliviana (Bolivian Workers' Center)

COPEI Christian Socialist Party, Venezuela (The original Spanish name, meaning Independent Committee for Political and Electoral Organization, is no longer used.)

CRAV Comisión para la Reforma Agraria y Vivienda (Agrarian Reform and Housing Commission)

CTP Confederación de Trabajadores del Perú (Workers' Confederation of Peru)

CTV Confederación de Trabajadores de Venezuela (Workers' Confederation of Venezuela)

DC Demócrata Cristiana (Christian Democratic party)

FCV Federación Campesina de Venezuela (Venezuelan *Campesino* Federation)

FENCAP Federación Nacional de Campesinos del Perú (National *Campesino* Federation of Peru)

FLN Frente de Liberación Nacional (National Liberation Front)

HAR *Hispanic American Report*

IDB Inter-American Development Bank

MIR Movimiento de la Izquierda Revolucionaria (Movement of the Revolutionary Left), Peru and Venezuela

MNR Movimiento Nacional Revolucionario (National Revolutionary Movement), Bolivia

PAP Partido Aprista Peruano (Peruvian Aprista party)

PDN Partido Democrático Nacional (National Democratic party), Venezuela

PIR Partido de la Izquierda Revolucionaria (Party of the Revolutionary Left), Bolivia

PLN Partido de Liberación Nacional (National Liberation Party), Costa Rica
POR Partido Obrero Revolucionario (Revolutionary Workers' party), Bolivia
PRD Partido Revolucionario Dominicano (Dominican Revolutionary party), Dominican Republic
PRI Partido Revolucionario Institucional (Institutional Revolutionary party), Mexico
SORO Special Operations Research Office
UNO Unión Nacional Odriísta (National Odriísta Union)
URD Unión Republicana Democrática (Democratic Republican Union), Venezuela

THE
POLITICS OF REFORM
IN PERU

I

THE APRISTA PARTY AND DEVELOPMENT

THE PROCESSES OF NATIONAL DEVELOPMENT are a major preoccupation of our time. They affect not only the less developed countries, as we once thought; they also concern the more highly developed portions of the world. The development phenomenon can be viewed from several angles.

This book is about one of those aspects, political development, as seen through the eyes of a political party. The Aprista party of Peru has had an unusually long history of involvement in development. The experiences of this party and of some of its counterparts in other Latin American countries can help to illuminate the question of how the development process begins.

THE DEVELOPMENT DILEMMA

Almost anyone can recognize a developed country on sight, but few can accurately describe how it got that way. And no one has said convincingly how to generate development in the variety of circumstances encountered around the world. Development cannot be easily prescribed, because it is complex and occurs in diverse settings.

In simplest terms, development permits a society to adjust continually to change, in meeting the demands of its members. At the same time, the demands themselves will undoubtedly be changing, while the conditions to which the society must respond are subjected to both internal and external influences. Scholars and bureaucrats try to reduce the complexity by viewing development in its economic, social, and political aspects.

Models of Development

The foreign assistance programs of the United States Government, for example, have undergone periodic shifts of emphasis. The different phases have concentrated on the transfer of techniques, capital investment, institutional development, and individual well-being.[1] Intersecting these divisions may be such emphases as the project approach, balance-of-payments gap, self-help, and human capital. Recently the capital market has been added as a superior device for the transfer of resources.[2]

These phases and criteria reflect alterations of policy objectives; they also reveal which development theories were entertained, with varying degrees of explicitness, at different times and places. They only re-emphasize the difficulty of stating a generally valid prescription for development, a lesson which has constantly to be rediscovered.

The economic aspect of development is often reduced to industrialization, especially when it emphasizes capital investment. It assumes that the energy release that is characteristic of development will be achieved by stimulating the productive process. Unless development is already incipient, the area of concern soon has to be broadened to include the supportive facilities, such as transport, power, and communications. Depending upon the market, but ultimately in any event, the next enlargement will probably be toward distributive and service activities.

Social infrastructure is another logical object of attention. An industry must employ technicians and skilled workers. Some can be brought from abroad, but both policy and economy commend the training and employment of local nationals for these jobs. Ideally they should be not only educated but also healthy, well-housed, and culturally satisfied. As the local population makes increased use of the products of industry, demands for social benefits such as these also will rise.

Development programs frequently evolve in this way, beginning with the aim of supplying the missing symptoms of modernity and working backward to prerequisites. However long the resulting shopping list may be, this is not the full story.

What passes for social development may be confined to welfare programs, which go mainly to meet the needs of individuals and families. Meeting these needs is highly significant, for it begins to get at the problem of change. Yet the mere consumption of industrial products does not result in new patterns of behavior compatible with modern life. Nor does

[1] Max F. Millikan, "The United States and Low-Income Countries," in *Agenda for the Nation*, ed. Kermit Gordon (Washington, D.C.: The Brookings Institution, 1968), pp. 515–16.

[2] David T. Kleinman, "Structuring Capital Markets for Efficient Use of Foreign Aid: The Case of Brazil," *Industrial Management Review* 10, no. 2 (Winter, 1969): 47–66.

the building of schools, hospitals, and housing projects do so, although they may gradually have those effects.

In a much broader sense, social development overlaps and encompasses political development. Its larger aspect is best understood in terms of how an individual changes in his relationships with others. Once broken out of traditional ways, he needs new values, perceptions, and roles to help him find his place in a different kind of culture. The effects are felt in all aspects of society, including economic and political development.

> . . . Development is much more than a technical operation, a series of innovations forced upon a society from outside or from the top, affecting only the pattern of organization of economic activities, the expansion of industries, the use of new tools, and the rise of productivity. Development is a living historical experiment. . . . What is developing is a social structure as a whole and as each one of its parts: economic types, stratification system, institutional patterns, values and norms, ideas and ideologies. . . .
> . . . Living in a transitional period of this scope, any decision is a political decision. . . . And social actions soon become political decisions. This is the phenomenology of development.[3]

Because the process is so complex and poorly understood, and so political, the initiation of development can be a critical point for study. Change does not occur spontaneously, although it sometimes so appears. Efforts to attribute certain examples of development to single causes tend to ignore the combination of circumstances that happened to be favorable. What that critical mass might be in any given situation is impossible to predict with certainty.

What is certain is that people who have already been jarred out of their traditional ways will be more receptive to other kinds of change than those whose conditions of life remain static. ". . . Men find it easier to adjust their beliefs to their actions than their actions to their beliefs."[4]

When it occurs on a substantial scale, random change can add up to social mobilization, which is one of the subprocesses of development. Deutsch explained it as "something that happens to large numbers of people in areas which undergo modernization, i.e., where advanced, nontraditional practices in culture, technology and economic life are introduced and accepted on a considerable scale."[5]

[3] L. A. Costa Pinto, "Portrait of Developing Man: The Processes of Social Changes in Latin America," in *The New Sociology: Essays in Social Science and Social Theory*, ed. Irving Louis Horowitz (New York: Oxford University Press, 1964), pp. 469–70.

[4] Dankwart A. Rustow, *A World of Nations: Problems of Political Modernization* (Washington, D.C.: The Brookings Institution, 1967), p. 233.

[5] Karl W. Deutsch, "Social Mobilization and Political Development," *American Political Science Review* 55, no. 3 (September, 1961): 493.

Social mobilization does not necessarily result in attainment of a new equilibrium. From a traditional world in which everyone has his place, and knows it, mobilization may produce a mass society. The most prominent characteristic of mass society is the individual's lack of a sense of belonging or of a knowledge of his identity in relation to others and to familiar social institutions and accepted values. In this condition the community, or some part of it, has been atomized, allowing it to be more easily manipulated for political purposes.[6]

In a continuous view of the modernization process, mobilization is only an intermediate step which prepares individuals for "acceptance of a modern or quasi-modern life." Integration is needed to make them full participants in the dominant society. People who have been shaken loose from traditional life patterns may be "mobilized but not yet fully integrated" into new styles.[7]

Politics of Development

The point at which social development becomes political is a matter of speculation. It could be said to occur when social contacts transcend the purely interpersonal relationships that loom largest in traditional folkways. Interaction among strangers, joined or divided by as little as a symbol, is certainly the stuff of politics. This is potentially true, regardless of the original purpose of the impersonal relationships, because political development need not take obviously political forms.

Farmers' organizations in the United States in the latter part of the nineteenth century became operating parts of the Populist movement, just as trade unions formed the nuclei of the socialist parties of Europe. Literary societies became catalysts of nationalism in some countries. Ostensibly organized to advance non-political interests, the associations lent themselves to political purposes and they were so used. Any form of customary participation in organized group action in one's own interest helps to form behavior patterns supportive of eventual overt political action.[8]

[6] William Kornhauser, *The Politics of Mass Society* (Glencoe, Ill.: The Free Press, 1959), pp. 30ff.

[7] K. H. Silvert, "Parties and the Masses," *The Annals* 358 (March, 1965): 102–3. See also Gino Germani, "Social Change and Intergroup Conflicts," in *The New Sociology*, ed. Horowitz, pp. 391–92, where the author distinguishes three aspects of integration: normative, psychosocial, and environmental.

[8] V. O. Key, Jr., *Politics, Parties and Pressure Groups*, 4th ed. (New York: Thomas Y. Crowell Co., 1958), pp. 170ff. Key presents a much more autonomous picture of pressure groups, based on United States experience, while noting that close collaboration is one extreme form of relationship among political parties.

The political aspect of development becomes more significant when an element of direction is added to volition. Normal social development occurs at its own pace, in response to the sum total of the impulses of individuals to change and to re-integrate their relationships in new ways. Directed change can originate with the state or from private initiative.

State-directed change is necessarily risky. The modern state enjoys, by definition, a monopoly of legitimate force. The temptation to rely excessively upon coercion as an implement of change can be overwhelming. The demands which development is supposed to serve can thereby become distorted by the constraints of a self-serving bureaucracy. In cybernetic terms, the feedback loop is severed and the system is driving blind.

Numerous opportunities can arise for political parties to influence the development process. Politics abhors the kind of vacuum created by the loss of traditional values and symbols, and the political entrepreneur, no less than the colonial trader, can find profit in transitional situations. Individual circumstances will help to determine whether parties of change take control of the state for purposes of reform. Such a situation is essentially different from that of state-directed change, if the party keeps its communication channels open in both directions. A party can serve this purpose even in the most authoritarian political systems. More common in Latin America, however, has been the condition in which reform parties do not gain control and governments are unwilling or unable to move vigorously in the direction of change.[9]

The Reluctant Regime

Official disinclination to promote development can have several causes. First, and perhaps most significant, is sheer intertia. Resistance to change need not be either conscious or conniving. It can be the result of mere ignorance or loyal attachment to the highest values of an outgrown culture. In any event, institutions, including governments, are not designed to bring about change; on the contrary, they enshrine stability.[10]

Changes of government do not often suffice to produce a regime favorable to development. Especially in Latin America, political parties are often personalist, ideologies are ephemeral, and constitutional norms are

[9] Rustow, *World of Nations*, p. 107. Costa Pinto, in "Portrait of Developing Man," pp. 465–66, asserts that direction by government is necessary in the case of delayed development in order to catch up when normal processes have been missed.

[10] Graham T. Allison, *Conceptual Models and the Cuban Missile Crisis: Rational Policy, Organization Process, and Bureaucratic Politics* (Santa Monica, Calif.: The RAND Corporation, P-3919, August, 1968). Also prepared for delivery at the 1968 Annual Meeting of The American Political Science Association, Washington Hilton Hotel, Washington, D.C., September 2–7, 1968.

easily disregarded or altered. Neither conventional politics nor so-called revolutions can be relied upon to do more than change the faces of the rulers.[11]

The reluctant regime is thus the typical case in Latin America. Circumstances might force upon a government an awareness of the imminence of change, but thereupon it finds itself already faced with the difficulties of development delayed beyond its time. Archaic social and economic institutions and values have persisted in most Latin American countries, sometimes being modified, but rarely destroyed, by successive shifts in internal and external conditions.

When a reluctant regime appears to conspire with private interests to divert change, it easily acquires the label of oligarchy. Refinement of the term has produced the concept of "system of interests," which permits a more precise understanding of the potential obstacles to change. Linked to traditional values as bases for the exclusion of large parts of the population from participation, the system nevertheless maintains competition within the circle of those enjoying access to power. Publicly espoused values relate to means rather than ends. Moreover, the rules of exclusion are flexible enough to permit the incorporation of segments of the excluded as they successfully challenge the system.[12]

The test, of course, is in the effectiveness of exclusion. In its extreme form, the oligarchic tendency amounts to "private government" in which "functional elites have set up their own informal political structures to act as control devices over their own activities and as offense units in the battle for political power." The results are usually of low visibility.[13]

A necessary condition for the maintenance of oligarchic control of the apparatus of government is also imbedded in the political culture. It is the custom of Latins in general to approach transactions with the state through an intermediary rather than directly. Even when an interest group has organized to present grievances to the government, it customarily acts

[11] George I. Blanksten, "The Politics of Latin America," in *The Politics of the Developing Areas*, ed. Gabriel A. Almond and James S. Coleman (Princeton: Princeton University Press, 1960), pp. 474, 496–97.

[12] Magali Sarfatti Larson and Arlene Eisen Bergman, *Social Stratification in Peru*, Politics of Modernization Series, no. 5 (Berkeley: University of California, Institute of International Studies, 1969), pp. 1–5. James L. Payne has commented on the vague use of the oligarchy concept in his "The Oligarchy Muddle" (Paper prepared for delivery at the 1967 Annual Meeting of the American Political Science Association, Chicago, September 5–9, 1967). Exclusion as a more exact criterion is consistent with Key's discussion of accountability of private power and of countervailing influences; see Key's *Politics, Parties and Pressure Groups*, pp. 110ff. and 142ff.

[13] Robert E. Scott, "Political Elites and Political Modernization: The Crisis of Transition," in *Elites in Latin America*, ed. Seymour Martin Lipset and Aldo Solari New York: Oxford University Press, 1967), p. 136 and *passim*.

indirectly. The result is a clientelistic political system, fragmentation of interest groups, and dilution of demands presented to the state.[14]

The general consequence of these structural and cultural characteristics is a dependency relationship of the "outs" toward the "ins." To the extent that open channels of political communication and interest articulation and aggregation exist, political parties and interest groups can function normally. If such channels are blocked, conventional politics can become a farce.

Political Parties of Change

Initiation of change is the most difficult problem of development. Political parties are the accepted vehicles for marshaling the will of the community. In conventional politics the functions of parties are to act as both intervening and dependent variables between the community and the state.

As an *intervening* variable, the party communicates popular demands to the state and conveys to the community its interpretation of the conduct of government. As a *dependent* variable, it is constrained and shaped by the substructure of the society it represents. These functions are conventional only because they emerged during the modernization of Europe, which proceeded "largely unconsciously and by means of unintended results." Transformations there occurred in a sequence extending over a space of six or seven centuries.[15]

In Asia, Africa, and Latin America thc pressures to keep pace or catch up with thc industrial world have accentuated the third function of political parties, the unconventional task of being the *independent* variable, by which the party exercises an autonomous influence not only upon the state but also in the community.[16] This function can be the critical one in the initiation of the social and political processes of development.

In the countries of early industrialization, development had its effects on politics; in the countries of delayed modernization, politics often has to take a hand in development. These reversals can be seen in terms of the doctrine (that is, ideologies and programs) and organization of political parties.

[14] William P. Mangin, "The Role of Regional Associations in the Adaptation of Rural Migrants to Cities in Peru," in *Contemporary Cultures and Societies of Latin America*, ed. Dwight B. Heath and Richard N. Adams (New York: Random House, 1965), p. 315; Larson and Bergman, *Social Stratification in Peru*, pp. 244ff., 284–86.

[15] Rustow, *World of Nations*, p. 107.

[16] David E. Apter, *The Politics of Modernization* (Chicago: The University of Chicago Press, 1965), pp. 181–82; see also his "Political Change" in *Comparative Politics*, ed. Harry Eckstein and David E. Apter (New York: Macmillan, The Free Press, 1963), pp. 549–55.

Doctrine of Reform

Traditional society is devoid of political ideology in the strict sense of that term. The pre-industrial world is organicist and holistic, in that beliefs and behavior are comprehensive, often theocratic in the Islamic sense. Ideologies exist, but they are not compartmentalized. The differentiation of social roles and areas of activity into religious, economic, social, and political segments opens the way for a specifically political ideology. Yet the tradition persists, for example, in one European country, where *non-political* is a code word for anyone who is conservative. It means that that person accepts traditional ends and means and sees no need for a separate political doctrine.

Ideology is thus ancillary to change and has a special utility in revolutionary symbolism. It can nevertheless be employed in other ways, and even to limit the scope of change. Industrial capitalism in the United States in the years 1880–1912 was able to define political democracy "in agreeable *economic* terms . . . as liberty of contract" and thus to establish its "ideological hegemony" in competition with Populism and middle-class movements for reform.[17]

The dominant ideology of the United States could almost be called an ideology of change. The fact that it facilitates entrepreneurial change more than social (and private investment more than public) is a product of the circumstances of its formative period. ("Everything's up to date in Kansas City" probably was not sung of the welfare system.) The "end of ideology" was a triumph of pragmatism. Means became ends in a mass-consumption society. Those who now protest the results seek to restore some of the values that have suffered from accelerated, overextended, and irresponsible change. Does this make them conservatives or reactionaries?

Ideological position is difficult to fix in the abstract, and only slightly less elusive on the basis of party behavior. In some circumstances a double standard may be needed to judge the status of parties of basically conflicting orientations. In place of the accustomed scale of ideologies from left to right, radical to conservative, there might to two such scales, placed parallel to each other. One would be for traditional parties and the other for modern parties. Parties could be placed in one category or the other according to whether they are organicist, static, and ritualistic, on the one hand, or relativist, self-adjusting, and rationalist, on the other. These characteristics reflect differences of attitude and expectation in relation to change.[18]

[17] Daniel Bell, *The End of Ideology* (New York: Macmillan, The Free Press, 1960), pp. 61–62.

[18] K. H. Silvert (Hanover, N.H.) to G. Hilliker, January 2, 1966.

Positions of particular parties along the respective scales would be determined by their programs as judged against their actions. Modern parties may differ little from one another as to the velocity and intensity of change proposed, but they can still be distinguished by the change they impose when in power. Traditional parties may verbally oppose change, or adopt limited definitions of the kinds of change permitted, yet actually impose considerable amounts of change when in power. Highly personalistic parties, such as those of Perón and Vargas, may qualify as left-traditionals on doctrinal grounds, but by their actions bring about some modernizing effects. An example is the present party of former President Odría in Peru, which profits from his record in office. By certain massive public works originated for paternalistic or technocratic reasons under his regime in the 1950s, Odría may have swelled the tide of social mobilization. Migration to the coastal cities increased as life there became more livable for the marginal workers dependent upon construction projects.

If traditional and modern parties are distinguished by differences of outlook, there should be no confusion between the two, even though their actions may have parallel effects. In the last analysis, personalist parties are recognizable by the cynicism of their leaders. For the totalitarian or authoritarian rightist leader, power becomes an end in itself, and ideology is only an instrument for domination and direction of the mass.[19]

Mass Organization

The functioning of parties in the development process will depend, of course, upon the conditions in which they operate. In Europe, mass-based parties began to replace elite or cadre parties as shifts occurred in the "social and political substructure" of the industrializing countries.[20] In the United States, the corresponding changes may have been the pre-industrial phenomenon of opening up the frontier from the term of Jackson until the turn of the century.

Those changes in substructure implied basic modifications in economic systems, something that has occurred only to a limited degree and in restricted areas of Latin America. The consequences for mass parties, there-

[19] Gino Germani, *Política y Sociedad en una Epoca de Transición* (Buenos Aires: Editorial Paidós, 1962), pp. 138–43, 157. Germani says that "the popular classes of a country—or certain subgroups thereof within the same country—will be disposed to support movements of authoritarian orientation (of Left or Right) in proportion to the retardation of their political integration and to the shock of their shift from the pre-industrial to the industrial society and of the process of 'fundamental democratization' " (*ibid.*, p. 142). He includes political participation in the last term.

[20] Maurice Duverger, *Political Parties*, trans. Barbara and Robert North, 2d English ed. (New York: John Wiley & Sons, 1959), p. 65.

fore, can be expected to differ from the European experience. Mass parties that operate in the absence of large and diversified labor forces, competitive consumer markets, and an achievement standard of social mobility run the risk of becoming the particularistic advocates of narrow clienteles.

Still different sociopolitical situations set apart Afro-Asian mass parties. First, many newly independent countries of Africa and Asia were led out of colonial status by popular revolutionary parties that carried nationalism, development, and often socialism under the same banner with independence. Thereafter, they faced the task of national integration against the barriers of cultural pluralism. Despite the racial diversity of Latin America, cultural fragmentation there has been less significant.[21] Moreover, while mass parties elsewhere typically operate as single-party regimes in power, in Latin America they have more frequently been opposition parties functioning in multiparty systems.

In a more general framework, parties operating in contexts of modernization can tend toward either the authoritarian or the democratic extreme while still retaining certain essential characteristics of parties of change. How they develop depends upon the interaction of parties and political systems.

Typically, coalitions are formed from a variety of particularistic associations joined in a common purpose. The institutionalization of loyalty and authority through cooperation can form the basis for parties of *representation*. They are pluralistic, tolerating and competing with other parties; representative in the sense of incorporating divergent views; and consitutional, abiding by preordained rules of the state. They tend to be found in, or to produce, reconciliation systems.

Coalitions can also become movements. A movement arises when it "suddenly gains a mass following around a particular ideology or heroic leadership," which greatly increases the "amount of non-rational excitement it can produce." From such movements parties of *solidarity* often emerge. They are monopolistic, seeking to eliminate other parties; directive, trying to change structural conditions to meet party goals; and extra-constitutional, subjecting the state to the party's will. Parties of solidarity have affinities for mobilization systems.[22]

These conflicting tendencies can be found within parties of change, and one or the other may dominate at different times. The main characteristics which they have in common, however, can be described for the group as a whole, with emphasis being placed on their similarities with early Soviet communism. The mass movement, as it has been called, is "typically

[21] Rustow, *World of Nations*, p. 216; Charles W. Anderson *et al.*, *Issues of Political Development* (Englewood Cliffs, N.J.: Prentice-Hall, 1967), pp. 18, 45–46.

[22] Apter, *Politics of Modernization*, pp. 202–12.

directed against a foreign colonial regime" or against "an indigenous order that is treated as though it were foreign." This is the mark of nationalism in Latin America, just as the foreign orientation of the czarist regime was condemned in Russia in 1917.[23]

A better basis for distinguishing the mass movement is its "revolutionary dynamism," especially if its other characteristics are purely nationalist in purpose. Modernization is often the longer-range objective and it involves "many elements of an internal social revolution" in opposition to old patterns. This sets it apart from nationalist movements, which are primarily devoted to maintenance of the status quo.[24]

Mass movements are distinctive also in the ways that they relate to supporters. A high degree of organized popular participation is typically achieved through "the enlisting of masses of people in the activities of trade unions, youth, professional and other organizations that are formally non-party in character but are operated under party guidance and supervision. . . ."[25] In mass parties a "multiplicity of organizations, each having some functional role to play in the community, is joined in some fashion within a political party. . . ."[26]

Given these characteristics, a more descriptive name would be the mass reform party. It includes the Aprista party of Peru and several other Latin American parties, which have the following features:

1. *Ideology* incorporating the goals of distributive justice and a view of the party's place in history independent of global political or religious connections.

2. *Programs* of action aimed at fundamental changes in the structures of society.

3. *Organization* of party-sponsored or affiliated support groups and maximum participation of members in party affairs.

Mass Reform Parties of Latin America

Since the late 1930s, the "popular parties" of Latin America have been conscious of their affinities. A sort of Latin American "Internationale" has been intermittently in the process of formation through the personal contacts of party leaders. The movement owed much, in a negative sense, to the regimes that had exiled, and thereby brought together, such reformers as Haya de la Torre (founder of APRA), Rómulo Betancourt of

[23] Robert C. Tucker, "Towards a Comparative Politics of Movement-Regimes," *American Political Science Review* 55, no. 2 (June, 1961): 283.

[24] *Ibid.*, pp. 286–87.

[25] *Ibid.*, p. 285.

[26] Apter, *Politics of Modernization*, p. 196.

Venezuela, and José Figueres of Costa Rica. Concrete collaborative efforts were begun in 1940, following interparty channels, but they resulted only in a series of meetings. Faltering attempts to organize a coordinating body of qualified parties, or governments, led finally to agreement among what were the hard-core parties of mass reform. The relationship was formalized in the "Declaration of Lima," signed in August, 1960, by the self-styled "League of Popular Parties."[27]

In his discussion of competitive party systems, Blanksten listed pragmatic, particularistic, and ideological parties, including in the last what he called the "agrarian-populist" or Aprista group of parties. These he characterized as being indigenous to the area and "seeking far-reaching social and economic change, usually including land reform and integration of the lower classes into the political process. . . . " Only three of Blanksten's five parties (the Peruvian, Venezuelan, and Costa Rican) signed the Lima declaration.[28] Alexander later offered a longer list of the "national revolutionary" parties within a broader category of "indigenous parties of change." To the Lima signatories he added the Institutional Revolutionary Party (PRI) of Mexico and PRD (Juan Bosch's party) in the Dominican Republic.[29] Both Alexander and Blanksten credit APRA with developing many of the ideas now shared by these parties. The three lists are compared in Table I–1. Other reform parties of Latin America might be added, but these are the ones that combined similar characteristics of ideology and program (at least in the late 1950s and early 1960s) without foreign ideological connections or excessively personalistic origins. Both Blanksten and Alexander mention, for example, the parties of Vargas and Perón, calling them "spurious ideological movements" or "personalist revolutionary parties."

This book will examine three parties as empirical standards against which to evaluate the strategies and methods of APRA. They are the Mexican Partido Revolucionario Institutional (PRI), the Bolivian Movimiento Nacional Revolucionario (MNR), and the Venezuelan Acción

[27] Harry Kantor, "La Colaboración entre los Partidos," *Panoramas* 12 (November-December, 1964): 67–76.

[28] Blanksten, "Politics of Latin America," pp. 485–86, 491–95; *Latino-américa Más Allá de sus Fronteras* (San Jose, Costa Rica: Ediciones Combate, 1960), pp. 109–15.

[29] Robert J. Alexander, "The Emergence of Modern Political Parties in Latin America," in *Politics of Change in Latin America*, ed. Joseph Maier and Richard W. Weatherhead (New York: Frederick A. Praeger, 1964), p. 119. See also Victor Alba, *Alliance Without Allies* (New York: Frederick A. Praeger, 1965), pp. 85ff., and Seymour Martin Lipset, "Political Cleavages in 'Developed' and 'Emerging' Politics," reprint no. 244 (Berkeley: University of California, Institutes of Industrial Relations and International Studies, 1964), p. 42, for somewhat similar selections of parties. Harry Kantor presents a list of thirteen "popular parties" in "Los Partidos Populares de América Latina," *Journal of Inter-American Studies* 6, no. 2 (April, 1964): 221–34.

TABLE I–1: MASS REFORM PARTIES OF LATIN AMERICA

	"Popular Parties" (Declaration of Lima)	"Agrarian-Populist" (Blanksten)	"National Revolutionary" (Alexander[a])
APRA (Peru)	x	x	x
AD (Venezuela)	x	x	x
PLN (Costa Rica)	x	x	x
MNR (Bolivia)	x		x
Febreristas (Paraguay)	x		x
PRI (Mexico)		x[b]	x
Auténticos (Cuba)		x	
PRD (Dominican Republic)			x

Sources: See notes 28 and 29 of this chapter.
[a] Alexander also included the Democratic party of Puerto Rico, not listed here.
[b] Included, with reservations, by the author.

Democrática (AD). Each of these countries presents a different background for the evolution and operation of mass reform parties.

Of the three countries, Bolivia is most similar to Peru, even though its urban-industrial sector is smaller. Peruvian problems of land and unassimilated Indian populations are much like those of Bolivia before the 1952 revolution. Both countries were considered in the early 1960s to have experienced, along with the majority of other Latin American countries, "low integration and extensive or very rapid mobilization." In these countries the most explosive social situations are to be anticipated, not only because of the pace of mobilization through urbanization or rural changes or both, but also because of persistent systems of archaic social stratification.

Mexico was in a comparable state of instability during the years of disorder that followed the 1910 revolution. It now has reached a condition of "expanded mobilization and integration in a state of equilibrium," although possibly half the population is still marginal to the national life. Chile and Brazil also are in this situation, each with different qualifications.

Venezuela is a country in which "mobilization started belatedly and proceeded at an extremely fast pace," due in large part to the development of oil and other resources. Integration is incomplete, as it is in Argentina, and conflicts in both countries tend to take violent forms. Particularly in Venezuela, the prospects of preserving democratic political and social structures are endangered by extremist alternatives.[30]

PRI is a point of reference for any mass reform party because it provided the revolutionary demonstration and inspiration to other popular

[30] Gino Germani, "Social Change," pp. 405–7.

movements in Latin America. Its initial ideology was rudimentary when the 1910 revolution began. The philosophical underpinnings were present, but they found scant articulation as preparation or justification for action; they were the property of the few. Even after fifty years the revolution has "no integrated and official ideology" beyond the general idea of progress and change.[31]

The slogans of the 1910 revolution were expressive by contrast. They revealed that it was primarily an act of protest, negativism, and violence. The many who took part in the revolution had no doubt of what they were opposing. "Bread and Freedom!" and "No re-election!" were meaningful words, even if there was no certainty as to the next step after destruction ended the old order. The formal program of PRI took shape slowly, however, being based on pragmatic experience, and the organizational form did not begin to emerge until almost twenty years after the revolution began. By then the party deserved to be called institutional.

The experience of MNR in Bolivia was comparable to that of PRI in Mexico in terms of revolutionary thoroughness, even though it was of short duration and involved less extreme violence. It was also similar in that party doctrine was sketchy. Although MNR was more than ten years old when it came to power in 1952, its ideology was eclectic, largely negative, and not highly formalized. Party goals had largely to be inferred from the acts of the new government.

In its organizational base MNR was better prepared and more quickly stabilized than PRI. Its principal support groups, however, were the miners' unions and the peasant syndicates, the leaders of which were personages in their own right whose primary loyalties were not to the party. Combined with the personalistic and opportunistic leadership style of MNR, these cleavages soon divided the party into warring factions that were easy prey for the military coup in 1964.

In contrast to the Mexican and the Bolivian revolutions, success was achieved in Venezuela by AD with minimal violence and unprecedented durability. The party's ideology and programs were slow in emerging, but by the time AD took power in 1958 they were more explicit than had been true for either of the other parties. The Venezuelan experience also varies from the others (even after making allowances for social and economic differences) in the breadth and stability of the organizational base built by AD.

Each of the parties came to power in different circumstances but later acquired greater similarity to the others. If Mexico and Bolivia are com-

[31] Robert E. Scott, *Mexican Government in Transition* (Urbana: University of Illinois Press, 1959), p. 100. The mass reform parties of Bolivia, Venezuela, and Mexico are discussed in more detail in Chapter VIII of the present volume.

parable in the completeness of their respective revolutions, Venezuela more closely resembles the Mexican revolution in its generally pragmatic program and ability to forge a sound institutional base.

In initial ideological emphases, the Mexican and Venezuelan parties were mainly political. The Bolivian MNR was at first nationalistic, aiming at seizure of the tin mines, and it soon added political and developmental acts by granting universal suffrage and redistributing the land of the large estates. The Venezuelan and Mexican parties eventually expanded into nationalist (oil exploitation) and developmental (agrarian reform) programs, although the Mexican action was delayed until the 1930s.

THE APRISTA PARTY

Neither revolutionary ideology nor mass-based politics was invented by APRA. Instead, the party was representative of a trend, already begun in Europe, where the Social Democratic parties most closely paralleled Aprista doctrine and organization. The party also had its counterparts in Latin America, although APRA was the first clearly to exhibit these characteristics.

The long history of APRA provides a rich store of experiences against the background of developing conditions in Peru. The fact that the party has never fully succeeded in reaching its goals only adds to that richness—failures teach more than successes.

Víctor Raúl Haya de la Torre, founder of APRA and still its chief, is also the author and principal expositor of *Aprismo*. He proclaimed APRA (American Popular Revolutionary Alliance), from exile in Mexico in 1924, as a kind of Pan-American movement of nationalism, reform, and integration. This was the international or "Maximum Program" of the movement.

Although it has not succeeded in this form, the international aspect of APRA was a prototype of the party's internal program and has had powerful indirect influences in Latin America. It was built around five points: anti-imperialism, economic and political unity of Latin America, nationalization of land and industry, internationalization of the Panama Canal, and the "solidarity with all oppressed people and classes of the world."[32]

Anti-imperialism was for Haya simply a defense against economic domination rather than an expression of eternal animosity. Economic determinism was his central theme. Unity of the American republics, through the use of a single currency and a common market, would help

[32] Felipe Cossío del Pomar, *Víctor Raúl* (Mexico, D.F.: Editorial Cultura, 1961), pp. 227–36. One holdover from the international aspirations of APRA is the leading part taken by Apristas such as Andrés Townsend Ezcurra in the Latin American Parliament (Parlamento Latinoamericano).

defend against imperialism. Political unity was not elaborated. Nationalization was considered necessary because of the inseparability of foreign imperialism and national feudalism. "The state cannot be controlled without revolutionizing the national economy, without the effective transformation of the feudal system of production, the dominant class of which controls the state, directly or indirectly, with support of imperialism."[33]

Haya's last two points were the source of political embarrassment in later years. Internationalization of the Panama Canal had to become "inter-Americanization" on the eve of World War II in order to avoid the stigma of favoring fascist penetration of the hemisphere. Of solidarity with "oppressed people" everywhere, little has been said by the Apristas, but their enemies have made much of it. It served as the pretext for repeated proscriptions of APRA as an international party prohibited by the constitution of 1933.[34]

The "Minimum Program" of APRA (for Peru alone) was formulated and proclaimed only in 1931, when Haya and other Apristas returned to Peru following the fall of President Leguía. It has since taken on almost the sanctity of the delivered word, along with various books and articles published by Haya before and after 1931. Haya presented the program as a speech to a large rally assembled in Lima on August 23, 1931, when he was the party's first candidate for president. The first Aprista National Congress adopted the speech as its own program, with little if any change, within a month after its delivery.[35]

El Jefe Máximo

Aprismo ranges from the simplest political slogan to the intricacies of Hegel, Marx, Einstein, and Sartre. "Only APRA will save Peru!" is a favorite popular appeal. But in the speeches and writings of Haya is found the philosophical reasoning of a man who, while eclectic, sought also to express his feeling for the uniqueness of Peru and Latin America. In fact, the latter is a name he refuses to use, preferring to call it "Indoamerica"

[33] *Ibid.*, p. 233.

[34] Harry Kantor, *The Ideology and Program of the Peruvian Aprista Movement* (Berkeley: University of California Press, 1953), p. 14. Unless otherwise noted, references to this basic work are to the original edition rather than to the Argentine edition, *El Movimiento Aprista Peruano* (Buenos Aires: Editorial Pleamar, 1964), or the 1966 revision in English.

[35] PAP, *El Plan del Aprismo* (Lima: Editorial Libertad, 1933), p. 80 and *passim*; Luís Alberto Sánchez, *Haya de la Torre y el APRA* (Santiago de Chile: Editorial del Pacífico, 1955), pp. 274–77. The continued validity of the 1931 speech is asserted by Sánchez ("*plan vigente aún*," *ibid.*, p. 274) and by Jesus Véliz Lizarraca ("*Transcribo la síntesis . . . por estar vigente*") in his *Principios Fundamentales del Aprismo: Filosofía, Doctrina, Programa* (Lima: Instituto de Estudios Apristas, 1956), p. 81.

to indicate the significance of indigenous contributions to the culture of the continent.[36]

The founder of APRA was born of parents financially distressed by the activities of foreign corporations, banks, and export houses. Revolutions and the disastrous war with Chile in 1879 had completed the impoverishment of families "of lineage" in the north. The year of Haya's birth, 1895, was also the year of Piérola's revolution, in which close relatives of the family found themselves on opposing sides.[37]

From his days as a student in Trujillo, largest city and cultural center of the Peruvian northern coast, Haya began taking up unpopular causes and radical movements. "I have always preferred doing to discussing. . . . I consider inseparable . . . the words *to do* and *to organize*; for I think that only in organizing one does, that is, one creates and builds permanently."[38]

In Lima to continue his education, Haya soon became involved in the kind of student agitation that broke out in several South American countries after the reform of the University of Córdoba, Argentina, in 1918. He attended a student congress in 1920 in Cuzco, where he had previously served a term as secretary to the prefect. One of the results of the congress was the organization of the "González Prada Peoples' Universities," adult evening schools in major cities where "workers studied social problems and learned to defend the rights of the Indians. . . ."[39]

Although the issue of university reform in Peru was a real one, the crisis for Haya de la Torre came on a religious issue. In 1923, President Augusto Leguía decided to consecrate the nation to the Sacred Heart of Jesus. In a university debate, Haya took occasion to object to the plan as a violation of the constitutional guarantee of freedom of conscience, threatening student and worker protests if the ceremony was carried out. The president persisted, the protesters marched and were fired upon, with fatalities, and the ceremony was cancelled. But soon afterward Haya was jailed and later that same year he was deported.[40]

Exile kept Haya and some of his fellow radicals out of Peru for the remainder of the twenties and Leguía's term as president. It was during this time that he traveled widely, staying for periods in Mexico, France, England, and the United States and visiting the Soviet Union and several other countries. Deeply impressed by the Mexican Revolution, he developed and refined his ideas, finally distinguishing his personal credo from Soviet communism.

[36] Sánchez, *Haya de la Torre*, p. 246.

[37] Cossío del Pomar, *Víctor Raúl*, pp. 21–24; he asserts that the Aprista leaders were mainly of middle-class origins (*ibid.*, p. 269).

[38] *Ibid.*, p. 84.

[39] *Ibid.*, pp. 107ff.; Kantor, *Peruvian Aprista Movement*, p. 8.

[40] Cossío del Pomar, *Víctor Raúl*, pp. 187ff.; Sánchez, *Haya de la Torre*, p. 119.

Led by Haya, the proto-Apristas of the 1920s drew their inspiration from various sources. Before going into exile, their Peruvian heroes were the nineteenth-century writers Manuel González Prada and Ricardo Palma, both anti-establishment and anticlerical social critics.

With his contemporaries, Haya shared important ideas: the Marxist conviction of José Carlos Mariátegui; Jorge Basadre's sense of the Peruvian historical perspective; Luís Valcárcel's reverence for the Indian; and the disgust with which novelists like Ciro Alegría viewed Peruvian society.[41] Haya came to know other Latin American writers and scholars, such as José Vasconcelos in Mexico, and Germán Arciniegas in Colombia. Still more numerous were his distinguished connections in the drawing rooms, union halls, and colleges of Europe and North America. Formed in times of involuntary exile, this cosmopolitan network of friendships became the target of voluntary periods of expatriation in later years.

Party Ideology

Setting aside the more deeply philosophical elements of Haya's ideology, and taking some liberties with the encyclopedic remains, the operative aspects of Aprismo as it relates to Peru can be reduced to three main themes:

1. "Authentic democracy," which can be interpreted as a call for a revolution of *social mobilization* and *political participation*. It is also called "responsible democracy" with "popular roots." It emphasizes the contrast between the exploiting and undemocratic "oligarchy" and APRA's championship of the underprivileged "three classes" of workers, farmers, and middle class.[42]

2. "Functional democracy" describes the Aprista revolution of *reason and scientific planning*. It is the harnessing of the state to the interests of the "national economy," as opposed to the sector of the economy which is foreign-oriented (although by 1931 Haya sought to control, rather than repel, foreign investment). Proposing a corporative fourth branch of government called the Economic Congress, APRA would establish "a new type of state based not on the citizen as quantity but on the citizen as quality."[43]

3. "The moral force of Aprismo" heralded the revolution of *crusading zeal* which would be required to support the more rational elements of

[41] John N. Plank, "Peru: A Study in the Problems of Nation-Forming" (Ph.D. diss., Harvard University, 1958), pp. 185–208; Sánchez, *Haya de la Torre*, pp. 146–68 and 252.

[42] PAP, *El Plan*, p. 1.

[43] *Ibid.*, p. 20.

doctrine. Haya said in 1931, "Beyond our economic, political, and social crisis, which demands an immediate solution, we have above all a moral crisis which demands, also immediately, a solution of national character." "*Aprismo*, then, is not a political banner; *Aprismo* . . . is a force that responds to a national yearning."[44]

The synthesis of these elements in contemporary party literature seems to stress the second, perhaps because it is the most tangible and operational of the three. Party doctrine explains it as "the concept of functional democracy, that is to say, the establishment of a rule of liberty of the people on the foundations of social justice according to the motto *bread with freedom*."[45]

Haya had recognized in 1931 the need to interrelate the rational and emotional elements of his ideology. He explained, "We are those who proclaim the need for a scientific government, a government of method, a government of discipline, but at the same time, [we are] those who invoke emotion, enthusiasm, faith, and decision in those who are called upon to impose such a government." He also sought to make explicit the revolutionary character of APRA by saying that "it brings to national politics for the first time new ideas, new men, and new methods."[46]

Aprista Programs

Descending from theory, APRA does not lack specific program proposals. To summarize all the ideas put forward by the party would be impossible; they could only be listed, for APRA has something to say on almost everything. Yet most of the Aprista program falls into broad categories, each with its salient features. These have been relatively constant since the early 1930s.

PUBLIC ADMINISTRATION

Reorganization of the state, stressing the adjustment of departmental and provincial boundaries to follow economic criteria; increasing regional autonomy in administrative and economic matters; organizing Congress and the municipalities functionally ("corporative" forms); giving voting rights to illiterates, women, and eighteen-year-olds; and generally decentralizing the exercise—but not the final control—of police power. (Women, including married women over eighteen, received the vote in 1955.)

---

44 *Ibid.*, pp. 30–31.

45 Véliz Lizarraca, *Principios*, p. 65. The idea of the Economic Congress was also the element of *Aprismo* that seemed to appeal most to a young Aprista who volunteered to explain the party to me in Lima in March, 1966. Article 182 of the constitution of 1933 provides for such a congress (or council), but it has never been implemented in law.

46 PAP, *El Plan*, pp. 1 and 34.

ECONOMIC AFFAIRS

Rationalization of the economy, with emphasis on the control of foreign capital investment; the substitution of direct taxes on land, inheritance, and higher incomes for indirect taxes on necessities; progressive nationalization of insurance (and transport, omitted from the 1956 program) and the earliest possible nationalization of mineral and petroleum industries; technical and financial aid to agriculture, mining, industry, and trade in exchange for government participation and observance of fair wage-hour practices; and the study and promotion of the country's economic development. (The 1956 APRA program dropped mention of certain controls.)

AGRICULTURE AND INDIAN AFFAIRS

Expropriation against just compensation of such estates as the state judges appropriate, whether for excessive size, absenteeism, irredeemable mortgages, location adjacent to cities, etc., and conversion to production for the domestic market; the promotion of small holdings and the creation of collective farms. (All of this language and several subsidiary proposals disappeared from the 1956 program, which substituted a proposal for general agrarian reform, taking into account a series of considerations ranging from property systems to taxation.)

Redemption of the Indian through his incorporation into the national life; the preservation and modernization of villages; the encouragement of native arts and crafts; the establishment of rural indigenous schools with Indian teachers; and the education of Indians in their own languages as well as in Spanish. (This was generalized by Sánchez and in the 1956 program, resulting in the loss of specificity more than of emphasis.)

LABOR

Establishment of the eight-hour day (six hours for sixteen-year-olds), one day of rest after every six days of work, from one to two weeks vacation annually with pay, and maternity leave for women before and after delivery. (These and numerous other demands were omitted from the 1956 program, probably because many had been enacted into law; instead it was proposed that labor laws in existence be more strictly enforced. Suggestions for equal pay for women, an institute of vocational studies, etc., were repeated.)

ARMED FORCES

Elaborate modernization of the armed forces, broadening activities and improving conditions of service without reducing the freedom of any of the branches (including the police) from political interference. (In the 1956 party program only the last assurance was reiterated, with a generalized pledge to "favor the constant improvement of the armed forces at all levels.")

CHURCH

Separation of church and state (not repeated in 1956).[47]

[47] This summary is based on PAP, *El Plan*, pp. 37–56, and on Véliz Lizarraca, *Principios*, pp. 85–95; see also Sánchez, *Haya de la Torre*, pp. 274–75 and 284–86, and Thomas R. Ford, *Man and Land in Peru* (Gainesville: University of Florida Press, 1955), pp. 122–23.

A summary can be illustrative only of the multiplicity of ideas—some of them so advanced as to be visionary in their day—contained in the 1931 program. Most of the emphasis remained unchanged through 1948. More recent publications have evidently seen wisdom in a broader approach, although not necessarily at the expense of detailed discussion within the party.[48]

Ideology and program were not the only distinguishing features of *Aprismo* when it emerged on the Latin American scene, nor were they enough to assure the survival of a political party in Peru. It was also necessary to organize, and APRA did so with characteristic imagination.

Organization

The Aprista conception of effective political organization can be traced to two sources. One was Haya's practical experience as a student leader. Although he undoubtedly was copying from abroad, he learned the value of disciplined numbers in the university politics that led to clashes with the authorities and of the need for group loyalties when he was jailed and in exile. In the crucial Sacred Heart protest, at least, the students also enlisted the participation of workers who were then in the early stages of organizing trade unions in Lima.

The second source of ideas on organization was observation of social democratic, communist, and fascist activities in Europe during the 1920s. As Aprista doctrine shows, Haya counted on the mass support of workers and other groups excluded from political participation by other means. Concurrent with the establishment of the party in 1931, support groups were promptly organized under Aprista leadership in fields such as labor and youth.

The result of the Apristas' adoption of a revolutionary doctrine and an organized mass base was to give the party an initial resemblance to the totalitarian parties of Europe in the 1930s. The fact that the comparison had some foundation is confirmed by the statement of Manuel Seoane, deputy to Haya, in a parliamentary debate of the early 1930s. He called APRA a "united front of the oppressed classes . . . which aims at the capture of the state. . . . For us the capture of the state means to convert the state into an instrument of doctrine."[49]

[48] The latter is a judgment based on the agenda of the 1957 National Congress of the Apristas; see PAP, *Directiva Orgánica del III Congreso Nacional del Partido Aprista* (Lima, 1957), pp. 9–12. The subject of intra- and interparty affairs is least mentioned in the doctrinal publications except in terms of "mystique" and an increasingly emphasized anticommunism.

[49] PAP, *Aprismo: El Manifiesto del Jefe del Aprismo a la Nación Peruana* (n.p., n.d., but probably late 1933 or early 1934), p. 95. See also Manuel Seoane, *Nuestros Fines*, 2d ed. (Lima: PAP, 1931), p. 18, where he wrote: "In Peru the main enemy is foreign capital" for the sake of external independence. "Our socialism, dialectically, therefore resolves itself into nationalism."

Summary

Aprista efforts to capture the presidency, as the best means of ensuring the implementation of its program, have not succeeded. The party has been outlawed during more than half of its forty years of formal existence. It has seldom had the opportunity even to present its own candidate for president, but its support for other candidates is often courted, even during periods of its illegality. Nevertheless, it can take credit for some of the advances made in Peru through its indirect power.

Especially since 1956, the party's longest period of unrestricted operation, APRA has had greater freedom, but it has also encountered several setbacks. Two of these were in the form of military coups; others were electoral losses. Two presidential, two congressional, and two municipal elections, as well as by-elections, were held in the sixties. Other opportunities took the form of potential bargains with parties and interest groups. Of greatest long-range significance, however, were the chances to organize political support groups in the manner peculiar to the mass reform party.

Had APRA won the 1931 election and retained power, Peru might have become a mobilization system and APRA its party of solidarity.[50] Haya was its prophet, and its supermen were the student and labor leaders returning from exile or prison. It claimed the total allegiance of individuals, demanded tight discipline, and sought to be a central force in the lives of its members. Had it gained power, it probably would have undertaken development projects using human investment in mass action. As it happened, APRA had no opportunity to share power until 1945, and then only briefly and imperfectly. In more favorable circumstances the party might have employed, as its adversaries charged, some degree of the coercion and manipulation of popular support which dominates the solidarity party's behavior, in order to bring about the desired "future state of affairs."

On the other hand, APRA also exhibited the characteristics of parties of representation. Haya early proclaimed that the party needed to "ask help of no one,"[51] but it soon resorted to political bargaining, a typical activity of representational parties. Sometime during or after the 1940s the party lost most of its monopolistic tendencies and began in earnest to work within the system rather than against it. Concurrently, the Peruvian political system was evolving in ways more congenial to the party of representation.

APRA presently has large, direct party membership; loose, pyramidal organization; easy discipline (though this is recent); and largely autono-

[50] See note 22 for Apter's typology, to which this discussion refers.
[51] PAP, *El Plan*, p. 31.

mous, functional affiliates related to the party locally—all of which are characteristic of the party of representation. It has always sought to provide education and entertainment as well as certain public services after the same style.

How APRA responded to the challenges presented by almost forty years of Peruvian politics will occupy most of my attention in this book. The period of legality since 1956 is of particular importance. Chapter II will outline the outstanding features of the society and politics of Peru, emphasizing those of special relevance to the mobilization and exclusion processes in relation to the system of interests.

The strategic choices presented to APRA in its pursuit of power are presented systematically in Chapter III. The framework for party decisions is first constructed in terms of attempts to win control of the executive and then analyzed for the preparatory actions implied and the alternative courses permitted by each strategy. The events of 1956–68 provide most of the background for showing what decisions were actually taken.

Chapters IV and V deal with Aprista organizing activities and methods in order to show what the party did and how well it succeeded in marshaling mass support of various kinds. Electoral results and interest-group allegiances are the main indicators of organizational support; party statements and actions suggest the techniques that were used. Both aspects are related to the context of Peruvian society and politics.

The tactics used by the party to promote the application of the Aprista program are the focus of Chapter VI. An assessment is made of the indirect influence of the party and is based on the enactment of legislation throughout its history. Certain substantive areas are surveyed in greater detail for their significance to development. The role of Congress as an instrument of power and reform is studied, with special attention being given to the periods of heaviest Aprista participation, 1945–48 and 1963–68. Chapter VII considers in still further detail the agrarian reform issue, which culminated in congressional adoption of the act of 1964.

Finally, in Chapter VIII the findings regarding APRA are compared with the experiences of the mass reform parties of Bolivia and Venezuela and against those of the Mexican Revolution. The perspective thus provided informs the summary discussion of the process by which political parties of the mass reform type serve as initiators of the development process.

II

SOCIETY AND POLITICS IN PERU

THE OPPORTUNITY FOR A POLITICAL PARTY to act effectively as an instigator of development depends very much upon the nature of the political system in which it operates. Conventional politics, as I have used the term, cannot function in an environment in which parties and interest groups are unable to perform a substantial proportion of the tasks that are peculiar to them.

This condition is typical of societies undergoing accelerated change. Traditional social structures do not generate demands consistent with the needs of newly mobilized elements of the population. Incipient, modern structures have not yet been formed, through the differentiation of individual roles or by the emergence of autonomous subsystems capable of processing such demands. Parties of change labor under serious handicaps.

In a transitional situation such as this, it follows that political calculations must be closely related to trends of social development. Any strategy that does not take account of projected currents of change is likely to be out-dated before it can be fully applied. Moreover, self-regenerative change can either be put to partisan use or become an obstacle to partisan gain, depending upon how the mass reform party responds to it.

Cultural aspects of change are equally significant, but they emerge at the psychological level. Individual attitudes and orientations are the essence of political participation. A voter is hardly capable of exercising a judgment, however, or even of feeling emotion on a political issue, until he becomes aware of himself as a member of the dominant community.

Usually he must first perceive of himself as being subject to the operation of free will as well as the object of blind fate.[1]

Structural and cultural change do not always coincide, nor do they proceed synchronously. Some traditional societies have had the advantage of a gradual secularization of attitudes, accompanying or preceding upheavals of social structure. This sequence tends to produce citizens who are psychologically participant before they accept, or demand, the behavioral modifications that are entailed in the differentiation of roles and structures.

In the world of delayed development the sequence is often the reverse. Shifts in behavior occur (around, if not to, the people involved) before changes in attitude. People who are still psychologically unprepared for modern life may be displaced by forces that require drastic alterations in their accustomed habits. They are in the predicament of the socially mobilized, but not yet culturally re-integrated, masses.[2]

Each of these conditions produces different kinds of social, and therefore political, dependency. The traditional who is excluded from the dominant society is able neither to act politically in his own interest nor to conceive of doing so. The literate peasant or laborer of nineteenth-century Europe or North America, however, was ready to take advantage of reform long before he organized to reduce his economic dependency. But the Latin American *campesino* may remain psychologically dependent long after he has become a plantation or factory wage-earner.

Peru is a country of tradition, which has also known more than a century of transition. The effects of uneven change on the Peruvian political system have not been widely documented. They must be seen largely in the superficial evidence of shifts in the society. This is the human environment in which the Aprista party has functioned. The physical environment is also significant.

The Physical Setting

It is a commonplace to say that geography influences everything in Peru. The usual description begins with the coast, climbs abruptly into the mountains, and descends into the broad jungle of the Amazon headwaters. For purposes of political analysis it is just as important to appreciate certain differences within the first two zones, which are the most thickly populated, as it is to know what divides the three.

The narrow coastal plain is mainly desert, but its broadest expanse is toward the north, where it is also less arid. More of the larger rivers lie

[1] Gabriel A. Almond and G. Bingham Powell, Jr., *Comparative Politics: A Developmental Approach* (Boston: Little, Brown & Co., 1966), pp. 21–57.

[2] Carlos Fuentes, *Washington Post Book Week*, April 24, 1966, pp. 3 and 14; Germani, "Social Change," p. 392.

to the north of Lima than to the south. In the south, spurs or ranges of hills often reach the sea, and the desert seems to invade the mountains.

The Peruvian sierra generally lacks the clear continuity of the Andean cordilleras in Ecuador and Colombia. Three ranges are identifiable, but the portions between the Bolivian border and Cerro de Pasco, in central Peru, appear to be joined at either end. The western cordillera parallels the coast, the central is rather complex, and the eastern is lower.

From the south the major rivers flow northward between the ranges until they near the central sierra in the Department of Junín, where they meet others and break through eastward to the Amazon Basin. Thus, access from the southern coast is limited and travel in the sierra is often parallel to the coastline. From Cerro de Pasco northward the three ranges reappear, the western soon subdividing and the eastern breaking up and diminishing in height, eventually to join the central cordillera near the northern border.

In the north the major intermontane rivers also flow northward and, except for the Santa in the Department of Ancash, turn eastward to the Amazon.[3] The northern sierra therefore tends to be narrower than the southern, and more easily penetrable.

The highlands of Peru are thus divided into at least two isolated regions by the physical "knot" near the juncture of the Departments of Lima, Pasco, Huánuco, and Ancash, whence rivers flow in all directions and roads join the coast, sierra, and selva, but not the central and northern parts of the sierra. The pre-Columbian "north highlands" have been recognized by anthropologists as one of the distinct subdivisions of the central Andes cultural unit. The rest of the Peruvian sierra is divided into the central highlands (from Huánuco to Cuzco) and the southern. The latter encompass the altiplano of southern Peru and parts of Bolivia.[4]

In general, the southern highlands are the least hospitable. Taking the use of Spanish as an indicator of acculturation, there are today three cultural areas, the highland portions of which are somewhat comparable to the three regions just outlined.

To the east of the mountains the selva is the least populated and exploited region of Peru. Four departments lie wholly in this zone, and four others that are generally thought of as highland (Cuzco, Junín, Pasco, and Huánuco) have more than half their territories in the selva.[5]

The physical divisions of Peru that have the greatest significance are the coast and the sierra. More than 89 percent of the population lives there.

[3] Ford, *Man and Land in Peru*, pp. 6, 57–64.

[4] Wendell C. Bennett and Junius B. Bird, *Andean Culture History*, Handbook Series, no. 15 (New York: American Museum of Natural History, 1960), pp. 96–100.

[5] Dario Sainte Marie S., ed., *Peru en Cifras: 1944–45* (Lima: Ediciones Internacionales, n.d.), p. 30.

Sociocultural differences that divide urban and rural life, and political distinctions that set the capital of Lima apart from all provincial areas, tend to reinforce the physical dichotomy.

Rural-Provincial-Sierra

The traditional feudal character of Peruvian society persists in the sierra, and its spirit is still present in most rural areas and provincial towns. More than half the total population lives in the sierra (rural and urban) or in rural areas (coastal-sierra-jungle). In the sierra alone almost 70 percent of the people are rural.[6]

The sierra is predominantly an area of subsistence agriculture, except for the grazing of sheep, alpacas, and llamas, which produces substantial wool exports. Minerals are mined in enclaves of limited extent and contribute to the commercialization of a few areas. Copper is normally Peru's largest single export by value (closely followed by fishmeal), amounting to about 20 percent of the total.

Migration has been draining people from most parts of the sierra for decades, mainly toward the coast, but also to some parts of the selva. Still, it was not enough to balance population growth in the sierra, for every department in the country experienced net increases in population between the 1940 and 1961 censuses.

The Indian

The largest population group in the country is composed of rural and largely traditional Indians. The Indian population not only is at the bottom of the class structure, but is almost completely isolated from it as a separate society. The inferior position of the Indian, however, tends to obscure his pursuit of a distinct way of life. For an Indian, whatever his personal attributes, is regarded as only an Indian. This is not caste exclusion; movement into the mestizo community is unrestricted by law or custom. The Indian has only to change his way of life—family ties and economic considerations permitting—to enter the bottom of the dominant structure.[7]

As long as he remains in his agricultural village or hacienda in the sierra, however, the Indian is likely to remain a non-participant in the market economy or national political life which revolve around the heavily

[6] CIDA, *Tenencia de la Tierra y Desarrollo Socio-Económico del Sector Agrícola: Perú* (Washington, D.C.: Unión Panamericana, 1966), pp. 250–51.

[7] Karl M. Schmitt and David D. Burks, *Evolution or Chaos: Dynamics of Latin American Government and Politics* (New York: Frederick A. Praeger, 1963), p. 91. The authors suggest the separateness of the Indian community by speaking of "horizontal" movement into western society.

urbanized, mestizo coast. The "Indian type" is "isolated . . . characterized by loyalty to a local community, local endogamy, lack of knowledge of life outside of the community or hacienda . . . and occupational and social ties to agriculture and land." Clothing and customs complete the picture: black ponchos for men, multiple skirts for women, locally made hats and sandals for both; coca-chewing by men, the carrying of swaddled babies by women; a diet of grain gruels and certain other "Indian" dishes.[8]

Even thus strictly defined, the Indian population is estimated at about one-third of the national total, or 3.5 million in 1961, including some who speak Spanish as a second language. All Indians are agriculturalists, but not all are any longer in actual or legal possession of land, either privately held or communal. The traditional and idealized situation is rare, that in which a group, numbering from twenty to a thousand families, retains possession of "ancestral" lands and cultivates or pastures a part or all in common. Much more usual are individual landholding or legal communities which have lost actual possession of land to a large estate, except as small parcels are ceded temporarily to individuals in return for various combinations of rent, labor, and crop shares.[9]

The Indian's relationship to the rest of the rural community is a demonstration of social dependency. At best, he is at the mercy of the mestizo; at worst, he is almost a serf tied to the land of a patron. The *latifundio* has been called "perhaps the greatest barrier to any change in this social system."[10]

Economic dependency is evident even in one of the more independent villages, where family heads still at times have to work for wages. If some Indians can leave their families, for the off season or longer, they earn

[8] William Mangin, "Sociological, Cultural and Political Characteristics of Some Rural Indians and Urban Migrants in Peru," prepared for the Wenner-Gren Foundation for Anthropological Research Symposium No. 26, August 27–September 8, 1964, p. 8; CIDA (*Tierra y Dessarrollo*, p. 123) estimates those "living under the communal regime" at between 2.5 and 4 million. Others put the figure as low as 1.5 million, probably using the strictly legal definition of Indian community. See Richard W. Patch, "How Communal are the Communities?" *American Universities Field Service Report*, RWP–5–'59, June 12, 1959, p. 10 (hereafter cited as *AUFS*). The 1940 census listed about 2,850,000 as "indigenous"; the 1961 census did not ask the racial question. See Union Panamericana, *Estudio Social de America Latina:* 1962 (Washington, D.C., 1964), pp. 180–82, and William W. Stein, *Hualcan: Life in the Highlands of Peru* (Ithaca, N.Y.: Cornell University Press, 1961), pp. 226–27. See also Allan R. Holmberg, "Changing Community Attitudes and Values in Peru: A Case Study in Guided Change," in Richard N. Adams *et al.*, *Social Change in Latin America Today* (New York: Harper & Row, for the Council on Foreign Relations, 1960), p. 68; he and others point out that the distinction is cultural, not primarily racial.

[9] Ford, *Man and Land in Peru*, pp. 72ff.; CIDA, *Tierra y Desarrollo*, pp. 122ff., also analyzed the tenure systems, but in more detail, by regions and sample cases, and examined the Indian communities as separate phenomena.

[10] Holmberg, "Changing Community Attitudes," pp. 73–74.

higher wages at distant points. In the long term, property binds them to the village. The landless, on the other hand, are obliged to rely on the nearby hacienda for their livelihood. An older son might go away to work, but eventually he must choose either the life of the displaced or the traditional values of wife and land in his home village.[11]

Relations with mestizos ordinarily are shunned by the Indians. Legal suits over land, however, are both a burden and source of hope to the communities and to individuals. Indians also seek "protectors" in the outside community through the relationship of *compadrazgo*. This is effective only so long as it does not conflict with relationships among mestizos.[12]

Change is not excluded from the sierra, but for the most part it occurs at the edges. From the coast, acculturation spreads inland along access routes and around enclaves of technological development (such as mines). Both the concentration of Indians in the sierra and the progression of change are strikingly revealed in the census statistics on languages. In Table II-1 the largest departments have been grouped by language characteristics into three categories. (Peru has 144 provinces and 23 departments plus the constitutional province of Callao.)

In the southern sierra, about 10 percent of the people speak Spanish exclusively. More than 60 percent speak only Indian languages (mostly Quechua, or Aymará in the far south). The other one-quarter to one-third are bilingual. All five of the contiguous, predominantly highland departments in the south fall into this group.

To a lesser extent, four central sierra departments retain a marked Indian influence but can only be termed mestizo in character. Spanish monolinguals do not exceed 40 percent in this area, while Indian speakers do not reach that proportion. Bilingual speakers fall in the range of from 30 to 50 percent. Here the tendency toward balance is most striking.

All other departments have predominantly Spanish-speaking populations, varying from 60 to 100 percent. All are coastal, northern sierra, or jungle departments. Some that have sierra provinces or receive many migrants include up to 12 percent Indian monolinguals and close to 30

[11] Stein, *Hualcan*, pp. 13–66 and *passim*.

[12] *Ibid.*, pp. 180, 201, 335; Richard W. Patch, "Life in a Peruvian Indian Community," *AUFS*, RWP-1-'62, January, 1962, p. 6. Both Stein (*Hualcan*, pp. 40–41) and Ford (*Man and Land in Peru*, pp. 89–90, 111) make interesting comparisons with early twentieth-century landlord-sharecropper relations in the southern United States. The *New York Times* made a similar point in 1962, observing that, "as we have discovered with integration in the United States, nothing is harder than a peaceful social transformation" such as the Alliance for Progress requires in Peruvian society (quoted in Richard H. Hawkins, Jr., "The Washington-Lima Crisis of 1962: A Historical Perspective," Senior Seminar in Foreign Policy, Foreign Service Institute, Washington, D.C., May, 1963.

TABLE II–1: LANGUAGE AREAS OF PERU

Department	1961 Population	Percentages in Department Speaking: Spanish Only[a]	Spanish-Indian (Bilingual)	Indian Only
Indian	2,300,000			
Apurímac		5	24	71
Ayacucho		6	28	66
Huancavelica		7	31	62
Puno		6	33	61
Cuzco		11	29	60
Mestizo	1,600,000			
Pasco		36	50	14
Junín		40	49	11
Huánuco		30	38	32
Ancash		34	30	36
Spanish[b]	6,000,000			
Piura		100	—	—
La Libertad		100	—	—
Cajamarca		98	2	—
Lambayeque		96	2	2
Callao		92	8	—
Ica		84	15	1
Lima		84	15	1
Loreto		83	12	5
Arequipa		67	25	8
Moquegua		60	28	12

Source: Magali Sarfatti Larson and Arlene Eisen Bergman, *Social Stratification in Peru*, Politics of Modernization Series, no. 5 (Berkeley: University of California, Institute of International Studies, 1969), pp. 363–64.

[a] Residual.

[b] Omitting five departments with a combined population of about 400,000 in 1961, all of which fall into the Spanish group.

percent bilinguals. Figure II–1 shows graphically the distinctive features of the three groupings, including the tendency toward greater diversity among departments within each group as acculturation increases.[13]

Some degree of change thus occurs independently of migration. Undoubtedly it happens very slowly. In the two decades between the 1940 and 1961 censuses, for example, none of the percentages defining the outer limits of the language areas in Table II–1 shifted by more than about twenty points. More rapid and drastic change requires migration toward the centers of the dominant culture.

[13] Language is not a perfect indicator of "Indianism" or of acculturation, but anthropologists come closer to agreement on this than on any other superficial test of identity.

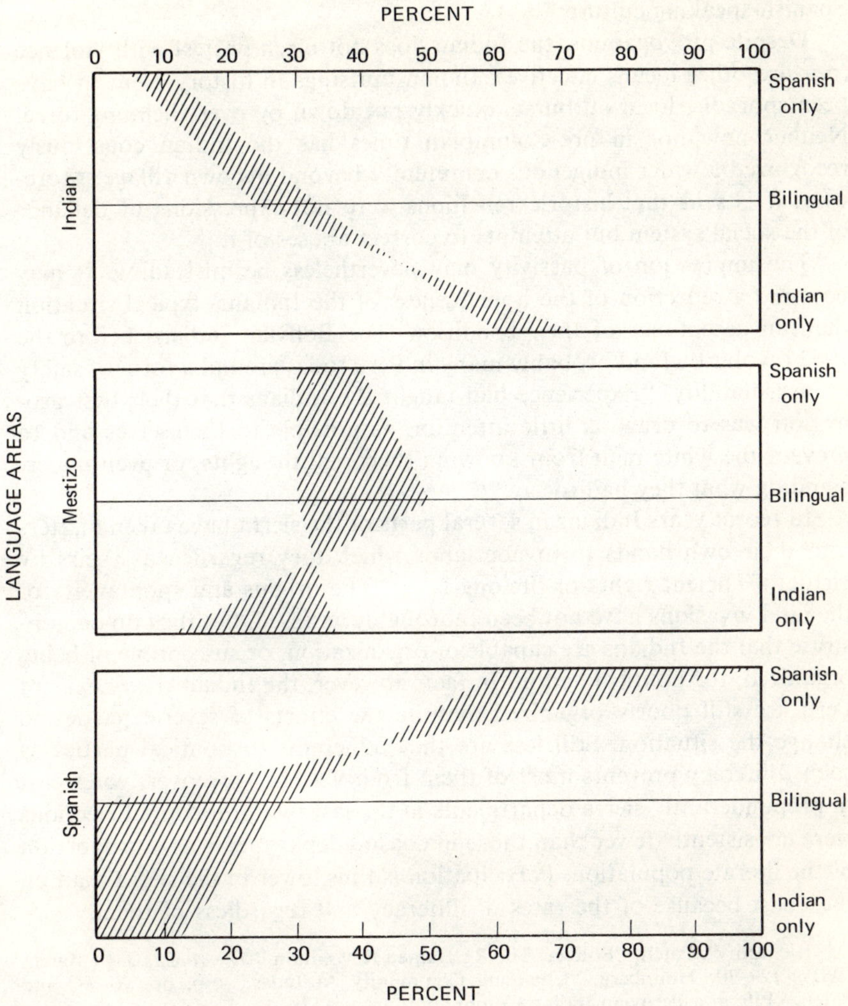

Note: Only the extreme values are plotted in each category.

FIGURE II–1. LANGUAGE PROFILES (FROM TABLE II–1)

Contrasting patterns of change have been found when comparing villages of Peru and Bolivia. In the Peruvian sierra the normal pattern of change requires an Indian to leave his home village, reject his Indian background, and enter the lowest level of mestizo society. In Bolivia, however, after the revolution of 1952, Indians underwent acculturation as entire communities began to "display behavior characteristics of the dominant Spanish-speaking culture."[14]

Despite provocations, the Indian does not often protest with violence (nor are other means effective). Indian uprisings in history seem to have been sporadic, local outbursts quickly put down by overwhelming force. Neither now nor in pre-Columbian times has the Indian consciously recognized a wider indigenous community beyond his own village. Moreover, it is said that historic rebellions were not expressions of defiance of the social system but attempts to correct abuses of it.[15]

The impression of passivity may nevertheless be misleading. It may be more a reflection of the hopelessness of the Indians' typical situation than an acceptance of their condition. The Bolivian Indians before the 1952 revolution (and probably many in Peru today) found a form of safety in inscrutability. "Experience had taught the Indians that their best protection was to draw as little attention as possible to themselves and to prevent the white man from knowing their real thoughts, or even understanding what they had to say."[16]

In recent years Indians in several parts of the sierra have taken matters into their own hands to invade lands which they regarded as theirs by virtue of ancient rights or lifelong labor. The origins and spontaneity of the land invasions have not been thoroughly assessed, but they do demonstrate that the Indians are capable of organization, or susceptible of being organized, for political action. In fact, however, the Indian *campesinos* of Peru are still poorly organized, despite the efforts of several parties to change the situation. Still less are they adherents to political parties as such. Illiteracy prevents most of them from voting. Moreover, votes cast in preponderantly sierra departments in the last two presidential elections were consistently fewer than those in coastal departments as a proportion of the literate population. Participation is thus lower in the sierra than on the coast because of the rates of illiteracy and regardless of them.[17]

[14] Richard W. Patch, "Bolivia: The Restrained Revolution," *The Annals* 334 (March, 1961): 129–30; Holmberg, "Changing Community Attitudes," esp. pp. 70–78; and Patch, "Life in a Peruvian Indian Community," esp. p. 28.

[15] Ciro Alegría has tellingly pictured the Indians' problem of protest in books such as *Broad and Alien Is the World*, trans. Harriet de Onis (New York: Farrar & Rinehart, 1941). See also Stein, *Hualcan*, p. 11; Plank, "Peru," pp. 56–57; and Larson and Bergman, *Social Stratification in Peru*, pp. 32–36. Information is scarce because of the lack of contemporary news reports. According to Jorge Basadre, the protests were peculiar to certain localities and were responses to flagrant abuses of land tenure (interview, Lima, March 1, 1966).

[16] Robert J. Alexander, *The Bolivian National Revolution* (New Brunswick, N.J.: Rutgers University Press, 1958), p. xiv.

[17] Calculated from Unión Panamericana, "El Censo de América," *Noticiero No. 91* (Washington, D.C.), October 12, 1964, and election data published in *La Prensa* (Lima), June 21, 1963, p. 2.

Provincial Lower Classes

The Indian *campesino* knows how to move toward the dominant society. He does not normally migrate directly to Lima, despite stories to that effect. He is more likely to move first to a nearby plantation or provincial town. If he stays, he becomes a cholo.

Cholos represent the transitional group moving toward the status of mestizo. Upward mobility is facilitated primarily by change of occupation. The shift may not be made in one generation, but the cholo can be sure that his children will enjoy mestizo status if they desire it.

To make the transition, the aspirant must learn Spanish, drop most of his Indian customs and clothing, and take up non-agricultural work. Identification with mestizos, at least by living in a non-Indian town or village or on the outskirts of a local capital, is crucial. "Yet . . . ties are not severed with home affairs" completely, and cholos may return to their home villages for fiestas.[18]

The migration from Indian to mestizo society generally flows from the sierra to the coast and to parts of the selva. The most remote sierra departments appear to have served as places of origin. They have experienced net migration losses ranging from 10 to more than 20 percent. Other departments, nearer the coast or having larger cities, serve as way stations, with turnover in both directions running from 10 to more than 20 percent, but with net losses of less than 10 percent. The Lima-Callao metropolis has been the major ultimate destination.[19]

This is the propulsive side of social mobilization which some writers claim is changing the nature of Peruvian society. Population pressures and the inelasticity of arable land in the highlands, combined with the attractions of the coast, exert a "push-pull" effect on those who find themselves at the crossover point of local disadvantage and freedom from binding obligations.[20]

Cultural change has also spread further into the provincial lower classes. In some parts of the northern sierra the process of Hispanization has produced a high level of true illiteracy (as opposed to the preliteracy of the Indians). In one of the most mountainous departments, where almost everyone speaks Spanish, only 45 percent of the population was counted

[18] Stein, *Hualcan*, pp. 226–27; Mangin, "Rural Indians and Urban Migrants," p. 9. The term "cholo" has several meanings, but I use it as quoted from Stein's text. Luís Valcárcel notes that family members of migrants already established in the city may come directly from the sierra (interview, Lima, March 2, 1966).

[19] Larson and Bergman, *Social Stratification in Peru*, p. 309.

[20] *Ibid.*, pp. 141, 62ff.; Francois Bourricaud, *Poder y Sociedad en el Perú Contemporáneo*, trans. Roberto Bixio (Buenos Aires: Sur, 1967), pp. 11ff.; Carlos A. Astiz, *Pressure Groups and Power Elites in Peruvian Politics* (Ithaca, N.Y.: Cornell University Press, 1969), p. 53.

as literate in 1961. This kind of social mobilization may relate to the economic process of "proletarianization" by which sierra peasants have lost or sold their possessions and gone to work permanently on haciendas or plantations.[21]

Psychological identity may be the key to the social status of the mobilized provincial lower classes. In the past the shift from lower-class cholo to middle-class mestizo has been primarily an economic, or occupational, change, just as the transition from Indian to cholo is a matter of dress and language.[22] Some recent studies also have revealed a tendency on the part of residents of certain sierra towns to call themselves Indians, or cholos, as frequently as mestizos.[23] This suggests that acculturation is not uniformly toward established racial stereotypes in sierra communities long exposed to outside influences.

Lower-class provincials generally are more likely to organize than are Indians. They make up most of the membership of the few *campesino* and trade-union organizations that are found in the provinces. Rarely would the average cholo attain the militancy of the miners or the sugar and petroleum workers. Even if they are literate and can vote, they retain most of the limitations of cultural immobilism and economic dependency upon mestizo society.

The Provincial Middle Class

The rural and provincial middle class is perhaps most easily identified. Objective standards, such as occupation or property, combine to set apart the groups that are neither affluent nor poverty-stricken. They range from 15 to 20 percent of the population as one moves from the most rural to the most urban departments outside the Lima-Callao area.[24]

Tax records indicate that a concentration of property within the most wealthy layers of the population in the 1920s tended to decrease from the coast to the isolated parts of the sierra. A kind of "downward mobility"

[21] CIDA, *Tierra y Desarrollo*, pp. 299–300. See also Jorge Basadre, *Historia de la República del Perú*, 5th ed., vol. 10 (Lima: Ediciones "Histórica," 1964), p. 4688; he states that "in the central sierra, in large part, and above all in the northern sierra the Indians have been 'Hispanized'."

[22] Plank, "Peru," pp. 119–20.

[23] William F. Whyte and Lawrence K. Williams, "The Use of Questionnaire Surveys for Community Studies of Culture Change and Economic Development" (Paper delivered at the Sixty-third Annual Meeting of the American Anthropological Association, Detroit, November 21, 1964), pp. 2–8, 14–19.

[24] Larson and Bergman, *Social Stratification in Peru*, pp. 370–79. Their data on social stratification were rearranged by ranking departments of the country according to rural-urban proportions to arrive at this approximation.

from wealthy provincial families into the "squirearchy," military officer corps, etc., may have produced this leveling tendency.[25]

Rural class divisions also can be seen in the statistics of farms of a size adequate to support a family. The actual number of such farms on the coast and in the sierra exceeds 10 percent of all farms in each region, but in neither does the total area in family farms exceed 5 percent of the respective totals. This means that the average single-family farm is considerably smaller than the regional mean for all farms. Multifamily farms (separate from estates) are still fewer, but on the average are larger than the regional mean.[26] These might be the property of the very small upper middle class.

White collar employees, the bulk of any urban middle class in Latin America, number some 323,000 in Peru. Of these, only 14 percent are located in "rural" areas. Public white collar employees are spread throughout the most rural departments in fairly uniform numbers. They comprise from 2 to 3 percent of the economically active population, compared to from 6 to 7 percent in Lima-Callao and a national average of about 4 percent.

Private white collar employees vary much more widely between rural and urban areas, falling to less than half the number of public employees in the most rural departments but outnumbering them by 50 percent for the whole country.[27] Taken together, these data help to confirm the expectation that the stable middle class in rural-provincial Peru is very small and is concentrated in conventional occupations.

Attitudes of the conventional middle class are comparable to those of the upper class. In a mestizo town in the north-central sierra, for example, a Peruvian anthropologist found a tendency to identify all the potential middle class as either "white" (which is a synonym for elite) or "white cholos" (including actual cholos).[28]

Undoubtedly most of the provincial middle class would fit the description of "groups which have the superficial characteristics of the middle

[25] David Chaplin, "Industrialization and the Distribution of Wealth in Peru," mimeographed (Madison: University of Wisconsin, Land Tenure Center, RP no. 18, July, 1966), pp. 17–20; telephone interview with David Chaplin, February 17, 1966; and *idem*, *The Peruvian Industrial Labor Force* (Princeton: Princeton University Press, 1967).

[26] CIDA, *Tierra y Desarrollo*, pp. 57, 109, 203. The definitions of family farms take account of differences in soils, moisture, and land uses among the three regions. Case investigations reported by CIDA further undermine any supposition that owners of family farms are, in general, middle class in attitude or well-being.

[27] Unión Panamericana, "El Censo de América," *Noticiero No. 93*, December 4, 1964, by calculation; Larson and Bergman, *Social Stratification in Peru*, p. 327.

[28] Humberto Ghersi Barrera, "El Indígena y el Mestizo en la Comunidad de Marcará," *Revista del Museo Nacional* (Lima) 29 (1960): 63–64, 126–27.

class" but lack the dynamic of reform generally associated with it elsewhere. Its attitudes are those of intrinsic conservatism, respect for hierarchy, admiration of the aristocracy, and a "vehement desire to rise and be accepted by those they regard as their superiors," in contrast to the European middle class, the emerging members of which had "a consciousness of independent status and . . . were anti-aristocratic and anti-traditionalist."[29]

The Provincial Upper Class

In contraposition to the Indian type in traditional Peruvian society stands the *hacendado*, aristocratic owner of the large estate from which landless workers draw a semifeudal existence outside the money economy of the country. The stereotype persists, but the estate owner is no longer the most significant economic power as such.

The dominance of sierra agriculture began to recede more than a century ago, with the export of guano and saltpeter and the entry of foreign capital to exploit the coastal deposits. José Carlos Mariátegui, the Marxist writer of the 1920s, described the new capitalist group. The members were linked in "origin and structure with the aristocracy," but within the capitalist class "the old aristocracy ceased to dominate as it had previously."[30]

On the coast the traditional landowner has almost disappeared because of the general process of modernization of sugar and cotton plantations.[31] Other influences have long been operating against the maintenance of a landed aristocracy in the sierra. Inheritance laws, and "the biologically variable sex ratio together with the dowry system," made it highly likely that a large estate would break up and pass from the aristocratic paternal line in several generations.[32]

[29] Claudio Véliz, "Obstáculos a la reforma en la América Latina," *Foro Internacional* (México, D.F.), January-March, 1964, quoted in Sacha Volman, "Quién Impondrá la Democracia?" *Panoramas* 3, no. 16 (July-August, 1965): 27–29. See also Larson and Bergman, *Social Stratification in Peru*, pp. 115–24.

[30] José Carlos Mariátegui, *Siete Ensayos de Interpretación de la Realidad Peruana* (Lima: Empresa Editora Amauta, 1964), pp. 17 and 21. The discovery of the coastal guano and saltpeter had two effects on the Peruvian economy which are still visible today. Their location accentuated the dualism between coast and sierra (unlike gold, silver, and other minerals that had attracted the Spaniards to the sierra), and the entry of foreign, especially British, capital gave the coastal region a strong position in the economy (*ibid.*, pp. 18 and 24).

[31] Ford, *Man and Land in Peru*, p. 67. See also CIDA, *Tierra y Desarrollo*, for a detailed analysis of tenure systems. Very large estates on the coast are considered to fall into either the *commercial* or the *transitional* category. "The so-called *traditional latifundio*, where the strongest vestiges of feudalism prevail . . . has no significance on the Peruvian coast, as opposed to the situation in the sierra where it is typical" (*ibid.*, p. 59).

[32] David Chaplin, "Socio-Economic Structural Changes in Twentieth Century Peru," mimeographed, 1963 (personal copy from the author), p. 11; see also Chaplin, "Wealth in Peru," p. 22.

The actual owner of a sierra estate is very likely to be a resident of the provincial, or even the national, capital. Some who acquire wealth by other means buy land for prestige or security.[33] Concentration of ownership continues, but its power is symbolic.

URBAN-CAPITAL-COASTAL

The dominant side of the Peruvian society, economy, and political system is seen in urban rather than rural life, the capital city of Lima in contrast to even the urban areas in the provinces, and the coastal region as opposed to the sierra. The Indian is the most numerous element of the rural-provincial-sierra population; the relatively few whites hold most of the economic power and have traditionally tended to dominate the country.

The Economic Elites

Our interest in the upper class is political. Studies of the political functioning of the so-called oligarchy, however, are hardly complete or precise enough to support useful discussion. Nor is the old aristocracy necessarily relevant politically. "Wealth and privilege" (social status) cannot be automatically equated with "power and prestige" (political influence), especially if the class system itself is not threatened.[34]

The economic basis is therefore the best available, and, to the extent that major economic interests would be threatened by reform, it is probably valid for this purpose. A key question is the extent to which differentiation of economic interests has produced a division of political interests, which would tend to reduce private resistance to reform.

The traditional linkage of family and property, Bell says, had economic, moral, and class justifications. When power (which in Peru no longer meant land) could not be transmitted to one's heirs, but came to reside in technical skills, the alliance between family and property should have broken down.[35] In Peru, one would expect to find in the entrepreneurial activities employing higher degrees of technology or managerial skills a differentiation of interest from that of the traditional aristocracy.

In fact, the capital needed to finance such technology has supplanted land as the necessary factor. Concentration of capital has tended to cancel out differentiation of economic activity. The process began with the pro-

[33] Chaplin, "Structural Changes." Chaplin traces one such migration from the southern sierra to Arequipa and Lima, and attributes it to rural violence late in the nineteenth century. Another current moved to Lima after 1920; see Ford, *Man and Land in Peru*, pp. 76–77.

[34] Bell, *End of Ideology*, p. 60.

[35] *Ibid.*, pp. 37–42.

vincial upper class, as already described. Sugar and cotton investments are now thought to dominate other sectors and even to have largely absorbed the recently developed fishmeal industry through banking, insurance, and trade. What was once viewed hopefully as the national bourgeoisie that would develop Peru and liberate it from foreign economic domination is now lumped with the traditional upper class as "export-oriented capital."[36]

The Peruvian upper class thus has an absorbing, rather than a blocking, effect on dynamic elements from below. This has prevented "the development of a completely separate, innovationally and socially oriented dynamic elite."[37] The result is a high degree of correspondence between social status and economic power. As in southern Europe, new forms of enterprise did not immediately break the tie between family and property, and anachronistic family businesses could persist.[38] In Peru, such family connections serve to create and re-inforce conglomerate business alliances which preserve the power of the upper class over the administration of wealth.[39]

The absorptive capacity of the economic elites is not confined to Peruvians. In common with Argentina, Chile, and Brazil, Peru has received a significant, though much smaller, group of immigrants from non-Iberian Europe. The surnames of such families can be identified in a number of the business activities already mentioned, which are thought to have succeeded due to the immigrants' "propensity to technological advance."[40] In the textile industry, for example, it was discovered that "very few of the owners and virtually none of the managers or technicians were *native Peruvians* in a cultural sense. . . . Peru experienced very little white immigration after 1800—but the few who came . . . did not have to acculturate fully as the price for acceptance and upward mobility and so they therefore

[36] Larson and Bergman, *Social Stratification in Peru*, pp. 258ff.

[37] Alvin Cohen, "The Technology/Elite Approach to the Developmental Process: Peruvian Case Study," *Economic Development and Cultural Change* 14, no. 3 (April, 1966) : 325–26; Larson and Bergman, *Social Stratification in Peru*, p. 290.

[38] Lipset, "Political Cleavages," pp. 28–29. Basadre (*Historia* 10 : 4699–733) stresses the drastic effects of price fluctuations, especially before World War I, in overturning traditional sources of power in favor of exporters and foreign capital, but states that "the society continued to be characterized by a seignorial structure."

[39] Bourricaud, *Poder y Sociedad*, pp. 32–42; Astiz, *Pressure Groups*, pp. 48–57, 190.

[40] Cohen, "Technology/Elite Approach," p. 7. He adds that the white, European origin of the immigrants facilitated their acceptance by the elite where lower-class, mestizo Peruvians might have had more difficulty. Distinguishing between this "economic elite" and the absorptive capacities of the "social elite," Cohen stresses the aristocratic practice of marrying within the group (*ibid.*, p. 8).

have exerted an influence out of all proportion to their numbers."[41] To the immigrant impact is added the cosmopolitan flavor of alien managers of foreign investments and the European orientation of the social elite.

Industry is included in the linkage. The largest group of industrial ownership interests apparently grew from small mercantile establishments by way of financial institutions, or from small factories. Some new industrialists have also acquired agricultural property. Those who lacked social status now enjoy it without discrimination due to origins. A medium-sized group with direct ties to the old aristocracy came to industry by way of coastal plantations and financial interests. A smaller group which went into manufacturing directly includes some who are highly important economically but not uniformly accepted socially.[42]

The size and significance of the industrial sector in the economy of Peru is open to question. Its impact through employment is limited by the fact that only about 4 percent of the labor force works in factories employing more than twenty workers. The industrial product (about one-fifth of the gross national product) is heavily concentrated in light consumer goods such as clothing, foodstuffs, beverages, etc. The administrators of domestic capital thus have not ventured generally into manufacturing for import substitution, nor are they likely to do so as long as the proceeds of exports are freely usable to finance imports.[43]

The Urban Middle Sectors

The Peruvian middle class is not as easily identified in the capital as it is in the provinces. By occupation it could be estimated at around 30 percent of the population of Lima-Callao and more than 20 percent in other leading cities. Dichotomous tendencies in social stratification, however, cause the middle class to be "neither well defined nor well developed.

[41] Chaplin, "Structural Changes," p. 3; see also Chaplin, "Wealth in Peru," pp. 24–25. Basadre (*Historia* 10: 4685–86, 4734) cites "the heterogeneous and mobile plutocracy which began to predominate . . ." but puts less stress on non-Iberian origins. He found many non-Spanish names in the post-1900 cabinets, however.

[42] These were preliminary indications from a survey by William P. Glade, University of Wisconsin, as relayed in a letter dated January 21, 1966, and supplemented by a telephone interview on February 17, 1966. See also William P. Glade, *The Latin American Economies: A Study of Their Institutional Evolution* (New York: American Book Co., 1969).

[43] Bourricaud, *Poder y Sociedad*, pp. 193–203; Astiz, *Pressure Groups*, pp. 61–64; William P. Glade and Jon G. Udell, "The Marketing Concept and Economic Development: Peru," *Journal of Inter-American Studies* 10, no. 4 (October, 1968): 533–46.

. . . It is almost without class feeling." Some question whether it exists at all as a functioning unit of the Peruvian system.[44]

As a product of change in the large cities, the middle class includes elements that are diverse if not actually antagonistic. In Latin America generally, and in Peru as well, it is divided into two groups. A very small, but growing, element is dynamic and technologically inclined, and provides many of the managers of industrial and business enterprises. The other element, the great majority, "continues vegetating in the professions" fighting for clientele, or is reduced to living as civil servants subject to political patronage.[45]

The basic differences in outlook between Latin American and other middle classes are summed up in the attitude of *huachafo*, the aping of the aristocracy and dissociation from the mass of workers and artisans, often without the economic means of maintaining the pretended level. In general, the middle class is characterized by the fragility of its economic independence and by close ties with the state.[46] These conditions have come to give the Latin American middle class a conformist, even parasitic, quality. It has increased in numbers and material comforts, but at the expense of the submerged masses, because over-all production has not kept pace with population growth.[47] The development of the middle class has been described in these terms:

> The cities of Latin America grew as they did on the income arising from the exports of primary products and foodstuffs. . . . Vast urban centres harboured a highly literate, perceptive, and self-conscious professional and bureaucratic middle class which also looked towards Europe for inspiration. . . .
> . . . Industrialization in Latin America is neither the product of the activities of a rising industrial bourgeoisie nor has it produced one. . . . The politically influential and now economically powerful urban middle class has moved on to conquer social prestige, the final summit in their ascent.[48]

Another segment of the middle class is the displaced provincial aristocracy which has moved to Lima or other coastal cities:

> The status in Lima of these provincials, separated from their old symbols and without means for the new, is precarious. . . . They buoy up their

[44] Schmitt and Burks, *Evolution or Chaos*, pp. 28–29; Richard W. Patch, "The Peruvian Elections of 1963," *AUFS*, RWP–1–'63, July, 1963.

[45] Eudocio Ravines, *La Gran Promesa* (Madrid: Aguilar, 1963), pp. 83–84.

[46] Basadre, *Historia* 10: 4746.

[47] Alba, *Alliance Without Allies*, p. 92.

[48] Claudio Véliz, ed., *Obstacles to Change in Latin America* (London: Oxford University Press, 1965), pp. 3–7. This is applicable to Peru, although written of Latin America in general.

struggling sense of position by bringing domestic servants direct from peonage on their old lands to Lima. . . . The young must not only profess but practice their professions in competiton with many others. They are forced to recognize that their status in the large hierarchy is low; but this does not destroy their belief in the hierarchy, their fatalism if they do not move up, their hope in upward mobility through help from family or friends (or party), or their faith in the formal act.[49]

Psychological, if not economic, dependence keeps middle-class professionals in the large cities:

Lima is in the process of becoming top heavy with lawyers who provoke disputes to stimulate business, physicians who are miserably paid but who remain in Lima rather than become "provincials" (where they are badly needed), and university professors who enter politics to supplement their meager stipends. . . . The result has been to inhibit the formation of a middle economic class and to force a hothouse growth of a professional class with an insufficient economic base.[50]

These evocative accounts suggest the continuation of a high degree of dependency among large sections of the conventional middle class. The more dynamic elements have not been well identified, much less enumerated. More important, in any event, may be the dynamism of the economically lower-class residents of the *barriadas* (shantytowns).

The Urban Lower Classes

Migration has been making of Lima and other coastal cities the fastest-growing large population centers in Peru. The attractions are only relative. The cities offer more than the precarious existence in the sierra, but they cannot really absorb most of the new arrivals.

The migrants get to the large cities mainly via provincial towns or the coastal and jungle plantations that hire for wages.[51] Lima-Callao alone

[49] Richard W. Patch, "New Techniques and Old Ideas: The Inertia of Attitudes as Observed in Peru," *AUFS*, RWP–5–'64, August, 1964, pp. 12–14.

[50] Richard W. Patch, "Life in a *Callejón*," *AUFS*, RWP–6–'61, June, 1961, p. 24.

[51] Guillermo Briones and José Mejía Valera, *El Obrero Industrial: Aspectos Sociales del Desarrollo Económico en el Perú* (Lima: Instituto de Investigaciones Sociológicas, Universidad Nacional de San Marcos, 1964), pp. 11–15. This survey of industrial workers in the Lima-Callao area showed that more than 60 percent of those sampled were born outside the Department of Lima. Of these, from 20 to 30 percent migrated to the city via one or more intermediate stops. Most of them had been in Lima for more than ten years, indicating that few recent migrants get work in industry. Chaplin found that textile workers come mainly from urbanized areas and that recent rural migrants concentrate in "entry occupations" such as construction, domestic work, or the armed services. See David Chaplin, "A Discussion of Major Issues Arising in the Recruitment of Industrial Labor in Peru," mimeographed (Madison: University of Wisconsin, Land Tenure Center, LTC no. 16, April, 1966), pp. 11–14; see also Mangin, "Rural Indians and Urban Migrants," p. 9.

gained more than one million residents between 1940 and 1961. The majority of the population of the capital is said to live in one kind of slum or another. Those who inhabit improvised *barriadas* in Lima-Callao are estimated at about 450,000. For the country as a whole the figure is put at more than 850,000 *barriada*-dwellers.[52]

A sketch of life in one of Lima's *callejones* (inner-city slums) presents a picture of overwhelming social disorganization and institutional breakdown. The men are distinguished neither by specific occupations or degrees of skill nor by origins on the coast or in the sierra. Their average stay in the *callejón* is more than ten years.

The mother is the only semistable family element. The supportive ties of ceremonial kinship have disappeared along with much of religious observance, and even drunkenness has changed from a social and ritual distribution of surplus wealth into a solitary means of losing consciousness. Most of the residents seem to aspire to rewards which are only material, or status (doctor, engineer) obtainable by large material expenditures."[53]

The move from the *callejón* to the *barriada* brings little or no physical improvement, and may represent a decline, but it appears to be a step toward a new integration into society. Family life still is by no means on a middle-class standard, but about three-fourths of the children in a typical *barriada* were in 1966 in the households of their own parents, and almost the same proportion of couples reported themselves formally married. The highest-paid residents might be regarded as having attained middle-class status.

Extended kinship groups are not as important in the *barriadas* as in the sierra villages, and residents have considerable choice among other contacts, including the *barriada* tenants' association, visiting in Lima, work-connected associations such as trade unions, regional-origin clubs, or visits to hometowns in the provinces. Almost ten years after the initial invasion of one *barriada* took place, a growing pride in the Indian language and culture was noted, together with a vague sense of group identity and the emergence of cholo and Indian leaders, all of which conveyed the impression of a community structure and movement.[54]

In the *callejones* and in the *barriadas*, parents hold exaggerated hopes for their children. Only 26 percent of a group of industrial workers sampled

[52] Mangin, "Rural Indians and Urban Migrants," pp. 3–4; Patch, "Life in a *Callejón*," pp. 1–3; CIDA, *Tierra y Desarrollo*, pp. 258–59. This does not include half a million in other dwellings regarded as marginal, nor does it take account of the prevailing rural housing and sanitary conditions. See Bourricaud, *Poder y Sociedad*, pp. 114–15, and Astiz, *Pressure Groups*, p. 220.

[53] This sketch summarizes Patch's account in "Life in a *Callejón*," pp. 1–3, 19–24.

[54] Mangin, "Rural Indians and Urban Migrants," esp. pp. 4–13, 22–37; William Mangin and Jerome Cohen, "Cultural and Psychological Characteristics of Mountain Migrants to Lima, Peru," *Sociologus* 14, no. 1 (1964): 81–88, esp. 84–86.

by Briones and Mejía Valera had attended secondary school, but age groups showed a marked progression. Almost three-fourths of them desired (possibly in the abstract) university education for their children. Of the first five vocations to which they would have their children aspire, only one (mechanic) was manual in nature; the others were doctor, engineer, lawyer, and professor.[55]

Thus, some of the vain aspirations of the middle class are shared by the lower classes. Moreover, there has been " 'too much' migration to the city in terms of available work. As a result the only occupations which seem to be able to 'give' endlessly, street vending, begging and domestic services, are being irrationally fractionalized to absorb the surplus."[56]

The valid distinction between the two elements of the urban lower class is that the *callejones* represent stability to the point of stagnation, from which there is no escape except by physical mobility. The *barriadas*, on the other hand, are transitional. The object of moving there is often to get tenuous title to, or at least possession of, a piece of land. *Barriadas* are progressively improved, through self-help or pressures for public services. To the extent that any exists, they seem to represent the dynamic element which strives for middle-class status.[57]

One of the apparent indicators of lower-class urban dynamism is the phenomenon of *criollismo*, by which mestizos of the city distinguish themselves from the recently arrived *indígena*. Popular "criollism" also provides a "source of prestige for determining relative status" within the mestizo group. Whether it is also "an integrating symbol . . . for mestizo culture" remains to be seen.[58]

Politics and Interest Groups

A political-party system can hardly be said to have existed in Peru prior to the 1960s, and even thereafter it has been relevant mainly in the cities. Certain names have persisted as party labels for extended periods, but only APRA, among existing parties of consequence (ignoring the splinters of the far Left), competed in elections earlier than 1956.

[55] Briones and Mejía Valera, *El Obrero*, pp. 58–80.

[56] Chaplin, "Structural Changes," pp. 8–9.

[57] Interviews with Jorge Basadre, March 1, 1966, and Luís Valcárcel, March 2, 1966. Dr. Basadre said that there are "many surprises" in the *barriadas*; e.g., some live there out of preference or to save rent money, and some have television sets and other luxury goods. Dr. Valcárcel also said that the *barriada*-dwellers are not all poor, although many may be illiterate.

[58] Ozzie G. Simmons, "The *Criollo* Outlook in the Mestizo Culture of Coastal Peru," in *Contemporary Cultures and Societies of Latin America*, ed. D. B. Heath and R. N. Adams (New York: Random House, 1965), pp. 526–28; Bourricaud, *Poder y Sociedad*, pp. 16ff.; Larson and Bergman, *Social Stratification in Peru*, pp. 171ff.

Politics of the Elites

The parties of the traditional upper class that once predominated in Peru have largely passed from the scene. Once, around the middle of the nineteenth century, the classic conservative-liberal division existed in Peru, representing at that time a polarization of upper-class opinion over Church privileges and reforms. That was the era of government by regional aristocracies and military *caudillos*.[59]

It was an upper-class reform party of another kind that next triumphed when the antimilitarist Civilistas elected Manuel Pardo the country's first non-military president in 1872. The shock of the 1879 War of the Pacific, the ensuing financial collapse, and opposition to military-supported civilian rule led to what is called the last successful popular movement in Peru. Led by Piérola and the new Democratic party, it soon fell before the consolidation of political power by the new, export-oriented, coastal enterprise.[60]

Parties of the early twentieth century were vestiges of the old elements, but they were basically personalist and never long survived their founders. Liberal currents were present,[61] but no coherent ideologies or programs emerged, and President Leguía in the twenties deliberately killed off the moribund party structure. Strains of the impending social mobilization were already evident, for example, in the alarm produced by the proto-Apristas and their philosophical progenitors.[62] Leguía resisted the efforts to organize the developing middle class.

By the 1930s, differentiation of economic interests was paralleled by new divisions in the upper-class political parties. Of this period it still could be accurately said that Latin American politics were for "limited stakes . . . disputed among articulate minorities," or "a contest between classes from which the masses are excluded."[63] An Aprista called the

[59] Francis Merriman Stanger, "Church and State in Peru During the First Century of Independence," in *The Conflict between Church and State in Latin America*, ed. Frederick B. Pike (New York: Alfred A. Knopf, 1964), pp. 145–48; Bourricaud, *Poder y Sociedad*, pp. 45ff.

[60] Víctor Villanueva, *El Militarismo en el Perú* (Lima: By the author, 1962), pp. 25–35; Mariátegui, *Siete Ensayos*, p. 20; Larson and Bergman, *Social Stratification in Peru*, p. 93.

[61] Villaneuva, *Militarismo*, pp. 39, 90–91. Of the presidents since World War I, only Benavides (1933–39) did not form his own party.

[62] Frederick B. Pike, "The Old and the New APRA in Peru: Myth and Reality," *Inter-American Economic Affairs* 18, no. 2 (August, 1964): 3–45, esp. 10–12. This article contains a useful brief summary of the intellectual history of liberalism in Peru. It poses the choice between liberal, laissez-faire gradualism and Aprista-type reform as contained in the party's original program.

[63] Luigi Einaudi, *Changing Contexts of Revolution in Latin America* (Santa Monica, Calif.: The RAND Corporation, P–3440, September, 1966), p. 5; Irving Louis Horowitz, "The Military Elites," in *Elites in Latin America*, ed. Lipset and Solari, p. 165.

election of 1939 a contest between the "fascist and agrarian nationalism" of Quesada and the "banking and industrial internationalism" of Manuel Prado.[64] He was describing the split which has already been discussed.

Also involved in the split were certain personal animosities. The best-known division persists after more than thirty years. It began with the refusal of Presidents Benavides and Prado to prosecute an Aprista who assassinated Antonio Miró Quesada in 1935. The Miró Quesada family, owners of *El Comercio*, a newspaper in Lima, can still be found vigorously opposing all things Aprista, and usually the views of those associated with the APRA.

Once free competition among mass-based parties was accepted, and definitely after 1956, the traditional party forms declined. By 1962 they had practically disappeared. The transition coincided with the appearance of Fernando Belaúnde Terry as a presidential contender and establishment of Acción Popular as a "respectable" party of reform.

The disappearance of the old parties also reflected the preference of upper-class and economic interests to operate "underground," i.e., through personal contact or openly through interest groups. In the agrarian-reform debate, for example, the Agrarian Society presented its case with full-page advertisements in the press. In open competition for votes, conservative forces could hardly hope to win with the traditional appeals. In direct access to the government, on the other hand, they had all the advantages of social connections, expert knowledge, financial resources, and key positions in the economy.[65]

To the extent that open political processes operate, they could be a defense against the preferred status of the system of interests. The breakdown of those processes is signaled by events such as politically motivated strikes, peasant land seizures, urban land invasions, congressional boycotts, and military coups. From these we infer that effective resistance to reform persists, even if only the reactions to it are visible. Changes in the political system, however, can be seen in the positions of the Church and the military, both institutional interest groups of traditional conservatism and recent evolution.

[64] Sánchez, *Haya de la Torre*, pp. 366–67.

[65] Carlos Zuzunaga Florez wrote that the elections of 1962 and 1963 proved that "the old traditional directing classes have now ceded to the influence of the middle class" (quoted in Pike, "Old and New APRA," p. 39). James L. Payne, *Labor and Politics in Peru* (New Haven, Conn.: Yale University Press, 1965), has disposed of the existence of an oligarchy by observing that employers do not consistently win labor disputes, explaining this by labor's ability to use the "trump card" of violence (pp. 272–77). A closer study, covering a period in which different political conditions prevailed, would seem necessary in order to determine more conclusively the power of the entrepreneurs working through personal or associational interest-group channels to influence decisions of government.

The Catholic Church

As the seat of the Spanish viceroy, Lima has always given corresponding status to the cardinal. Church privileges became subjects of elite controversy soon after independence. Members of the clergy for a time even took an active part in politics. Until the decline of such issues later in the nineteenth century, there was a kind of "bipolar balance of power" between Church and state in Peru.[66]

Some forty years ago it was predicted that anticlericalism would increase. It has not happened. The modicum of reform that did occur, led at times by prominent clergymen, may have averted a more concerted protest. The Church at a certain point is thought to have found discretion in the fact that "overwhelming majorities in congress favored the reforms and made them effective over the heads of reluctant executives."[67]

The official charitable agency of the state, Beneficéncia Pública, played a major role in early efforts to undercut the Church's secular power. It did so by duplicating the charitable activities of the Church and by serving as an alternative recipient of land (through bequests, etc.). It now has probably as much property as the Church and in some areas more than the dioceses and orders combined.[68] The government also has direct leverage on the Church through payment of clerical salaries and maintenance of buildings.

Demands made early in this century for separation of Church and state did not excite much popular interest in Peru. Student federations alone (and APRA, to which they gave rise) seemed to have responded to the appeals of González Prada, a new type of reformer who was both anticlerical and irreligious. It remained for the Church itself to realize its human responsibilities.

Recent recognition of serious faults in the Church in Peru have deeper roots than is generally conceded. The Eucharistic Congress of 1934 in Lima and the rise of Catholic Action are said to have "played a part in the resurgence of the faith." A more direct concern for the "whole man" began with a 1958 statement. It has been called "the most important post-

[66] Frederick B. Pike, "The Catholic Church and Modernization in Peru and Chile," *Journal of International Affairs* 20, no. 2 (1966): 272–88.

[67] Stanger, "Church and State in Peru," reviewed the situation; see pp. 143–53. Basadre has observed that Peru has never had an extremely belligerent anti-clericalism; see his *Historia*, 10: 4746.

[68] Chaplin, "Structural Changes," pp. 12–13; *idem*, "A Discussion of Major Isues," p. 7; CIDA, *Tierra y Desarrollo*, p. 18.

war joint pastoral letter dealing with social justice" and the forerunner of activist moves by Roman Catholics elsewhere.[69]

Some activities of the Church in Peru have been widely praised. In 1962, holdings of the Church in the Department of Cuzco were subdivided and sold at half-value. In the same department the Maryknoll Fathers have maintained a school which in three years trained 1,500 "volunteer catechists" for service among the Indians. As recently as early 1969 a statement issued by Peruvian bishops was praised by one of the most reformist magazines of Lima.[70]

The impact of Church humanitarianism is nevertheless questioned. A most sympathetic observer says that Peruvian churchmen lack understanding of social and economic problems and are prone to stress easy solutions and to slide over the need for work and sacrifice. Less charitable is the view that the Church sanctifies, not always consciously, the "upper-class ideology" of the status quo, which is otherwise missing in the Peruvian culture. Church prohibitions on mass political power, for example, mean that social betterment must not go so far as to endanger the existing structure.[71]

Armed Forces

The military has been more active than the Church in Peruvian politics, but this, too, has been changing in character. In 1961 Peru was classed among the seven Latin countries in which the armed forces were in transition between domination of, and withdrawal from, politics. But the military "still looms large," a judgment borne out by two subsequent coups.[72]

The military coups of 1962 and 1968 both interrupted constitutional terms of office of presidents elected in unprecedented freedom. Those events are still the best indicators of the current military role in politics. A former officer has said that the history of militarism in Peru is "a social phenomenon" reflecting "contradictions of the society." He divided its development into three phases:

1. *Caudillismo*—from independence until the latter part of the nineteenth century, with the military officer as political entrepreneur;

[69] William J. Coleman, *Latin-American Catholocism: A Self-Evaluation* (Maryknoll, N.Y.: World Horizon Reports, 1958), pp. 28–29. This is based on the 1953 Chimbote Assembly.

[70] John J. Considine, ed., *The Church in the New Latin America* (Notre Dame, Ind.: Fides Publishers, 1964), p. 216. See also *Oiga* (Lima), January 31, 1969, pp. 12–14, 38.

[71] Pike, "Church and Modernization," pp. 279ff.; Astiz, *Pressure Groups*, pp. 174–76.

[72] Edwin Lieuwen, *Arms and Politics in Latin America* (New York: Frederick A. Praeger, 1961), p. 163.

2. *Civilismo*—submission of the military to the purposes of the "oligarchy," notably in 1914 and 1948, to recover threatened privileges of the "extractive" sector of the economy;

3. *Constitutionalism*—assertion (as in 1962 and 1968) of the need and duty to monitor "the crisis and disorientation of the political parties . . . without the power to find a path to their goals."[73]

To these can now be added the reformist current. In neither of the latest coups, however, was the picture unmixed.

The 1962–63 junta was predominantly, and ultimately in its conduct, constitutionalist. It kept its promise to rule for only one year and to hold new elections. Yet internal differences during that year forced the removal of General Pérez Godoy, possibly because he opposed new elections. Another view is that the "traditional upper-class" strove successfully during 1962–63 to dissuade the officer corps from undertaking reforms.[74]

In contrast to the previous coup, the emphasis of the 1968 seizure was definitely reformist. While the theme of the military as a "popular force" was present in 1962 and 1968, the leaders of the latter regime were more explicit. They announced that they intended to retire from the government only "when the revolution's reforms are irreversible." Relative anonymity and institutional unity were shown in both coups of the past decade, as opposed to former evidence of personal ambitions and the desire to preserve the status quo.[75]

Changes in the political behavior of the Peruvian military have been attributed to various causes. An idealistic reform element appeared as early as the 1940s. As in some other countries, young officers organized a secret military society which was opposed to oligarchy and dedicated to "collectivity."

The officer corps was reacting against army politics and "service to extractive industries." Popular rule was seen as the remedy, for the sake of military morale as much as national interests. The conspirators resolved to work for revolution, but independently of political parties. The goals proved premature and the movement was short-lived. It allegedly assisted

[73] Villanueva, *Militarismo*, pp. 12–13.

[74] Cesar Martín, *Dichos y Hechos de la Política Peruana* (Lima: By the author, 1963); M. Guillermo Ramírez y Berrios, *Examen Espectral de las Elecciones de 9 de Junio de 1963* (Lima: By the author, 1963); see also Patch, "Elections of 1963."

[75] Luigi Einaudi, *The Peruvian Military: A Summary Political Analysis* (Santa Monica, Calif.: The RAND Corporation, RM-6048-RC, May, 1969), p. 12; Jose Yglesias, "Report from Peru: The Reformers in Brass Hats," *New York Times Magazine*, December 14, 1969, p. 58. On the other hand, War and Prime Minister Ernesto Montagne was quoted shortly after the coup as saying that the Velasco regime would not retain power "indefinitely," but would set a date for elections "at the opportune time" (*La Crónica* (Lima), December 17,1968, p. 3). See also Bourricaud, *Poder y Sociedad*, pp. 311–13, and Arnold Payne, *The Peruvian Coup d'Etat of 1962: The Overthrow of Manual Prado* (Washington, D.C.: Operations and Policy Research, Inc., 1968), p. 60.

in two abortive uprisings, in 1945 and 1948, in which rebellious military garrisons were deserted by their Aprista sponsors.[76]

The reformist current reappeared in 1958 with the establishment of the Center for Higher Military Studies, or CAEM (Centro de Altos Estudios Militares). There the officer corps began to take a deeper interest in national problems through the study of modern schools of economics and sociology. CAEM doctrine stated that, the "fundamental goal of the state being the welfare of the nation . . . the armed forces have as their mission the safeguarding of the social well-being. . . ."[77]

The emergence of reform as a goal of the Peruvian Army is explained in part by its sociocultural isolation from other national groups. Officers came largely from non-aristocratic families, some of them of the impoverished middle class (which also bore Haya de la Torre). Sons were often forced to enter military service, sometimes at enlisted ranks, for lack of any other choice. While 94 percent of Peruvian corporation directors were born on the coast, the majority of generals were not. Most of the generals, moreover, cannot enter the elite society of Lima, which adds to their sense of apartness.

Isolation of the military is further increased by professionalization, which represents an achievement orientation that is alien to both the aristocratic and the popular versions of "criollism." It is revealed in surprising ways. Officers agree, for example, on the need for a military role in national development, even if they disagree on the subject of authoritarian rule versus abstention from politics.[78]

The radical option showed signs of emerging in the military even before 1962, but it was brushed aside as the "Nasserism" of a small group of colonels. Later, democratization of the military was deliberately promoted under Belaúnde through civic action projects that brought the army, at least, into direct touch with the rural population.

Finally, the 1968 coup has been traced in part to military dissatisfaction with past accomplishments. The view that the junta of 1962–63 had not gone far enough in reform was combined with revulsion at the impotence of subsequent civilian rule. The experience of suppressing guerrilla bands in the sierra in the mid-1960s may also have aroused the sympathies of some officers.[79]

[76] Víctor Villanueva, *La Tragedia de un Pueblo y un Partido*, 3d ed. (Lima: n.p., 1957), pp. 30–32, 213–14; *idem*, *Militarismo*, p. 15.

[77] Luís Mercier Vega, *Roads to Power in Latin America*, trans. Robert Rowland (New York: Frederick A. Praeger, 1969), p. 51; Bourricaud, *Poder y Sociedad*, p. 321

[78] Einaudi, "Peruvian Military," pp. 6–8; see also John M. Goshko's series of articles in the *Washington Post*, December 14–18, 1969.

[79] Einaudi, "Peruvian Military," pp. 10–16; Frederick N. Pike, *The Modern History of Peru* (New York: Frederick A. Praeger, 1967), pp. 315–16.

Like the Church, the army has thus ostensibly joined the forces of change. Being the most independent of interest groups in Peru, the military undoubtedly can pursue a reform program as long as it is not divided or weakened by factionalism. Organized and trained for purposeful action, it is potentially more effective than the Church in a developmental role. Whatever results flow directly from the 1968 coup, however, the military has now changed the basic political equation in Peru. The implications for party-initiated reform are fundamental.

The Political Parties

The development of a party system in Peru is recent and somewhat amorphous. As recently as 1958, politics and government in Peru were called "epiphenomenal . . . superficial, symptomatic."[80] There was nevertheless a considerable degree of stability and structure in the election results of the sixties. Regionalism has been one of the bases of party strength, as has the support of interest groups of varying degrees of formal organization.

Class appeal was the basis on which APRA and the older parties of the Left won initial support. In the fifties and sixties it began to yield to heterogeneous tendencies. A broadening of the ideological base reflects the limitations of class appeal. It also follows from the fact that all parties are now in one way or another "reformist." Each of the major new parties—Acción Popular (AP) of Belaúnde, the Christian Democratic Party (DC), and the Unión Nacional Odriísta of former President Odría (UNO)—had some success during the sixties in developing trade-union, or at least worker, support, even though APRA maintained the dominant lead.[81]

The formation of the new parties and the attraction of diversified support were made possible by the rapid urbanization and the accompanying expansion of the middle and lower classes. Mobilization of the availables was not an unmixed blessing, however, and, combined with ambiguities of doctrine, organization, and leadership, it had divisive effects in all the parties.

Heterogeneity is most apparent in UNO. One of its leaders is a prosperous sugar cane planter, but this does not prevent it from winning the votes of large numbers of lower-class urban voters. As the name "Odriísta" indicates, the party is built on the record Odría made as president, when he spent freely for public works in Lima and his native Piura.

[80] Plank, "Peru," p. 216.
[81] J. Payne, *Labor and Politics in Peru*, pp. 101, 116ff.

Ironically, the "Unión Nacional" in Odría's party name originally came from a "non-political" attempt at politics by González Prada, the radical thinker of a half-century earlier. Personalist appeals were completed by the image of Señora Odría. She gained genuine popularity as first lady through her concern for the poor, and in 1963 even ran (unsuccessfully) for mayor of Lima on the APRA/UNO ticket.[82] Defections in UNO in mid-1967 gave the government alliance a temporary majority in Congress, which was later upset. A lasting split occurred in UNO early in 1968, however, and by July the APRA/UNO coalition had ruptured.

Belaúnde's AP probably appealed most to the "dynamic" middle class of unknown proportions. Many of his supporters must have been modernizing bureaucrats, professional people, and business innovators whose careers or aspirations resembled those of Belaúnde himself. His father, Rafael, was independent enough to be exiled for a time, during which Fernando was educated in the United States as an architect. His uncle, Víctor Andrés, was a prominent writer, politician, and Catholic layman.

To this background of respectability, Belaúnde added enough of the flair of a visionary to lend very broad support to his kind of "pragmatic populism."[83] Some AP members proved too radical, however, to be accommodated within the party in power. Opposition politics was aimed at embarrassing the president with evidence of radical tendencies of some of his appointees. The combination of aristocratic and extremist elements led, finally, to the split in AP that preceded Belaúnde's removal from office.

To a marked degree, DC combined similar elements of upper-class origins and radical position. This and the coincidence of regional strengths in Lima and Arequipa contributed to the very weak showing of the party in competition with AP in 1962. Allied with Belaúnde in his successful 1963 campaign, the party reaped a reward of cabinet posts. Soon divided over policy issues, DC left the alliance after the November, 1967, by-elections.[84]

Summary

It is apparent that Peruvian society and politics are not immune to change. The process of social mobilization is not irresistible, but neither is the system of interests immovable. The task of the mass reform party

[82] Enrique Chirinos Soto, *El Perú Frente a Junio de 1962* (Lima: Ediciones del Sol, 1962), p. 31; Villanueva, *Militarismo*, p. 214.

[83] The label was used by John N. Plank in a lecture at the Foreign Service Institute, Department of State, on May 12, 1966. He applies it to AP in Peru and to PRI in Mexico because of their emphasis on mystique over ideology and their care in maintaining cordial relations with the armed forces.

[84] The normally pro-government *Expreso* called into question the directions being taken by DC as early as the 1966 budget crisis (March 11, 1966, pp. 2 and 10).

is to identify the areas of change, to take advantage of those that offer opportunities, and to hasten the processes that seem promising.

The sectors of society that are most pertinent in the planning of political reform strategies are arranged below according to the alternative sequences of structural-cultural change already discussed. Dependent or liberated status in either or both dimensions is, of course, only relative to the previous positions or attitudes.

Estimated Psychosocial Conditions of Certain Sectors of Peruvian Society

	SOCIAL STRUCTURE	
CULTURE	*Dependent*	*Liberated*
Dependent	Sierra Indians Inner-City Slum Residents	Conventional Middle Class
Liberated	*Barriada* Residents Urban *Criollos*	Dynamic Middle Class

The consequences of social and cultural change could be seen in the political system. First, the traditional elite parties were replaced by mass parties, all dedicated in some measure to development and reform. They brought politics to a different level of discourse and placed new tasks before interest groups of all kinds. Second, the overt goals of the two basic institutional interest groups, the Church and the army, were transformed to point in the direction of reform.

Some movement is not necessarily enough to start the accelerated processes of development. It is possible that Peru has "missed" its revolution, by virtue of the very flexibility of the system of interests, which permitted some of the pressure to escape without changing the system itself.[85] Or demands for economic equality may have been diverted into channels of nationalism as an acceptable substitute for redistribution of the bases of political influence. The inadequacy of social forces as autonomous instruments of reform was, in any event, demonstrated by the breakdown of the open political system. The extent to which political parties might have influenced the outcome can be seen in an examination of the actions of the Apristas.

[85] Chaplin, "Structural Changes," p. 12; Bell, *End of Ideology*, pp. 61–62.

III

APRA'S STRATEGIC CHOICES

CONTROL OF THE APPARATUS of the state is the object of politics in Latin America. In Peru, control of the executive has traditionally been the primary key to political power. Despite a balanced constitutional distribution of authority, the machinery of government is almost exclusively dominated by the president.[1]

Whether the presidency is the *only* key to power is a separate question. It is generally assumed that executive control is both *necessary* and *sufficient* to allow a reform party to apply its program more quickly and fully than by any other means. APRA therefore made the election of its candidate to the presidency its first and central objective.

THE STATE

The president is considered "omni-competent," which enhances his influence, and "omni-responsible," which adds to his risks.[2] Within limits, the executive is positively or negatively moved by three main institutions of government. In order of influence, they are the military, Congress, and the bureaucracy, each with its peculiar role. The military, historically a toppler of governments and an obstacle to reform, has shown signs of becoming a promoter of change. At the other extreme is the bureaucracy, often incompetent and wholly subject to favoritism and family connec-

[1] William S. Stokes, *Latin American Politics* (New York: Thomas Y. Crowell Co., 1959), pp. 385ff.

[2] James L. Payne, "Peru: The Politics of Structured Violence," *Journal of Politics* 27, no. 2 (May, 1965): 362–74, esp. 366.

tions. Yet it has a potential as an instrument of change which, with rationalization of governmental organization and a degree of civil service reform, could be realized in the future.

The immunity of the bureaucracy from popular influence is symptomatic of Peruvian traditionalism. It is related to the central control of local functions through the power of appointment. The introduction of municipal elections in 1963 promised a devolution of responsibilities for certain governmental and developmental processes to the localities. This kind of building from the grass roots was behind Belaúnde's idea of *Cooperación Popular*.[3]

Coalition control of Congress in the periods 1945–48 and 1963–68 was the nearest APRA came to the formal exercise of power. Congress has been largely subservient to the executive, however, as is indicated by the occasions (e.g., 1933, 1936, 1948) when a coup was followed by congressional legitimation of the new president.

To a greater degree than perhaps any of its Latin American counterparts, the Peruvian Congress has strong constitutional prerogatives which have been neglected in practice.[4] Twice since World War II the Apristas have tried to revive the power of Congress, but without real success. Far more typical is the historical record of laws enacted but left partly or wholly unenforced by the executive.[5]

In the 1945–48 period, APRA set out deliberately to "restore the majesty of the parliament." It had so pledged itself in helping to elect the president and a supporting majority in Congress. But poor relations with that president and a boycott of the Senate by a conservative minority blocked the effort. The Apristas succeeded only in establishing some legislative history before they were put out of office by the Odría coup.

Two main issues in Congress during that time were the presidential veto and congressional investigative powers. From 1963 to 1968, by contrast, the questions of cabinet confidence and appropriation powers dominated Congress, although another congressional boycott occurred, investigations were held, and Congress acceded to a presidential veto as late as 1967. In 1968, as in 1948, APRA's control of Congress was interrupted by a military coup.

The state is one of the environments of politics. In authoritarian states, it is the dominant one. Its popular support notwithstanding, APRA could

[3] See the discussion of this approach as it enters into U.S. foreign assistance policy, for example, in David Hapgood, ed., *The Role of Popular Participation in Development* (Cambridge, Mass.: M.I.T. Center for International Studies, for the Agency for International Development, 1968).

[4] Lieuwen, *Arms and Politics*, p. 429; Interview with Enrique Chirinos Soto, Lima, March 3, 1966.

[5] For example, see Ford, *Man and Land in Peru*, pp. 78, 84, 125–26.

not make its congressional power effective without taking account of the crucial power of the executive. Upon default or defeat of civilian executive authority, the military takes control.

Nature of Choices

The combination of two circumstances—the presidency as a necessary ingredient and the military as a potentially negative one—presented APRA with a complex of strategic choices in place of the otherwise clear and simple tasks of a reform party. The choices have a symmetry about them which not only is based on logical relationships but also can be seen in the actual history of Aprista decisions. They divide naturally into two distinct routes to power.

A *strong* and a *weak* approach are open to APRA. Both are directed at ultimate control of the executive by means of the presidential election. These are the choices in the area of non-violence and reform, for the revolutionary alternative was rejected, or set aside; the party's freedom to revert to it was impaired by the decisions attendant upon adopting the course of reform.

The strong approach to power has been to seek the election of an Aprista presidential candidate. The other way is through indirect election, or Aprista support of another candidate for the presidency, which implies an admission of weakness or the presence of some critical factor foreclosing the strong, direct approach.

Time constraints influence the party's decision. The strong path might be chosen to take advantage of temporary popular support or in acknowledgment of waning advantages. The weak option, on the other hand, could be a way of buying time in which to build strength for a future change of strategy.

Risk is implied in both dimensions of APRA's strategic choices. The strong approach is an "all or nothing" gamble. Greater security lies in election coalitions, at least in the short run. But APRA has also to recognize certain watersheds between *preparation* and *commitment*. One kind of commitment is implied in any move from an organizational phase to active campaigning by either route. Another appears at the point of choice—whether direct or indirect—between the two election approaches.

Figure III–1 portrays the relationships already sketched, as well as subsidiary considerations. It presents the proposition that strategic decisions, once made, limit the party's discretion in tactics.

The preparatory phases involve minimal risks and commitments. Organizing the party's popular base, however, involves some choice, at least between conventional and unconventional methods. The degree and

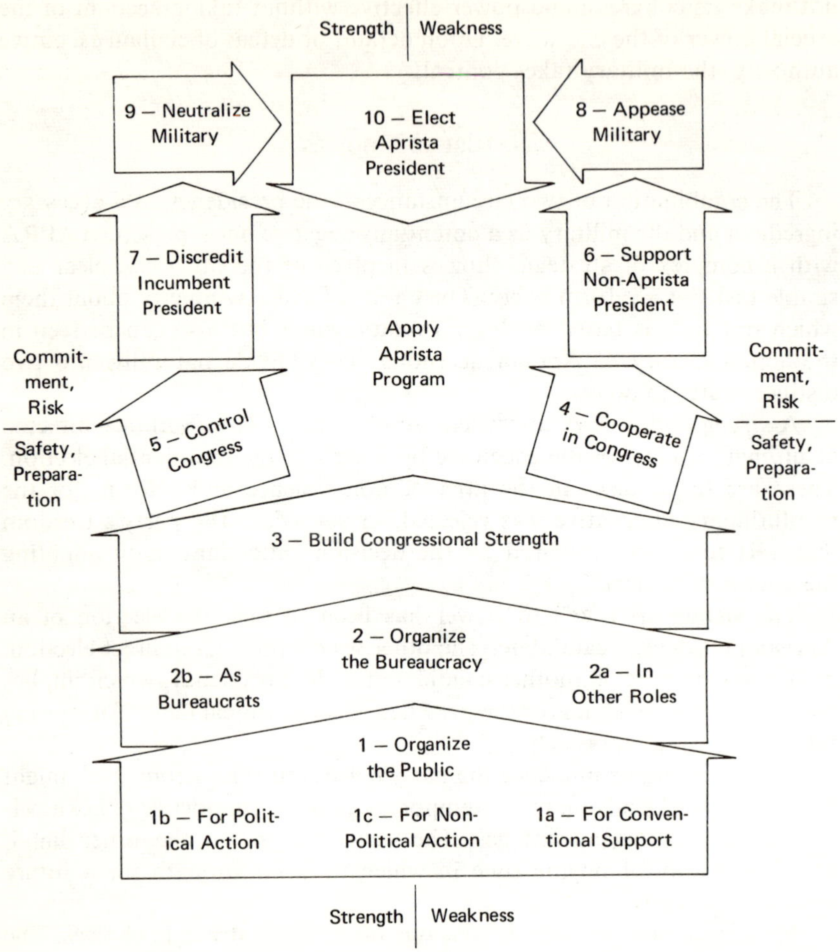

FIGURE III–1. STRATEGIC CHOICES IN APRA'S SEARCH FOR POWER

kind of member activism and involvement may prove to be critical in either a positive or a negative sense. A basic assessment is required of the party's relationship with the *community*, and of the political system and direction of its development.

The same kind of decision is needed with respect to organization within the bureaucracy. The risk increases in this direction because of the sensitivity and unconventional character of any attempt to politicize state employes. This choice involves an assessment of the nature of APRA's relationship to the *state*, and particularly to the social structures, which might allow or impede the use of the bureaucracy for partisan purposes.

In the next level of preparatory activity, the Congress, the party must take positions in its relationships with other *political parties*. It has to decide whether to try to control Congress—independently or in coalition—or to cooperate under the leadership of another party.

These preparatory decisions affect the eventual choice of strong or weak approaches to the presidency and the nature and amount of support the party can expect in its efforts to apply its program. The crucial decision on a presidential candidate must be made, however, in light of the party's relationship to the military. Then the party passes a "point of no return," at least for the current election campaign. Ideally, the military factor should enter into the strong-weak calculation at an early stage. That is, unless the party is assured of means to neutralize the military (as a probable antagonist) from strength, it would be wiser not to embark on the strong course.

Choice of either route to the presidency greatly diminishes the party's freedom later to resort to the other, partly because the nature of some preparatory activities are peculiarly suited to one strategy or the other. It is fairly clear that adoption of the indirect approach, being an implicit admission of weakness, reduces the chance that the party could later in the same campaign plausibly shift to a strong, direct strategy. It is less obvious whether or not a party can successfully shift from a strong to a weak strategy. The result may depend heavily upon the nature of the party supported. Aprista experiences afford some empirical evidence of the impracticality, at least for a mass reform party, of either this or the opposite change of strategy.

Table III–1 summarizes the changes of government in which APRA was involved during a period of almost forty years. Appendix A recounts in greater detail how each of the stages shown in the table were encountered.

In its organized existence, legal and illegal, APRA has seen a total of thirteen selections of a president or junta, two of which (1936 and 1962) were shortly thereafter cancelled by arbitrary action supported with force. The other eleven were formal changes of government, two of which were mere extensions of power by the incumbent presidents (1936 and 1950).

With Haya de la Torre as its candidate, APRA took an active part in three elections (1931, 1962, 1963) and supported non-Aprista candidates in three others. In the first of these (1936), victory was denied by congressional action; in the other two the Aprista-supported candidates won (1945 and 1956) and gave APRA a measure of indirect influence on the executive. The party was prepared to participate indirectly also in the 1939

TABLE III–1: CHANGES OF GOVERNMENT IN PERU, 1931–68

	APRA's Role in Presidential Elections When			Coups and Elections by Congress
Year	Active	Supporting Other Party	Inactive	
1931	Sánchez Cerro over Haya, who claimed fraud			
1933	———	———	———	Assassination; Congress named Benavides
1936	———	Eguiguren leading, but	———	Congress extended Benavides' term
1939	———	———	Manuel Prado over Quesada; APRA boycott	
1945	———	Bustamante over Ureta		
1948	———	———	———	Odría's revolt
1950	———	———	Odría elected as sole candidate	
1956	———	Manuel Prado over Belaúnde and Lavalle		
1962	Haya plurality over Belaúnde and Odría, but	———	———	Military coup intervened
1963	Belaúnde over Haya and Odría			
1968	———	———	———	Military coup; 1969 election cancelled

election, but withdrew its support from the "official" candidate when the newspaper of his rival was forcibly closed down.[6]

THE COURSE OF EVENTS

Convivencia

In 1956 APRA resorted for the third time to the indirect route to control of the executive, through a *convivencia* (coexistence) agreement with former President Manual Prado. The party could not have advanced its

[6] Sánchez, *Haya de la Torre*, pp. 365–68; Villanueva, *Militarismo*, p. 98; Chirinos, *El Perú*. Other data in the foregoing summary are based on the same sources and are in general agreement on the essential facts.

own candidate, because only by supporting that of another party did it obtain assurances that it would be restored to legal status.[7]

The restoration of legality did not occur prior to the 1956 election, however, so APRA could not run candidates for Congress as it had in 1945. Aprista expectations and tactics in the *convivencia* also departed in other respects from the party's 1945–48 experiences. Then it had "taken power" in a flush of victory and had regarded the indirect control of the executive as an opportunity to apply a large part of its program. By 1948 it was disillusioned, both in the tractability of President Bustamante and in the utility of its majority-within-the-majority in Congress.[8]

APRA viewed the election of Prado, on the other hand, as a closely calculated risk. In 1956 "the essential thing was to keep a democratic government in power for the next six years so that the Aprista party might win the 1962 elections and at least have a chance to carry out its program." Besides trying not to rock the boat, therefore, the party sought to give Prado no more support than was needed to keep his regime in office and avoided responsibility for the regime's acts.[9] Thus, indirect control in this instance was seen as a means of bringing about conditions favorable to later direct control rather than as an opportunity to apply the Aprista program immediately. APRA's limited objective of preserving political freedom during most of that period was achieved.[10]

Aprista moderation had other aspects, however, and earlier roots. The inference is that during the early fifties Haya (while claiming political asylum in the Colombian Embassy) had decided on a change of policy which was resisted at lower party levels. The main evidence is the long letter that Manuel Seoane sent to Haya in June, 1954, on behalf of the Aprista exiles. It protested Haya's article in *Life* magazine, which the exiles said compromised the party program and alienated APRA from the masses.

[7] Robert J. Alexander, *Prophets of the Revolution* (New York: Macmillan Co., 1962), pp. 103–4. In the absence of Haya, Prialé had also negotiated with Odría, who was unwilling to legalize APRA before the election. Fernando Belaúnde Terry (who ran a close second to Prado) had publicly committed himself to legalizing the party if elected, but he was ignored; he was running on an essentially Aprista platform. The charge was made that Odría rigged the election in favor of Prado after he decided that his own candidate, Lavalle, could not win; see Villanueva, *Militarismo*, pp. 139ff. This would hardly have seemed necessary in the circumstances.

[8] Sánchez, *Haya de la Torre*, pp. 385ff. Aprista achievements in that Congress are discussed in Chapter VI of the present volume.

[9] Alexander, *Prophets*, pp. 105–6. Villanueva, otherwise highly critical of APRA, says that its support of the Prado government was "only superficial" (*Militarismo*, p. 144).

[10] J. Payne, "Politics of Structured Violence," pp. 362, 364. Even anti-Apristas like Villanueva concur, while complaining of "economic dictatorship" (*Militarismo*, pp. 142ff.). The only charge of political repression arose because the Communists were outlawed during most of 1961.

In addition to being blamed on Haya's attitude toward the United States, however, the dissension has been attributed to a split between the 1930 and 1950 generations, a split which also appeared in Venezuela. Younger party leaders, some of whom later defected from both APRA and Venezuela's Acción Democrática, were not merely more radical but also looked with concern beyond the acquisition and retention of power to the problems of future program application.[11]

Mere association with the wartime dictator Prado, however, was enough to alienate some Apristas, both leaders and rank and file, and certain exiled leaders never returned from abroad after 1956. Soon APRA's position became still more difficult, especially among students, when the successful Cuban revolution provided a new banner for communism in Latin America.[12]

The strength of internal party dissension may have been underestimated in 1956. In any event it seems to have been separated from strategic consideratons. APRA could hardly have declined to support some presidential candidate. Moreover, it had to pick the winner if it wished to be assured of legal status for the next six years. The strategic choice was unavoidable, although the tactical decision may have been faulty.

In retrospect, the party probably would have done better had it joined Belaúnde in 1956 (when he needed Aprista support) and tried to make of him another Bustamante, who had failed ten years earlier. But Belaúnde was a long shot in 1956 and an "arms-length" alliance with Prado seemed the most secure course.

Although for the most part the party avoided accepting positions of responsibility under Prado, it was still blamed by the opposition for the faults of his administration. With the fall of world market prices at the end of the Korean War, the economic situation was basically disadvantageous, but the Prado administration has been called a "do-nothing regime" which "presided over perhaps the six most wasted years" in twentieth-century Peru. Despite these handicaps, APRA was optimistic that Haya would win the presidency in 1962.[13]

[11] Villanueva, *Tragedia*, pp. 224–57; Astiz, *Pressure Groups*, p. 100; Einaudi, "Changing Contexts," pp. 24–26.

[12] Richard W. Patch, "Fidelismo in Peruvian Universities—I," *AUFS*, RWP–2–'61, January, 1961. Part II appeared as RWP-3-'61, February, 1961.

[13] Pike, "Old and New APRA," p. 37; Kantor, *El Movimiento Aprista*, pp. 13–15. Richard W. Patch ("The Peruvian Elections of 1962 and Their Amendment," *AUFS*, RWP–6–'62, September, 1962, p. 9) wrote: "Nothing positive was accomplished either by Prado or by APRA." An Aprista leader of an earlier period places the effective congressional strength of APRA at a higher figure, but agrees that it had suffered great damage during the Odría era (Interview G, 1966—a few interviews omit names where identification might prove embarrassing).

1962 Campaign

The fact that APRA did not win the presidency in 1962 has been attributed to a complex of causes. Superficially, its failure can be blamed on the intervention of the military or lack of the decisive one-third of the popular vote, or on both.

Each explanation, however, raises further questions: Would the military have intervened if Haya had received the constitutional plurality? Was it Haya personally to whom the military objected, or would Manuel Seoane (APRA's vice-presidential candidate) or some other Aprista have had the same difficulty? Was it APRA's later agreement—when faced with deadlock—to throw the presidency to Odría, and the prospect of Odría and APRA running the government, which led the military to intervene? Or was the military sincerely concerned over the apparent breakdown of orderly government caused by prolonged uncertainty amid charges of fraud? Would APRA have shown more strength in the election had it maintained a less quiescent posture during the Prado period or during the election campaign? Did it feel too sure of automatic majority support? Most of these questions can have no answers, but it is worthwhile to look briefly at events leading up to 1962.

During the *convivencia*, APRA had to define its "good behavior" as a balance between conflicting demands. On the one hand stood a presumed military opposition to eventual election of an Aprista president. Changes in the military attitude, which were then in progress, were not easily projected. On the other hand arose the demands of APRA's constituencies, which no longer expressed merely inchoate and latent interests. Organized labor during this period enjoyed relative freedom after intense repression by Odría. It was also a period of rising living costs and growing wage demands expressed through Aprista-led trade unions.[14]

During this time the unions engaged in "political bargaining"; through strikes and semiviolent demonstrations they sufficiently threatened the tenure of the president to get satisfaction by executive decree. Aprista leaders obviously had to hold their trade-union demands to a level adequate to get reasonable worker benefits, yet not so extreme as to bring about military intervention. They "struck a productive balance" between

[14] Official recognition of labor organizations in Peru had been slow until 1945, when 200 were so recognized. The number more than doubled in the first two years of Bustamante's presidency, then rose slowly to about 550 in 1956, and again doubled by the end of 1962. See U.S. Department of Labor, *Labor in Peru* (Washington, D.C.: BLS Report no. 262, February, 1964), p. 52. See also J. Payne, *Labor and Politics in Peru*, pp. 52–54; Villanueva, *Militarismo*, p. 142; and Sánchez, *Haya de la Torre*, pp. 460–61.

party and workers' interests, but at a cost which was paid in the elections of 1962 and 1963.[15]

More difficult were the demands of other groups in which the party did not have a dominant voice. The strike of public school teachers, for example, succeeded (with some violence) in obtaining from Congress salary increases financed by a cigarette tax. The teachers' independent association attracted what seemed to be widespread, spontaneous public support, but with no particular help from APRA or the Aprista-led Workers' Confederation of Peru (Confederación de Trabajadores del Perú—CTP).[16]

Rural violence posed a similar yet more serious problem for APRA. An expert study of Peruvian land tenure charts the shift from isolated incidents of peasant invasions in the late fifties to their concentration and intensification in the central sierra and the southeastern valleys in the early sixties. After some indecision the party took a "hard-line" position favoring repressive measures by the military. An anti-Aprista writer commented that Haya had neglected to tell his followers that APRA, "in order to become a governing party, had to forget—or at least temporarily silence—its revolutionary proclamations."[17]

In the 1962 election campaign the Apristas faced a situation that involved one basic change. Calculations of a mass reform party tend to assume the absence of strong competition from another reform party of comparable goals and popular support. Several new parties appeared in 1962, the most notable of which was Acción Popular.

Belaúnde's candidacy may have seemed like a temporary phenomenon in 1956, one which Apristas assumed would not survive the reappearance of their party. Contrary to tradition and expectations, however, Belaúnde campaigned throughout the six years of Prado's regime and was more

[15] This concept is presented by J. Payne in both *Labor and Politics in Peru* and "Politics of Structured Violence." It is based on the intensity of conflict over the presidency and the ability and readiness of the armed forces to intervene to replace a president who proves unable to prevent violence. "Political bargaining" is examined by Payne primarily as a trade-union tool, an alternative to collective (economic) bargaining or legal enactment, rather than as a means of mobilizing organized labor for political ends, which is the focus of this inquiry (*Labor and Politics in Peru*, pp. 93, 116–24). Villanueva stresses Prado's indifference to social needs and police brutality in dealing with labor troubles and land invasions, in which he says 100 died in the six years (*Militarismo*, pp. 142–43).

[16] J. Payne, *Labor and Politics in Peru*, pp. 236–51; see also Bourricaud, *Poder y Sociedad*, p. 106, concerning the abandonment of the Bank Employees' Union in 1959.

[17] CIDA, *Tierra y Desarrollo*, pp. 394–98; Villanueva, *Militarismo*, p. 144; Ramírez, *Elecciones*, p. 20.

active in 1962 than any other candidate.[18] The result was that he built up substantial strength, especially in areas of relative Aprista weakness. The Apristas were inclined to view him as an upstart who would be no match for Haya de la Torre in 1962.

The attitude of Prado on the presidential succession of 1962 also needs to be considered. Unfriendly Peruvian analysts accuse him of mounting an apparatus for fraudulently delivering the presidency to APRA, or even of conspiring to lay the foundation for a last-minute coup continuing his own regime.[19] All appearances, however, were either that Prado was indifferent to the results in 1962 or that he conceded the presidency to APRA but was unable to help it win. Few congressional candidates closely associated with Prado appeared in the campaign.

Registration irregularities were actually discovered and corrected before the election. This by no means satisfied the anti-Apristas, who concentrated their fire on the new election law adopted "under pressure" in 1961. Well in advance of the June 10 election, protests over anticipated frauds were raised by "all the political parties . . . except the Apristas, who relied upon official support."[20] The anti-Aprista press and the armed forces joined the chorus.

It was left to the military, finally, to press the objections. As early as May 26 the three military officers holding the cabinet portfolios of war, navy, and air complained to the Elections Board. The Navy minister was quoted on two occasions outside of Peru as saying that APRA would not be permitted to take power if Haya won.[21]

Thus it was evident before the voting that Haya faced a definite element of military opposition even if he was elected. Belaúnde seemed confident of the outcome. He had told a journalist that it was "free elections or

[18] Ramirez, *Elecciones*, pp. 16, 35, 81–85, and *passim;* Martin, *Política Peruana*, pp. 13, 25–32, 130; Enrique Chirinos Soto, *Cuenta y Balance de las Elecciones de 1962* (Lima: Ediciones Perú, 1962), p. 31; Patch, "Elections of 1963."

[19] Ramírez, in his frankly pro-Belaúnde review, portrays the Apristas as simply trying to replace the Prado regime without changing it, although he concedes that APRA had avoided sharing responsibility for its actions. He blames the Elections Board (Jurado Nacional de Elecciones) for actually rigging the vote in favor of APRA. See *Elecciones*, pp. 55ff. Villanueva agrees with all of this and accuses Prado (and later Odría) of double-crossing APRA by encouraging the armed forces to uncover the fraud, intervene, and annul the election; see *Militarismo*, pp. 198ff. and 221–22. Bourricaud explains that the switching of ballot boxes was still easy in 1956 because votes were not tabulated at the polling places or in the presence of the candidates' poll watchers. The reform of 1961 corrected this. See *Poder y Sociedad*, pp. 283–84.

[20] Villanueva, *Militarismo*, pp. 193–94.

[21] *Ibid.*, p. 203; Ramírez, *Elecciones*, pp. 51–52.

inevitable revolution" and that he would expect the armed forces to give their allegiance "only to the legitimate winners."[22]

The 1962 Military Coup

After the voting on June 10, the pace quickened, until the coup of July 18. Election results showed no one with the constitutional one-third plurality required for election. Congress would elect the president. Negotiations proceeded on at least three circuits, the interconnections of which are not clear.

1. Interparty discussions began at once on the election of a president in Congress. APRA held the key position because the total of Belaúnde's and Odría's members did not represent a majority. The Apristas' approach was finally rejected by Belaúnde, presumably because of his confidence in military support.[23]

Turning next to Odría, the Apristas seemed to concede frustration when, on July 4, Haya announced laconically that he had been "vetoed" for the presidency and was declining it in the interests of "defense of the constitution and the law." The effect was not official until July 17, however, when Odría delivered what sounded like an acceptance speech on television; it obviously was based on assurances of Apristá support.[24] The next morning the junta had assumed power.

2. The military pressure on the Elections Board continued during the interparty negotiations. On June 11, the day after the election, the Ministry of War routinely certified the orderliness of the procedure. After one month's delay, on July 12 the Joint Command (*Comando Conjunto*) of the armed forces issued a communique denying ties with any presidential candidate. The Navy minister formally resigned the same day (and the

[22] Martín, *Política Peruana*, pp. 76–77.

[23] Patch, "Elections of 1962," pp. 12–13; Chirinos, *Cuenta y Balance*, p. 75; Terry L. McCoy, "The Peruvian Aprista Party, 1948–63" (Master's thesis, Tulane University, 1964), pp. 85–86.

[24] Martín, *Política Peruana*, pp. 35–36. Martín does not say who vetoed Haya or how it was done, but Ramírez attributes it to "the army" (*Elecciones*, p. 67). Martín suggests that APRA continued trying to garner support for Haya even after his July 4 renunciation and that the agreement to elect Odría president and Seoane vice-president might have succeeded had not APRA delayed so long. As it was, Odría learned just before he went on the air that the coup was planned for the next day (see *Política Peruana*, pp. 49–52). Chirinos is explicit in saying that President Prado was given the news by the three defense ministers (*Cuenta y Balance*, pp. 71–72). See also Villanueva, *Militarismo*, pp. 213–15, and Patch, "Elections of 1962," p. 13.

Prado government accepted on July 17).[25] As late as July 16 the armed forces were still presenting evidence of vote frauds to the Elections Board.[26]

3. Belaúnde announced his victory in an unexpected television appearance on the day following the election. The vote still had not been counted officially. Once the result was announced, and the likelihood of an Aprista-Odriísta deal was recognized, Belaúnde assumed a posture of defiance.[27]

On July 11 Belaúnde returned to his native Arequipa (starting point of several past revolts). The press reported that barricades were being put up in front of his party office there. In succeeding days he publicly appealed for the formation of a miltary junta, saying that he could not be responsible for the attitude of the people of Arequipa and that the Prado regime might shortly be overthrown if it did not listen to his proposals.[28]

Meanwhile, Prado had tried in June to remove the commander of the air force, Pedro Vargas Prada, only to be faced with a virtual officers' strike which threatened to spread to the armed forces generally. Army officers commanding the major regions of Peru were assembled in Lima in the first days of July to pay annual homage to the military victims of the Aprista revolt of 1932 in Trujillo. The opportunity to coordinate views and actions was ideal.[29] On the eve of the coup, conferences occurred in which the members of the Joint Command seemed to predominate, but in which at least two other institutions, the Church and the conservative press, were represented.[30]

[25] Ramírez, *Elecciones*, p. 52; Martín, *Política Peruana*, pp. 37 and 45. These developments and earlier assurances of War Minister Cuadra Ravines that the election results would be respected may have given APRA grounds for hope; see Chirinos, *Cuenta y Balance*, p. 71.

[26] Villanueva, *Militarismo*, pp. 212, 216–17; Chirinos, *Cuenta y Balance*, p. 76.

[27] It was later explained that the information came from a high-ranking military officer (Martín, *Política Peruana*, pp. 33–34). The account states that "almost official" figures gave him one-third of the votes and that he was so "very well informed" that his supporters announced his victory (Ramírez, *Elecciones*, pp. 57, 61).

[28] Villanueva, *Militarismo*, p. 227; Martín, *Política Peruana*, pp. 37, 39–40. Another version said that Belaúnde wanted the cardinal to preside over a "court of honor" to overrule the Elections Board (Chirinos, *Cuenta y Balance*, pp. 73–74).

[29] Ramírez, *Elecciones*, pp. 63–66. Villanueva described this seriocomic situation as a "convention" such as other kinds of organizations hold. He recounted also the modern method used by the "high command" some months before the elections for polling the opinions of the officer corps while protecting the anonymity of respondents! He did not know the results but presumed they were in accord with the action ultimately taken (i.e., on July 18). See *Militarismo*, pp. 209–11.

The Vargas Prada transfer, mentioned above, was an unsuccessful attempt at "neutralization by transfer" of military officers. It was practiced by Cárdenas *after* he assumed the presidency of Mexico, but benefitted from the special circumstances of the Mexican Revolution. See Alexander, *Prophets*, pp. 36–38.

[30] Ramírez states that Archbishop Cardinal Landázuri and Carlos Miró Quesada, publisher of *El Comercio*, were present; see *Elecciones*, pp. 66–70.

Following the overnight coup of July 17–18, APRA called an indefinite, general strike. The fact that it was delayed until Monday, July 23, suggests a number of flaws. The lapse may indicate, first, that the need to react to a coup had not been foreseen and, second, that there was resistance in the trade unions concerned. In any event, the strike was a failure.

The Elections Board, on the other hand, repeatedly refused to concede irregularities. Its position is sustained by observers and by the similarity of results, department by department, in the 1963 elections, which were under the control of the military junta and a new Elections Board.[31]

Hindsight

Pursuing direct control of the executive, APRA was blocked primarily by the military, which in turn was supported by a complex of other forces. The party switched back to a belated, and probably wasted, effort at indirect rule. Understandably, the Apristas spent the six weeks following the election mainly in efforts to combat charges of fraud, but they also sought congressional votes to make Haya president.

The facts that became available to the party during that critical period, however, threw considerable doubt on its ability to reach its main goal. Developments were of such fundamental significance that they seemed to invalidate the basic strategy of seeking Haya's election to the presidency and even to impair the soundness of the resort to indirect control.

The military obviously had not been neutralized. Its behavior showed that the armed forces were still strongly anti-Aprista. The question for APRA was not so much whether the military would step in as when and how. The pretense that might be used for intervention was of secondary importance to the Apristas once it became apparent that the military was both deeply concerned and united enough to act.

[31] Raymond Estep, *The Latin American Nations Today* (Maxwell Air Force Base, Ala.: Air University, Aerospace Studies Institute, 1964). Estep says that 3,000 labor leaders pledged themselves *not* to respect the strike call (*ibid.*, p. 236); see also Patch, "Elections of 1962," p. 4. APRA did send out small groups of street demonstrators on July 18, but the police handled them with restraint and did not even make any arrests. Of these forays and the strike call, Villanueva says that the Apristas wanted to show popular repudiation of the junta but failed even to saddle it with a charge of "bloody repression" (*Militarismo*, pp. 222–24). See also McCoy, "Aprista Party, 1948–63," pp. 88–89.

In response to military messages dated July 17, the Elections Board the same day certified the results to Congress (Martín, *Política Peruana*, pp. 19–20, 40–43). Critics of the board stress that, although supposedly independent, it was actually partial to the regime in power and that the armed forces, although formally guaranteeing the fairness of the elections, actually could take responsibility under the law only for maintaining order at the polls and for the safe custody of sealed ballot boxes. See Villanueva, *Militarismo*, pp. 196–97; 205–7: Patch, "Elections of 1962," p. 5; *idem*, "Elections of 1963," p. 9.

The abortive agreement by APRA to support Odría for president raised other questions. It would have been a combination of weaknesses—APRA's reduced popular support added to Odría's loss of military support. Nor would an alliance with Odría have been another arms length *convivencia*. The Apristas could not have avoided responsibility for executive acts while both helping to elect a former opponent and holding the largest block of congressional seats. The outcome would have resembled the situation of 1945–48. The dissimilarity of Aprista and Odriísta programs would have revived the dilemma in which APRA had either to sacrifice its program or to face a completely contradictory set of conditions in Congress. Neither prospect would have offered much as a base from which to revert, someday, to its original goal of electing an Aprista president.

1963: Repeat Performance

The revelations of June-July, 1962, notwithstanding, APRA approached the 1963 election as if it were a replay of the first attempt, which it very nearly was. This time, however, important differences worked against the party:

1. The advantage of official sponsorship, which APRA had enjoyed in 1962, was transferred to Belaúnde (balanced, of course, by the Apristas' acquisition of opposition status in relation to the junta). This was especially true after March, 1963, when General Lindley replaced Pérez Godoy as head of the junta. Lindley set about revising the elections law, shifting army commanders, and replacing civilian officials from prefects down to municipal authorities. A complete revision of voter registration rolls was carried out for the first time in twenty years.[32]

2. APRA undoubtedly suffered in 1963 from intangible factors such as the absence of Manuel Seoane as a vice-presidential candidate, rank-and-file disillusionment over the 1962 agreement to support Odría (who was again the opponent of Haya in 1963), the demonstration of Aprista weakness in the abortive general strike, and the suspicion that the armed forces might again veto Haya's election if he should win.

3. The decisive statistical factor in the 1963 election, however, was Belaúnde's ability to build alliances between the two elections from among

[32] Martín, *Política Peruana*, pp. 63–64; Patch, "Elections of 1963," p. 13. Neither this nor the introduction of the "distribution sum" (*cifra repartidora*) in the congressional vote seemed to work against APRA as anticipated; Haya's presidential vote increased by more than 65,000, and APRA picked up two senators and seven deputies in Lima, where it had none in 1962. See Ramírez, *Elecciones*, p. 81, and Martín, *Política Peruana*, p. 135. The purging of voter lists decreased them sharply, but the losses were about equal in the departments of APRA and AP majorities; Larson and Bergman, *Social Stratification in Peru*, p. 380.

the also-rans of 1962. These were the Christian Democratic, National Liberation Front, Socialist, and Social Progressive parties, candidates of which had received a total of more than 6 percent of the 1962 vote. In addition, following the death of Pope John XXIII, Belaúnde is believed to have received the clerical endorsement, which had formerly gone to Odría.[33]

In contrast to Belaúnde's successful maneuvers, and to their own previous willingness to make alliances, the Apristas stood alone in 1963; they even lost from their congressional lists a few successful 1962 candidates who were elected independently the second time around.[34]

The party thought it was necessary to demonstrate the dimensions of Aprista strength in circumstances that were free from suspicion of fraud, and to test the junta's commitment to free elections. All this was reinforced by the fact that only the candidacy of Haya could unite the party in 1963. On the issues, APRA seemed to adopt a more militant line in 1963, but Haya campaigned only in the north.[35]

Opposition Politics

The period of Belaúnde's administration (1963–68) was one of parliamentary and electoral politics. Left with no claim to executive power, APRA chose in 1963 to make the most of its plurality of seats in Congress. In coalition with Odría's UNO, it shared control of Congress for five years. The period was highlighted by such issues as agrarian reform, guerrilla operation in the sierra, negative control of the executive by means of appropriation power, congressional inquiries, the censure of objectionable ministers, and the exposure of corruption. Conflict between the development and stabilization of the economy, together with the nationalization of oil, gradually intensified the problems leading to Belaúnde's overthrow by the military on October 3, 1968.

Aprista conduct in this period has been widely attacked as obstructionist and subservient to the "oligarchy." Moral judgments are useless, however, in amoral situations. In an apologia for AP which was written before the 1968 coup, one observer described the problem in terms that might apply also to an opposition party: "The complexities of the constitutional procedure and the ability of all sides to hide their true goals and actions from the average Peruvian voter (who has only an elementary

[33] Patch, "Elections of 1963," p. 11; Martín, *Política Peruana*, pp. 134–35.

[34] See Martín, *Política Peruana*, pp. 29–32, and Ramírez, *Elecciones*, pp. 82–84, for deputies from Ancash and Madre de Dios representing MDP (Movimiento Democrático Peruano—Prado's party) and from Piura representing UR (Unión Revolucionaria—once the party of Sánchez Cerro).

[35] McCoy, "Aprista Party, 1948–63," pp. 91–92; Martín, *Política Peruana*, p. 119.

education), plus the contempt and cynicism with which politics and politicians are viewed, make it extremely difficult to maintain popular support while in power, except by unusual charisma or by dramatic improvements."[36]

APRA's fortunes at the popular level suffered early reversals in the municipal elections that Belaúnde called in December, 1963. It is difficult to assign party labels to all candidates in a local election. It is still more dangerous to base conclusions on national totals in such elections, or to compare them with presidential election results. (Geographic concentration of votes, characteristic of APRA and UNO, carries handicaps in this kind of mathematics, compared with the dispersion that favored AP.)

One calculation nevertheless shows the APRA/UNO coalition in the first municipal elections getting only 44 percent of the total national vote, compared to combined totals of around 60 percent in the 1962 and 1963 presidential elections. AP/DC candidates, by contrast, got almost 47 percent in the municipal vote, against totals of between 30 and 40 percent in the 1962–63 national elections.

The Lima mayoralty race in December, 1963, illuminated the situation more clearly. It was an overwhelming victory for Christian Democrat Luís Bedoya Reyes, the AP/DC candidate, against the wife of former President Odría, backed by APRA/UNO. Three years later, nationwide municipal elections brought the opposing coalition back toward parity, but still did not reflect the congressional division of strengths.[37]

Concurrently with demonstrations of popular support, however, AP and DC were experiencing growing divisions within the governing alliance and within the two parties. Both were split along reformist-moderate lines, and each faction had its prominent leader. The strain within DC broke in February, 1967, when Bedoya Reyes led the conservative elements out of the party to form a new "Christian Popular" party. When Belaúnde sought the support of this faction in the by-elections of November, 1967, the original DC, headed by Héctor Cornejo Chávez, second vice-president of the republic, left the cabinet.[38]

The leader of the AP reformist wing was Vice-President Edgardo Seoane, professional agronomist and brother of the late deputy leader of APRA. Impatient with the frustration of development efforts, and in favor of a hard line against the APRA/UNO opposition in Congress, Seoane was rankling. Upon being elected secretary general of AP in 1967,

[36] Astiz, *Pressure Groups*, p. 122.
[37] *Ibid.*, pp. 110–11.
[38] *Ibid.*, p. 127; *New York Times*, November 14, 1967, p. 33.

he promised to add reform and social justice to the public works being built by the government.[39]

Already having been mentioned as AP's candidate for president in 1969, Seoane became more open in his criticism of foreign investments in extractive industry and physical infrastructure. He was named both foreign and prime minister on September 7, 1967, in the aftermath of the boycott of the Senate by government members, but he continued in office only until November.[40] In the same month, the stability of the government parties was further shaken by losses to APRA/UNO in the by-elections for certain municipal and congressional seats.[41]

Meanwhile, economic deterioration was proceeding. By 1967, inflation had reached 30 percent in three years without any change in the exchange rate or limitation on convertibility. In 1966 Belaúnde had imposed tighter internal credit controls. In 1967 he cut credit available to foreign firms and raised customs duties on consumer goods. He finally decided on devaluation of the sol on September 1, 1967, ending what some condemned as a conspiracy of upper-class business interests.[42]

The devaluation crisis had its repercussions in politics. Tax reforms which might have combatted inflation while financing development were opposed by APRA/UNO. The need for a working arrangement brought Belaúnde and Haya into conference in October. Later, it is claimed, they reached an understanding that gave Belaúnde the cooperation of Congress in exchange for his appointment of a "technical" cabinet representing orthodox management of the economy by coastal business interests.[43]

Each of these events widened the breach in AP's ranks. Seoane was chosen as the 1969 presidential candidate. By mid-1968 there was a pitched battle for physical control of the national party headquarters, which Belaúnde won with police aid. By then, however, the military officers who organized the coup must have been near decision, if not already making plans. On October 3 Belaúnde was deported and General Juan Velasco Alvarado assumed the presidency.

Various explanations are given for the 1968 coup. Ostensibly, the case of the "missing page" of the International Petroleum Corporation contract was the provocation and the trigger. Other reasons were of longer standing. Among the military grievances are cited the need in this period to clear

[39] Astiz, *Pressure Groups*, pp. 117–18.

[40] *Journal of Commerce*, August 17, 1967; *New York Times*, September 8, 1967, p. 3, and October 18, 1967, p. 4.

[41] PAP, "Amplio Triunfo Obtuvo La Oposición en el Perú," (News release, n.p., n.d., received November 28, 1967).

[42] *New York Times*, August 13, 1967; *Los Angeles Times*, August 23, 1967; Astiz, *Pressure Groups*, pp. 118ff.

[43] *New York Times*, October 25, 1967, p. 14.

promotions with the Aprista-led Congress and the army's small share of budget relative to its strength in manpower.[44] Traditional military dislike of APRA and concern that AP and DC factionalism might permit an Aprista victory in the 1969 presidential elections are also generally accepted. The paradox is suggested, however, that the military opposed APRA in 1968 for its moderation rather than its radicalism. More generally, the coup is attributed to military disillusionment with civilian rule, and particularly with Belaúnde, who seemed so promising in 1963.[45] If one concedes the influence of the CAEM studies of civilian problems, it is easy to conclude that the officers had decided that this was no way to run a government.

Whatever its origins and directions, the 1968 coup brought to a close APRA's twelve-year search for power and left no indication as to when or on what terms the search would be renewed. Without abolishing political parties, the Velasco regime postponed elections indefinitely, dissolved Congress, and replaced the elected municipal councils. APRA responded by condemning the coup and adopting a defiant posture.[46] Parties were free to operate, but they had no immediate functions.

Critique

Aprista actions have been traced through the events of the 1956–68 period in terms that can be related to my strategic model for peaceful ascent to power. Obviously, the party failed to reach its objective. Some of the reasons are evident in the choices the party made.

Even before 1956, Harry Kantor wrote, "The *Aprista* ideology has its weaknesses, the most conspicuous its neglect of a method of achieving power. . . ."[47] The inadequacy of the party's strategy can be seen in its community, party, and state relationships.

It was apparent by 1962 that APRA had lost popular support from its former standing as the reputed majority party. Later it may have slipped further. Its losses appear to have been less the result of an oppressive, unyielding conspiracy, however, than of the evolution of society and the political system. APRA either failed to recognize the changes that were occurring or was unable to cope with them.

In the party system of Peru the new development after 1956 was the legitimation of development as a subject of party politics and the dis-

[44] Astiz, *Pressure Groups*, pp. 265–68.

[45] Einaudi, "Peruvian Military," pp. 11–12, 16.

[46] George W. Grayson, Jr., "Peru's Military Government," *Current History* 58, no. 342 (February, 1970): 70.

[47] Harry Kantor, "Aprismo: Peru's Indigenous Political Theory," in *The Dynamics of Change in Latin American Politics*, ed. John D. Martz (Englewood Cliffs, N.J.: Prentice-Hall, 1965), p. 86.

appearance of old parties overtly dedicated to resisting change. APRA never fully came to terms with its most avid imitators, and one result was the disintegration of the other moderate parties in the final year of Belaúnde's administration.

APRA's actions in relation to the state tended to be inconsistent. To all appearances the party lacked significant allies in the civil service or the military officer corps. Either could have been useful; the latter was indispensable. The only strength APRA had in the state apparatus was in Congress. This power was used in ways that may have been psychologically satisfying, and by some standards possibly even high minded. But from the standpoint of practical politics the party seemed to be fighting the last war in Congress.

As it turned out, tactics that may have been aimed at pleasing the military missed their target because many of the present generation of senior officers had moved on. They reached the spot where APRA once had been. Sometime between 1948 and 1968, APRA and the army had traded places.

If these are accurate assessments, APRA's mistakes are easily identified. In one sense the party confused strategy and tactics. It neglected to keep its short-range decisions within the limits imposed by its long-range plans and capabilities. Stated differently, APRA did not recognize the essential weakness of its position or take effective steps to correct it. Or, I should say, APRA failed at times to see its weakness. At other times its weaknesses were admitted, tacitly, by the actions taken.

This inconsistency between reality and aspiration can be seen in Figure III–2. It shows the alternations that occurred during the 1956–68 period between strong and weak acts of the party. If one were to prescribe, with the clarity of hindsight, what the party should have done within the situation as it existed, one would begin with pursuit of a weak strategy, or the indirect approach to power. Such an approach would have had to continue until certain prerequisites of the strong approach were acquired.

In a weak strategy, APRA would have seized one of its several opportunities to combine with Belaúnde. The first was in 1956, when the Apristas evidently decided that Belaúnde could not win the presidency, even with their help (another admission of weakness), or that he could not legalize APRA if he did win. By 1962, doubts about Belaúnde's popular strength and his influence with the military could have been discounted.

By then, however, APRA was intent upon electing its own candidate, even though it had no assurances (on the contrary, it had serious reasons to doubt) that the army would let him take office. In 1962 the critical element of the strong course, neutralization of the military, would have entailed the willingness and capability of President Prado to cooperate effectively, and subsequent plans for subordinating the military to civilian control. Neither of these was available.

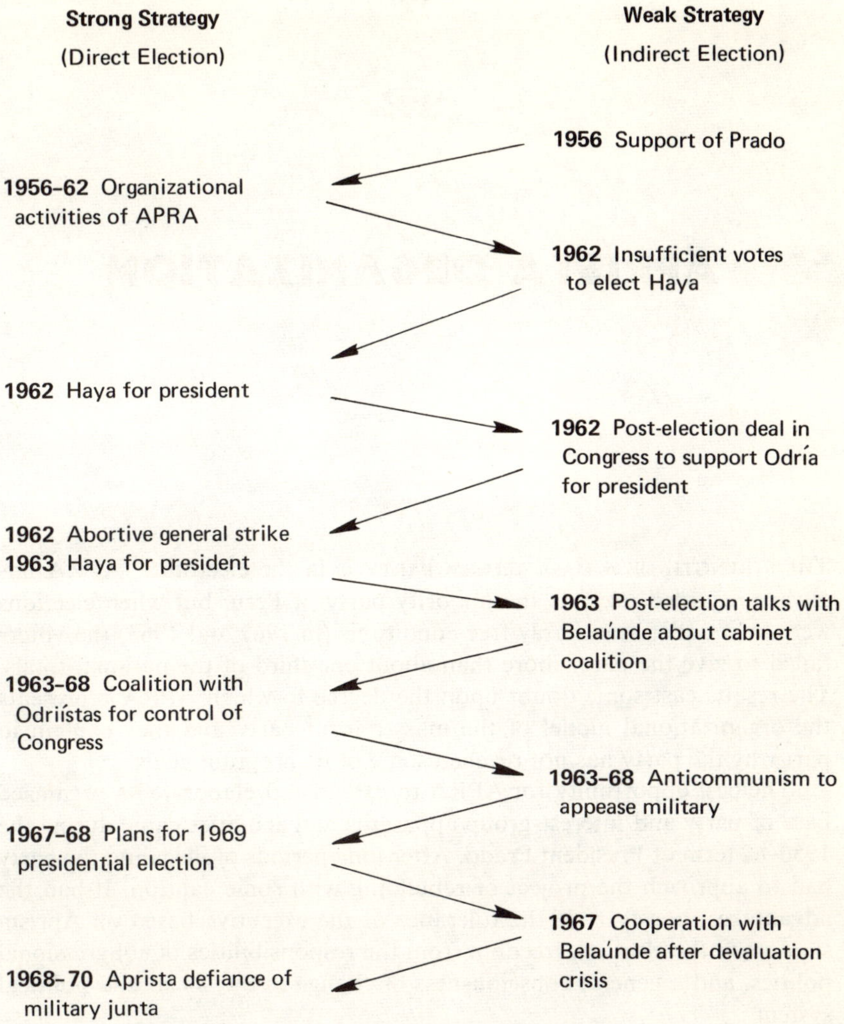

FIGURE III–2. ALTERNATION OF STRATEGIES BY APRA, 1956–68

In 1963 the same situation and opportunities were present before the election campaign, except that APRA now knew its weaknesses in all sectors—community, party system, and state. After the election, as in the pre-coup negotiations a year earlier, APRA probably could have come to terms with Belaúnde if it had accurately assessed its own position. Their coalition might have made the ensuing five years and beyond much different in terms of effective reform. Instead, rapprochement with Belaúnde was put off until his administration was beyond help.

IV

APRISTA ORGANIZATION

THE STRENGTH OF A MASS REFORM PARTY is in the electorate. APRA has always regarded itself as the majority party of Peru, but when elections were held under reasonably free conditions (in 1962 and 1963) the voters failed to give the party more than about one-third of the national totals. The results cast some doubt upon the degree to which APRA represents the organizational model of the mass reform party and they explain in part why the party has not reached some of its program goals.

The best opportunity for APRA to extend and elaborate its organized base of party and interest-group apparatus and activities came during the 1956–62 term of President Prado. After long periods of illegality, the party had to approach the project of rebuilding with some caution. It had the advantages, however, of the tolerance of the executive based on Aprista support in the election, freedom from the responsibilities of congressional politics, and a general consciousness of change in the social and political system.

The relative freedom of action accorded APRA in this period was illustrated by the use that it made of "political bargaining" in trade-union affairs, where the party had always been strong. The question of organization, however, is directed not to the *use* of existing strength so much as it is to the *extension* of it. In such fields as organized labor and in other geographic and functional areas of the country, APRA faced the task of perfecting and measuring its popular strength during the Prado administration, which was preparatory to determining its strategy for the next election and beyond.

In the building of political infrastructure, the basic choice as seen in Figure III–1 must be between conventional and unconventional politics. APRA was determined in 1956 to avoid violence and to work within the system that was offering it a chance to bring about reform. This need not have meant a renunciation of unconventional methods, however, nor by any means the neglect of contingent preparations for the future use of peaceful, unconventional means. In fact, this was how the active management of the party seems to have viewed its tasks in 1956. How well it succeeded in the following six years can be seen in the times of testing that came during the middle sixties.

A Regional Party?

APRA has always been strongest in the area of its origins. So much of its history during the thirties, forties, and fifties was spent underground, however, that it was not exclusively identified with the north but came to symbolize a force of national proportions.

The true distribution of its followers throughout Peru was further obscured by its repeated use of the strategy of indirect control of the executive. Only in 1962 and 1963 (for the first times since 1931) did APRA present its own candidate for the presidency and thereby obtain a pair of reasonably reliable voting patterns. These provide surprisingly consistent data from which to judge the degree to which APRA is more a regional than a mass party.

Contradicting the majority party thesis of APRA is the theory that the party has never commanded more than about one-third of the national electorate, and that this (1) has been relatively constant over time and (2) represents the only true party vote in Peru. The rest of the national vote is thought to be equally divided, one-third of the total being identified with opposition to the regime in power (*renovación*), the other third being tied to the traditional voter (*conservador*).

By this reasoning APRA did not lose support in 1962 but was simply reduced to its hard-core vote for the first time since 1931. Over the years, by combining its one-third of the electorate with one or the other of the opposition and traditional groups, it had seemed to be more potent than it was. In 1945 it joined the opposition to elect Bustamante; in 1956 it helped the traditional group (as did outgoing President Odría, finally), while the opposition vote went to Belaúnde.

The distribution of the supposedly stable thirds began to be evident in the elections of 1945 and 1956, in which the die-hard traditionals voted for Ureta and Lavalle, respectively. If this thesis is correct, Prado may have gotten few votes other than those of the Apristas in 1956. Belaúnde's appearance that year marked the beginning of the consistent patterns that became more evident in 1962 and 1963, when his support seemed to change from one of opposition to one of reform and when Odría's was one of traditional opinion without class limitations.[1]

The four presidential elections conducted in relative freedom since World War II show the following vote totals:[2]

Year	APRA-supported Candidates		Acción Popular (Belaúnde)	Other Candidates of Note	
1945	Bustamante	300,000*	—	Ureta	150,000
1956	Prado	568,000	458,000	Lavalle	223,000
1962	Haya	557,000	544,000	Odría	481,000
1963	Haya	624,000	709,000	Odría	463,000

* Approximate number

The geographic distribution of election results can be viewed from several angles in an effort to discern characteristics in any one election and from one election to another. Most striking is the factor showing stability in the dominant positions of Haya de la Torre and Belaúnde in different departments.

Polarization

Simply in terms of major sources of continuing support, certain departments of Peru overwhelmingly favored one or the other leading candidate in 1962 and 1963. Haya de la Torre received absolute majorities in the three northern departments of Cajamarca, La Libertad and Lambayeque in both elections and suffered almost no loss in his share of the total between the two elections. (In the central department of Pasco he also had majorities but dropped slightly in his 1963 share of the vote.) This is the core of the area known to APRA as the "Solid North." In the same way, Belaúnde received solid support in Cuzco, Puno, and Moquegua in 1962 and 1963. These two opposing blocs of contiguous departments represent

[1] Chirinos, *Cuenta y Balance*, esp. pp. 22–38. Written in 1962 after the elections of that year, this assessment is most interesting because of its source. Chirinos became known as a "friend" of APRA while he was also a writer for *La Prensa*, president of the journalists' association, and a practicing attorney. Although he did not claim that his formula remained valid for the future, his claims for its stability were supported by the similarity of election results in 1962 and 1963. He later was elected deputy from Lima on the APRA/UNO ticket in the November, 1967, by-elections.

[2] Data for 1945 are from Sánchez, *Haya de la Torre*, p. 396; for 1956, from César Francisco Macera and Alfonso de Souza Ferreira, *El Proceso Electoral de 1956* (Lima: By the authors, n.d.), p. 20; and for 1962 and 1963, from *La Prensa*, June 21, 1963, p. 2. Votes for other candidates not listed totaled about 109,000 in 1962 and 19,000 in 1963.

the extremes of Aprista strength and weakness, respectively, as shown on Figure IV–1. Both shade off into areas, generally contiguous as well, in which Haya or Belaúnde enjoyed pluralities, but not majorities, in both elections. In summary, the listing of departments by leading party majorities and pluralities is as follows:

	Majorities	Pluralities
APRA	Cajamarca, La Libertad, Lambayeque, Pasco	Ancash, Huánuco, San Martín, Amazonas, Ica
AP	Cuzco, Puno, Moquegua	Arequipa, Ayacucho, Huancavelica, Junín, Madre de Dios, Loreto

Concentrations

The effect of polarization between the two main contenders for the presidency was to reveal the proportions of their respective totals which were dependent upon a concentration, rather than a dispersion, of popular support. APRA, for example, exhibited a high degree of concentrated support. In 1963 it got almost half of its total vote from departments that it consistently dominated, and more than one-fourth from areas where it held absolute majorities.

AP, on the other hand, was less dependent upon concentrations of strength. In 1963 it received less than one-third of its total from departments it dominated, and about 10 percent from majority departments (in coalition with DC). The third leading party, UNO, was the most parochial, getting 64 percent of its 1963 vote in the four jurisdictions (Lima, Callao, Piura, and Tacna) where it received pluralities in 1962 (and, except for Lima, in 1963).

The relative importance of each of these areas for the two leading candidates in the 1963 election is shown by the following totals:

	Aprista Votes		AP/DC Votes	
	Thousands	Percent	Thousands	Percent
Departments producing *majorities* in 1962 and 1963	175	28	73	10
Departments producing *pluralities* in 1962 and 1963	111	18	153	21
Totals in these areas	286	46	226	31
National totals	624	100	723	100

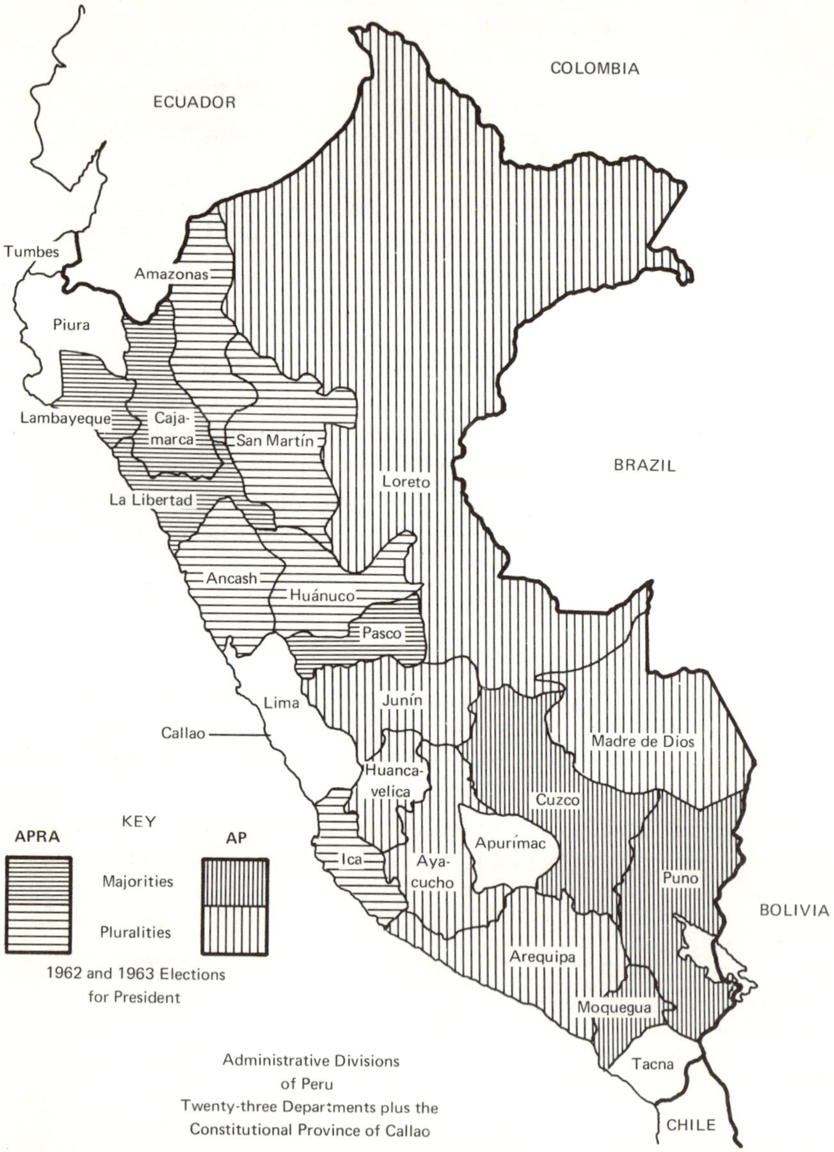

FIGURE IV–1. REGIONAL CONCENTRATIONS OF APRA AND AP STRENGTH, 1962 AND 1963 ELECTIONS

Regional Contrasts

Considering only the Aprista vote, the degree of its concentration in the North becomes still more apparent. For this purpose the other departments—i.e., those not Aprista-dominated—can be regrouped in terms of geographic location. The Lima-Callao metropolitan area and environs form the largest source of votes, while the rest of the southern and central coast, sierra, and selva divide into two regions, as indicated in Table IV–1.

TABLE IV–1: REGIONALISM IN THE 1963 PRESIDENTIAL ELECTION

Regions	Total Vote for President (thousands)	APRA Vote (thousands)	APRA Vote as Percentage of Regional Totals	APRA Vote as Percentage of APRA Total
A. "Solid North" (coast, sierra, selva, south to Pasco and including Ica)	488	286	57	46
B. Lima (Department) and Callao	786	211	27	34
C. South-central sierra and eastern Selva	222	68	30	11
D. Far South (coast and sierra)	320	59	18	10
Totals	1,815	624	34	100

Although APRA got 57 percent of the regional vote in the North, the total number of voters there did not loom large in the country as a whole. The Aprista share was large enough, however, to form a solid base of 46 percent of the party's national vote in 1963. The Lima-Callao area is important from any point of view. It supplied almost half the voters in 1963 and, although APRA received less than 30 percent of them, they represented another one-third of the national total for the party. The other two areas are not highly significant individually, and are even less so to APRA, yet they supply almost one-third of the voters for the whole country. Figure IV–2 shows these contrasts graphically.

The parallels between the Aprista North in Peru and the historically Democratic Solid South in the United States are striking. APRA relies upon this region of concentrated strength for its base of support. In 1962 and 1963 the North plus minority Aprista strength in all other areas came very close to electing Haya to the presidency.

The potential significance of Lima-Callao to the party lies in its present preponderance of dynamic interest groups; that of the rest of the Center-

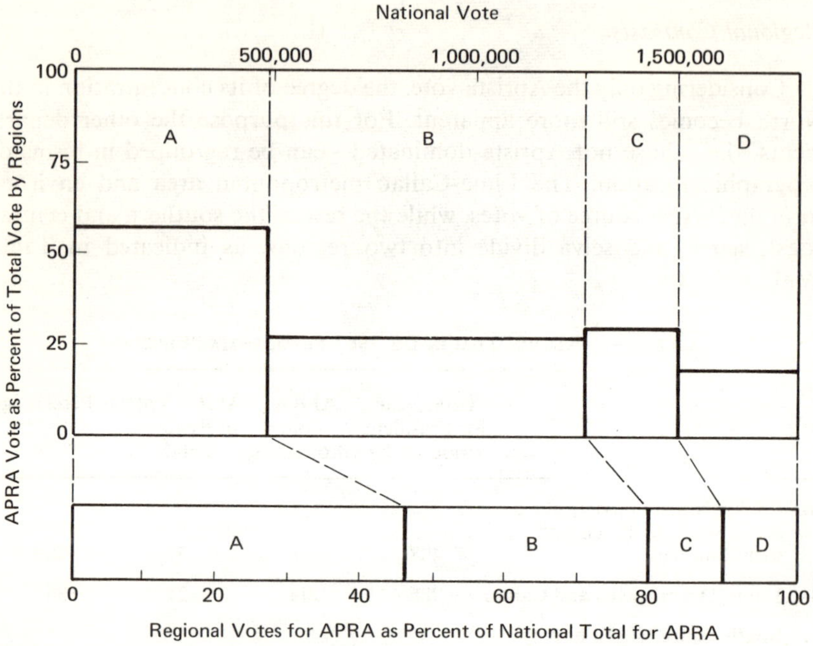

FIGURE IV–2. REGIONALISM IN THE 1963 PRESIDENTIAL ELECTION

South lies in the future development it undoubtedly will undergo to make fuller use of its under-utilized human and physical resources. The parallel with the Democratic party breaks down because Haya failed to perform Franklin D. Roosevelt's feat of combining big-city strength with a dependable provincial base.

Continuity

A further factor of some interest was the ability of APRA to maintain or increase its popular support between elections. Comparisons are made between the elections of 1956 and 1962 to show the effects of the change from indirect to direct strategy, and between those of 1962 and 1963 to suggest where Haya failed to stay abreast of Belaúnde in the decisive contest.

The concept of vote trading is used here as a simplification of statistical presentation on the assumption that marginal changes in the individual candidate's share of the departmental voting totals actually reflects an equivalent shift of voter preference. This may not always be true—for example, when the number of registered voters or participants changes markedly between elections.

In 1962 Haya was able to increase the share of departmental votes Prado had received in five places. These included the four Aprista majority departments, plus one in which APRA won a plurality. In the three places of greatest Aprista strength, Belaúnde lost over-all about as much as Haya gained. In the other two departments, Haya gained less than Belaúnde lost between the elections. In seven other departments, Haya fell somewhat below Prado's share of the vote. Belaúnde's gains in these places in 1962 were, with few exceptions, directly proportional to Aprista strength. In the four departments in which APRA was generally strongest, Belaúnde gained; in the three others, where Aprista strength was minor, he lost.

Thus, in 1962 Haya was able to hold or improve upon the record of the Aprista-supported candidate of 1956 in twelve departments. The results were to increase the polarization of strength between APRA and AP, and the concentration of voter support for APRA alone. Where Haya was weakest, the votes lost by Belaúnde went to Odría or other minor candidates. In the rest of the country, Haya failed to equal the record of Prado in 1956, and the directions and beneficiaries of the vote trading were mixed. Belaúnde lost votes to minor candidates in Lima and Arequipa. In only four departments in the entire country did he appear to take votes directly from Haya. These were in four of the southern sierra departments where, with one exception, Belaúnde dominated.

The 1963 election results were not markedly different from those of 1962. This was especially true in areas of greatest Aprista strength. Belaúnde won back in 1963 some of the votes he had lost to minor parties the previous year, both in the largest cities and in the sierra departments of the South. Aprista gains occurred in its areas of strength and, to a lesser extent, in some of the urban and rural strongholds of Belaúnde (see Appendix B).

Dynamics

The question arises whether changes in voting preferences between elections may have been related to migration, especially between the 1956 and 1962 elections. Statistics are available which show migration to Lima by department of origin, and migration through all departments, up to 1962.[3]

Migration to Lima during this period totaled almost 800,000 people. More of them (344,000) came from departments dominated by APRA than came from those in which AP won pluralities in 1962–63 (294,000). Taking into account the degrees of party strength in each department, however, the theoretical advantage for APRA remains unchanged. It could

[3] Larson and Bergman, *Social Stratification in Peru*, pp. 306–11.

not be said from this evidence, therefore, that the difficulty APRA encountered in capturing the burgeoning capital vote stemmed from differential rates of migration from areas of partisan concentration.

Approximately the same conclusion can be drawn from an examination of the statistics for net growth of all departments. Absolute growth in areas of Aprista dominance totaled almost 1,200,000, while in AP areas it was less than 900,000. Since 1940 the Aprista departments had grown by more than 50 percent, compared to less than half that rate in AP departments. The population of the rest of the country, however, had increased by 75 percent. When APRA and AP voting strengths were used to weight the population increases department by department, there was little by which to choose between the two.

A Labor Party?

The functional sources of strength upon which APRA depends are still fundamentally those to which Haya de la Torre appealed in 1931—the workers, *campesinos*, and the middle class.[4] Each of these sectors, however, presented the party with different problems of organization and communication. Only among the workers, through trade unionism, can APRA be said to dominate, and even there regionalism seems to override the functional factor when they conflict. A tendency toward particularism is thus evident, although not without qualifications.

The Working Class

The fact that APRA is almost synonymous with trade unionism in Peru hardly requires demonstration. It is shown by the way in which trade unionism has prospered in periods of APRA's legality and stagnated while the party was underground, as before 1945 and from 1948 to 1956. It is apparent also in the durability of trade unionists who are also long-term Apristas in firm positions of leadership in the Confederación de Trabajadores del Perú (CTP).[5]

[4] PAP, *Aprismo*, p. 20.

[5] U.S. Department of Labor, *Labor in Peru*, p. 52; see also Robert J. Alexander, *Organized Labor in Latin America* (New York: Macmillan, The Free Press, 1965), pp. 116–22. J. Payne, in his *Labor and Politics in Peru*, dealt with this question under the peculiar conditions of the 1956–62 *convivencia*. Two others also surveyed the history of APRA-labor interaction: Moises Poblete Troncoso and Ben G. Burnett, *The Rise of the Latin American Labor Movement* (New Haven, Conn.: College & University Press, 1960), pp. 89–92; and John J. Crowley, Jr., "Labor and Political Parties in Latin America: Three Examples" (Paper prepared at the University of Wisconsin, for the Foreign Service Institute, May, 1960), pp. 42–53.

What is not so clear is the precise effect of the preponderance of Aprista influence in CTP in the political arena. To assess this aspect it is necessary to gauge Aprista influence in the trade unions, to trace its regional influence, and to suggest some of the effects the relationship has on the party itself.

The first of these is relatively easy. The effective membership of trade unions under "extremist" control (i.e., some form or faction of communism in Peru) was estimated at only about 50,000 in 1957, the year after the Apristas returned from exile. Four years later it had been cut in half, while the total number of recognized unions had almost doubled. As of the end of 1963, at least three-fourths of the union members in Peru, estimated at between 200,000 and 400,000, belonged to CTP unions. Qualified observers estimate that Aprista labor strength increased after 1963.[6]

Against these figures, the proportion of the non-agricultural work force that was organized was calculated in 1962 at only 15 percent, compared to 30 percent in the United States. Investigators looking only at factories, which are the most "organizable," however, find that they are practically all organized. The unorganized workers probably are in small shops. Manufacturing employs less than 20 percent of the active population.[7]

Other sectors of labor are in some cases larger or better paid than factory workers, but by the dispersed locations or non-homogeneous nature of their work they are less likely to be as readily mobilizable for political purposes. The largest factories are for the most part located in the Lima-Callao area or elsewhere in populous centers of political activity on the Peruvian coast.

The key significance of organized labor made the trade unions ready instruments for political purposes under certain conditions. There is probably no question that (1) Aprista control of trade unions is the best *potential* weapon the party has in times of political crisis, and (2) that APRA enjoys a greater *degree* of such control than any other party or, in the number of adherents, all other parties combined. In the commitment

[6] J. Payne, *Labor and Politics in Peru*, pp. 100–101. Payne estimates at 329,000 the number of union members who could be reliably called out on strike when, by implication, their immediate interests were not affected. U.S. Department of Labor, *Labor in Peru*, pp. 52–53, is the source of the other statistics. See also Gladys Delmas, "Peru's New Politics: The Hit-or-Miss Approach," *The Reporter*, October 24, 1963, who stated that "the labor movement in Peru is overwhelmingly Aprista; Belaúnde has no strength there at all. . . . " (pp. 35–38).

[7] J. Payne, *Labor and Politics in Peru*, p. 131. Payne considered only private firms of more than fifty employees. In a sample of factory workers in the Lime-Callao area, it was found that about 64 percent attended union meetings and more than 55 percent took part in union elections (see Briones and Mejía Valera, *El Obrero*, p. 54). This suggests a higher degree of participation by factory workers than is indicated by the 15 percent over-all figure (IDB, *Social Progress Trust Fund: Fifth Annual Report, 1965* [Washington, D.C., 1966], pp. 524–25).

of this power, however, APRA must also reckon with its effect on over-all party strategy, and for most of the period since 1960 such use has been inappropriate to, or actually in conflict with, its basic aims.

A further influence on the relationship of Aprista trade-union strength to the party's political power lies in its geographic distribution. This is most apparent in APRA's control of regional federations of CTP. Of seventeen such unions (having an estimated total membership of 160,000 in 1963), five, or 58 percent of the total membership, came from departments in which APRA was dominant and Haya received majorities in 1963. Three unions, with an additional 34 percent of the membership, represented areas (Lima, Callao, Junín) where Haya got more than 25 percent of the 1963 vote. Four other regional unions, under extremist direction and declining to memberships of 2,000 or less by 1962, all came from departments in which Haya lost in 1962 and 1963.[8]

Aprista trade-union strength thus is considerable, but it nevertheless seems to follow the regional pattern revealed in the presidential elections. It probably does not exceed a disciplined party membership of more than 100,000. With family members and others, this might reach a maximum voting power of 200,000, or not more than one-third of the some 600,000 votes Haya received in 1963.

The significant question for the party is probably less "What can the trade unions do for us?" than "What must the party do for the trade unions?" The tendency to assume that the trade unions are in danger of being subverted to political ends ignores the fact that the Apristas have not been willing, or perhaps able, to use their CTP influence to achieve political objectives. On the other hand, the political behavior of the party is necessarily strongly influenced by the fact that CTP is the party's functional base, just as the North is its geographic base.

The rank-and-file union member in Peru undoubtedly sees his interests mainly in the attack on "specific, immediate grievance" rather than indirectly through promotion of the political aims of a party. The tensions that exist, therefore, are likely to depend upon the status of the party that is dominant in the trade unions. When APRA was supporting Prado, it was accused by workers and by its opponents of being too conservative; as it found itself in opposition to the government, a change to greater advocacy of strikes was conceivable, although not expected to follow automatically. In fact, some increase in strikes did occur during the period of the 1962–63 military junta, but this may have been due as much to management's ineptness in labor relations as to deliberate Aprista policy.[9]

[8] U.S. Department of Labor, *Labor in Peru*, pp. 54–55; J. Payne, *Labor and Politics in Peru*, p. 101. The membership figures tend to be inflated.

[9] J. Payne, *Labor and Politics in Peru*, pp. 92–94, 123–24; U.S. Department of Labor, *Labor in Peru*, pp. 62–63.

The problem that may be represented by labor's pre-eminent position in APRA is what Alba has called labor's reconciliation to the situation. He states that the proletariat becomes conformist and "a parasite on the people" after it has improved its position at the expense of the "great submerged masses," forgets them, and "collaborates with the very groups that keep the masses submerged."[10]

In situations such as those in which APRA finds itself, the party must constantly choose between incremental benefits for its active supporters and constituents, organized in trade unions capable of independent action, and basic reforms for the benefit of retarded sectors of the society which may or may not be politically active. If it follows the former tendency at the expense of the latter (though they may not always be in conflict), the reform party tends to transform itself into a particularistic tool of an interest group. If so, it is no longer a "mass" party.

A Middle-Class Party?

APRA is a party of middle-class origins. Its first leaders, and most of those long prominent in the party, were drawn together as leaders of university reform and protest while students in Trujillo or Lima. Their family backgrounds were not typically bourgeois, however; more than likely they resembled that of Haya de la Torre, aristocratic in tradition but reduced to modest circumstances by the political and financial upheavals of the late nineteenth century. The student leaders of the early twenties had a toe hold in the developing middle class, thanks partly to the fact that they were studying for professions.[11] University student bodies have since become much more diversified.

Some would say that APRA is not only a party of middle-class origins but also one of middle-class interests, and that it has aimed at becoming such a party from the beginning. The plausibility of this thesis is based on the ideological antecedents of *Aprismo.* Before Haya de la Torre was twenty, for example, Víctor Andrés Belaúnde put forth the idea that the insecurity and impoverishment of the middle class explained many of Peru's problems.

APRA, then, was born of a rivalry between the student agitators and President Leguía. Leguía wanted to bind the middle class to him by means of technocratic development, and he succeeded in "fostering a new, self-conscious and assertive middle sector, as a countervailing force to the aristocracy." By his investment policies, however, Leguía antagonized the

[10] Alba, *Alliance Without Allies*, p. 107.

[11] Cossío del Pomar, *Víctor Raúl*, pp. 19–25. Sánchez says that only five of the twenty-two Aprista members of the 1931–32 constituent Congress were from the working class (*congresales obreros*); see his *Haya de la Torre*, pp. 284 and 286.

middle class and in the late twenties further weakened its economic position until it was radicalized sufficiently to support the Apristas.[12]

The current middle-class appeal of APRA can be judged by the drop of Aprista strength in 1962 below expectations in Lima-Callao, the point of greatest middle-class concentration in Peru and also the urban area of greatest absolute growth in recent years. APRA's hopes for the capital area were undoubtedly based not only on the results of 1956, when President Prado was narrowly shaded by Belaúnde in the city of Lima, but also on more remote times when Aprista strength there was matched only by the parties of the extreme Left and the conservative Right.

APRA publicly admitted (in its magazine of August, 1962) being surprised by the drop, saying that the result was difficult to explain, even discounting "various factors, such as attrition due to support of *Pradismo*, the presence of unpopular names on the parliamentary list, the millions spent by Odría on television and other propaganda media, the support of the *barriadas*, etc. . . ."[13]

The party should not have been surprised. Between 1940 and 1961 the combined populations of Lima and Callao increased by more than one million persons. This was more than one-fourth of the total Peruvian population increase in the same period. Votes cast in the Department of Lima, plus Callao, rose by 34 percent between the 1956 and 1962 elections. These were two of the key jurisdictions in which Haya's 1962 strength did not even equal that of Prado when APRA supported him in 1956.

Several developments had changed the political situation in Lima by 1962. APRA retained its ideology of change and its image of radicalism and, for some, violence. Those of the middle class who found fulfillment and security in their new status were fearful of the threats posed by such a party; they were of the conventional middle class. Others retained or acquired a taste for reform after the ineffectual government of the fifties under Odría and Prado, while signs of urban change were accumulating on every side. These were people of the dynamic middle sectors, extending from lower to upper income levels, who were disillusioned with the moderate stance which APRA seemed to have adopted in the preceding decade or two. Among them were some former Apristas.

The largest numerical rise in the voting populations of Lima-Callao probably came from the *barriada*-dwellers. Without being highly partisan, they are nevertheless politically organized and active in their own interests. APRA quite obviously did not succeed in capturing a large proportion of this vote. Instead it went heavily to former President Odría, who ran ahead of all candidates in Lima in 1962 and in Callao in 1962 and 1963.

[12] Pike, *History of Peru*, pp. 218, 240–41.

[13] *Presente* (Lima) 6, no. 86 : 7.

Although APRA is known to have had some members active in the politics of the *barriada* tenant councils, there is no indication that it made a special play for *barriada* votes, as Odría did. In a settlement studied by Mangin, the campaigns of 1958, 1959, and 1960 were nonpartisan, but regional slogans were used which failed to disguise national party affiliations.

A still broader opportunity was open to the political parties through the regional associations, which were estimated to number more than 1,000 in Lima alone. These range from the rich and highly exclusive departmental societies to the much more numerous, sometimes affiliated, provincial clubs. The extent of participation by recent migrants is not clear. Within the limits of their goals, membership, and customary methods, however, the regional associations would appear to be an underexploited source of political party expansion, not only in the capital, but also, through hometown ties, into the provinces.[14]

In a broader sense, APRA faced other kinds of problems in the capital area beginning in 1962, when it was for the first time openly in competition with two other parties of reform. Belaúnde's Acción Popular (AP) and the new Christian Democratic party (DC) now enjoyed the psychological advantage of opposition status with respect to the outgoing Prado administration, which APRA had helped put into office.

Both AP and DC candidates had other advantages. Fernando Belaúnde and Héctor Cornejo Chávez were products of the provincial (*arequipeño*) upper middle class, one an architect and the other a lawyer. Each had strong followings among the professions and white-collar occupations, yet both presented reform programs that rivaled that of APRA. The real surprise was that these respectable reform candidates did not do better in 1962. Belaúnde fell below his 1956 proportion of the Lima vote, but maintained his position in Callao. Cornejo drew only between 2 and 3 percent of the votes. The votes they failed to get went not to Haya, but to Odría and the minor leftist candidates.

APRA fared only slightly better in Lima in the 1963 presidential elections. In combination with UNO in the succeeding municipal and by-elections of December, 1963 and 1966, the party found it hard to account for coalition strength, which fell to some 40 percent or less of the total, compared with separate presidential votes that had totaled almost 60 percent. Only in the November, 1967, by-election, when both the governing

[14] Mangin, "Rural Indians and Urban Migrants," p. 33; *idem*, "Regional Associations," *passim;* Larson and Bergman, *Social Stratification in Peru*, pp. 244–46; Astiz, *Pressure Groups*, pp. 224–25. Luís Valcárcel estimated in 1966 that there were more than 1,000 provincial clubs of various kinds in Lima. He commented that they are stratified, those of highest status being organized by departments, and the lower-class clubs attaching to smaller communities or localities. Interview, March 2, 1966.

alliance and DC were deeply divided and a strong leftist candidate was running, did the APRA/UNO coalition win a congressional seat in Lima, by plurality.

Thus, for the political party there are several avenues into the middle class. Middle-class origins, shared by almost all the party leaders, offer no assurance of success. Student politics is perhaps the next most useful point of attack. Increasingly, white-collar and professional organizations have attracted the attention of at least the two largest parties, APRA and Acción Popular. Finally, and perhaps the least generally exploited in the past, are the groupings based on place of residence—notably the tenant councils in the *barriadas*, but also other unofficial urban associations and the official governing bodies of municipalities which were popularly elected after 1963.

Students and Youth

From its beginnings, APRA has enjoyed strong, organized support from youth. In the past decade, however, following the advent of Castroism, APRA has lost its initial and long-standing dominance of university student politics. After initially supporting Castro's movement in 1958, the Aprista students at Lima's San Marcos University came to oppose him because of his communist allegiance. Not long afterward they lost decisive control of the student body.

In 1959 the Apristas were narrowly defeated by a coalition of Castroites and Christian Democrats. Thereafter the Castroites—using "independent" labels to advantage—were strong enough to win repeatedly without assistance. APRA also lost some of its leaders, among them two student leaders from Trujillo who broke away in 1958 to form APRA Rebelde, which later became the Movimiento de la Izquierda Revolucionaria (MIR), making Castroite inroads even in Trujillo, the alma mater of Haya de la Torre.[15]

Aprista student losses were repeated in other Peruvian universities, sometimes because of coalitions between Communists and Acción Popular, until in October, 1963, APRA did not even present a slate of officers at the National Student Congress. Only two of the twenty-one university delegations at that meeting were Aprista; the rest had pro-Communist majorities.

Some revival of APRA's student strength occurred in 1964–65, but in general the Communists remained dominant. The Apristas could hope to influence student politics in most universities only through combinations

[15] Patch, "Fidelismo in Peruvian Universities—I and II"; Einaudi, "Changing Contexts of Revolution," p. 22.

with other parties, including in some instances even one or another of the Moscow, Peking, or Cuban Communist factions.[16]

Efforts to explain the decline in Aprista student support have emphasized the party's new image of moderation in contrast to the radicalism that fed on Castroism and, for a time, on Peruvian peasant unrest and guerrilla activities. The decline is also laid in part to the changing character of student bodies. Some 48,000 students were enrolled in thirty universities in 1964, compared to only 4,000 in seven institutions in 1940.

There has always been the tendency on the part of aristocratic and conservative families (except in Arequipa) to send their sons abroad to study, or, if to Lima, to the Catholic University rather than to San Marcos or the technical schools. The provincial universities have been regarded as the least desirable, and they have been expanded greatly in recent years. The expansion of educational opportunities for students of lower economic status, and the tendency to flood the job market with professionals, has increased the students' radical propensities.[17]

In contrast to the trade unions, the hostage value of which tended to impose demands on the party, university students ask only that the party give it moral support and an activist ideology. Aprista losses in the artificial world of student politics have probably resulted more from student disillusionment with the party's actions than from defects of organizational effort or political maneuver.

After experiencing reverses in the universities, APRA showed concern for its future by giving renewed attention to youth activities, which was only a return to its traditional emphasis. One of the earliest party pamphlets read in part like a youngster's catechism and explained that the object of "these litanies" was to understand "the meaning of youth in action."[18]

The youth section of APRA, one of the elements which gives APRA the distinctive characteristics of a mass party, was first formed in 1934. Years of underground existence, however, undoubtedly limited Aprista youth

[16] *HAR* 16 (1963): 992; Delmas, "Peru's New Politics," p. 38; Terry L. McCoy, "The Peruvian Aprista Party, 1965," mimeographed field research report (Madison: University of Wisconsin, 1965), p. 10; *HAR* 18, no. 6 (1965): 541–42. A split between the Moscow and Peking factions in San Marcos, Lima, permitted APRA to win there in 1964 and to get into position to regain the rectorship (with the help of independent votes) in 1966; see *Expreso*, March 13, 1966, p. 2.

[17] Patch, "Fidelismo in Peruvian Universities—I," pp. 12–13; interviews with Jorge Basadre, March 1, 1966, and Nilo Arroba, rector of the University of Huancayo, March 12, 1966. See Ravines, *La Gran Promesa*, pp. 100–103, on the phenomenon in Latin America; Pike, *History of Peru*, p. 304; Einaudi, "Changing Contexts of Revolution," pp. 11ff.

[18] PAP, *4 Aspectos Importantes del Aprismo* (n.p.: Editorial Manco Capac, 1933), p. 36; see also the youth code in Kantor, *Peruvian Aprista Movement*, app. C, p. 135.

recruiting largely to the families of dedicated members. Some observers blame such limitations on the "aging leadership" of APRA and similar long-standing movements, and try to gauge the youthfulness of the turnout at Aprista rallies.[19]

Claims that APRA is no longer attracting young people found a mark, judging from items in the party newspaper which stress success in the recruiting of young people and the crowds which gather at the *coloquios* (question-and-answer sessions) given by Haya as often as twice weekly from time to time in the auditorium of the Lima *Casa del Pueblo*. Whether these are the youth activities best calculated to attract outsiders is questionable.

White-Collar Associations

After student politics, APRA's next most important route into the middle class lies in the white-collar trade unions and the professional associations. Moreover, these probably hold a greater long-run promise for the party than does student politics. Although the unions are part of CTP, they present political problems that are closer to those of the professional associations. In fact, it is difficult to draw a clear line between these two, in contrast to the deep psychological gap that divides the manual and intellectual workers.

At the lower end of this range of middle-class groups are those associations which formally identify themselves as unions. They are generally to be found in the Confederación Sindical de Empleados Particulares del Perú (CSEPP). In 1961 it affiliated with CTP and was strongly led by an Aprista. As the strongest organization in the field, it represented a political asset to the party. It is composed of diverse elements, however, and like most white-collar unions it probably does not arouse the enthusiasm of the whole white-collar group.

Among the independent white-collar unions is the National Union of Bank Clerks, which came under extremist control in 1958 and joined the competing confederation. The Lima Union of Trolley Operators (regarded as white-collar workers) was captured by Odriístas in 1962. The strongest regional federation in the field is in Arequipa, which, as a city, votes overwhelmingly for parties other than APRA. Although the major parties—AP, DC, and UNO—have made sorties into this field (where they should be very much at home), they are latecomers and are now disorganized by

[19] Sánchez, *Haya de la Torre*, pp. 336, 346–47, 378. The name of the youth section was twice changed before it became Juventud Aprista Peruana (JAP) in 1944. See also Alba, *Alliance Without Allies*, pp. 87–91; "Peruvian Salute to Party Leader Hints Time Has Passed Him By," *Washington Post*, March 23, 1966.

internal splits. They probably represent no greater over-all threat to Aprista domination of *organized* white-collar workers than do the small extremist parties.

Better organized, but standing outside the trade-union framework, are the public school teachers grouped into several competing or overlapping organizations. The major one, Federación Nacional de Educadores del Perú (FENEP), dates from 1960, with roots going back only to the mid-fifties. It includes primary, secondary, and certain specialized teachers.

The teachers' organizations are well-financed and cohesive, as shown by the success of their strike during the latter part of Prado's regime, which gave them salary increases financed by a cigarette tax. At that time, FENEP called on CTP for support similar to that which it was already getting from the extremists. It was not forthcoming, evidently because of the Aprista fear of endangering the stability of the government and the technicality that teachers, as government employees, are not allowed to strike.[20]

Teachers' associations burgeoned in the sixties, with one Aprista-oriented group, Sindicato Peruano de Educadores Secundarios (SINPES), in competition with another proclaiming the same initials. The idea of strikes and union activity was still under debate in the pro-government press early in 1966, following an indication by the minister of education that teachers' associations should present to him their credentials. The ensuing discussion of a possible supervised vote to determine representation questions probably was not unrelated to the parallel threats by APRA to censure the minister for other reasons. APRA is considered to have substantial strength among the public school teachers, although in the opinion of a Peruvian observer it is greater among primary than among secondary teachers.[21]

In the closely related area of civil servants' organizations, the ban on strike activities carries much more weight. Probably as a result, APRA was not highly influential in the first confederation of public employees Asociación Nacional de Servidores Civiles del Estado (ANSCE). The party failed, for example, to avert a strike call which ostensibly was in sympathy with the striking postal workers but which actually was aimed at the Prado government. The government quickly discharged a large number of leaders, but it later recognized the association. Since political and family patronage is still prevalent in the civil service, significant organiza-

[20] J. Payne, *Labor and Politics in Peru*, pp. 124–25, 174–86, 237–51. The law of 1950 (during Odría's term) prohibited strikes by civil servants; U.S. Department of Labor, *Labor in Peru*, p. 50.

[21] *Expreso*, March 4, 1966, p. 2, and March 9, 1966, p. 11; *El Comercio*, March 3, 1966, p. 4; interview with Sra. Luz Landázuri de Maurtua, March 11, 1966.

tional activity must await the conclusion of reforms. Aprista leaders reject the suggestion that the civil service could be an area of politically motivated trade-union action.[22]

In the more strictly professional field, associations have long been the object of Aprista attention. Most other major parties have followed suit, as in trade unionism. The Apristas are therefore stronger in the older professions, while AP and DC tend to dominate among the economists, architects (former President Belaúnde's profession), social workers, etc. The medical profession is divided between Apristas and AP. Control might be a dubious advantage for either party in view of the physicians' strong insistence on their own, particularistic interests against what was viewed as socialization of medicine under Prado.[23]

Journalists likewise can be divided by party loyalties, although a close associate of APRA was president of their association in the mid-sixties and actively defended leftist writers accused of subversion. He claimed that an independent profession of Peruvian journalists had grown up during the fifties, and even that a journalistic revolution had occurred. The press does have an independence and a power in the middle sectors which rivals that of the entrepreneurs.[24] It is doubtful, however, that the influence is wielded as much by working journalists as by the proprietors, whose interests are intertwined with those of the economic elites.

The evidence of continuing competition for the middle-class vote by way of professional associations can be seen, almost any day, in the meeting notices in the Lima press. Usually they simply announce that the *agrupacion* of this or that profession in such-and-such a party is meeting. Or they may be of key significance, such as one stating that the president of the Peruvian Engineer Society had joined Acción Popular in a "simple ceremony at which the secretary general of that party presided."[25]

The over-all impression that emerges from a study of APRA's attempts to woo and hold the middle class is extremely mixed. The efforts certainly are not as successful as they once were, and in some sectors they seem to have failed.[26] The faults in this area probably lie not in the nature or

[22] J. Payne, *Labor and Politics in Peru*, pp. 233–37; interview with Andrés Townsend Ezcurra, March 2, 1966.

[23] Interviews with Sra. de Maurtua (March 11, 1966) and Townsend (March 2, 1966).

[24] Interview with Enrique Chirinos Soto, March 16, 1966. See also Chirinos, *El Perú*, pp. 83–84 (n. 6), 107, and 129; Ramírez, *Elecciones*, pp. 26–29.

[25] *La Prensa*, March 11, 1966, p. 2; *La Tribuna*, July 18, 1963, p. 2. The latter includes notices of meetings of Aprista groups of lawyers, obstetricians, doctors, and primary teachers.

[26] An Aprista leader agreed that AD in Venezuela had been aided by what the Marxists call "the leading section of the bourgeoisie." APRA—by implication—had not. Interview F, March, 1966.

intensity of the effort so much as in the nature of the party and the tendency of the middle class to outgrow it. The appeals that attract support in the regions of firm Aprista strength are no longer those which necessarily win votes in Lima; the techniques that succeed in the trade unions probably are not those best suited to the middle class, whether it be the dynamic or the lethargic sector thereof.

The middle sectors of Peruvian urban life are an arena for the practice of conventional politics. Especially at lower income levels and in new professions, the functions of a party as an intervening and dependent variable are made-to-order for situations in which large numbers of people have left traditional habits, perceive new wants, and are prepared to organize to present group demands to the government.

To organize this kind of raw material is neither radical nor difficult. It requires that clear distinctions be drawn between the preparation and commitment of organized political power, as well as among different kinds of goals and the methods of attaining them. The important point, however, is that psychological change is proceeding. For some individuals it has gone rather far; for others it is just beginning. But the two are in close contact, and the mechanisms for advancing the process exist. They will operate, regardless of the party's decisions or those of anyone else.

Such circumstances were, for APRA, the great opportunity of the late 1950s and early sixties. The task may not have been congenial to Apristas of the old school. There may have been a threat of dilution of *esprit*. Certainly there would have been a characteristic temptation to commit to action, for the sake of short-range objectives, forces which might be unready and which would have a greater political impact when fully organized. On the other hand, there were risks inherent even in conventional politics, risks that were pursued to the limit in favorable circumstances. The alternative of conserving the existing bases of Aprista strength undoubtedly had strong support. The danger of antagonizing the armed forces had to be assessed. The degree to which the adoption of truly extensive organizing tactics could change the nature of APRA probably was viewed with apprehension.

The goals of such an organizing effort would have to go beyond the satisfaction of the simple, immediate needs of the middle sectors, although that would be a way of improving its chances of success. To provide trash-collection service, with or without the help of the government, to align the streets of a squatter settlement, or to organize a school—these are fruits of organized effort, and they improve the eventual political impact of a group.

The methods used in organizing would have to develop by stages. In the beginning, undoubtedly the main reliance would be upon intermediaries carrying the group's demands to those who could meet them. These cannot be the only avenues, because the traditional process leaves the group too vulnerable to delays and red tape. For the party, however, mere assistance to the accustomed methods of presenting demands would improve its ability later to introduce more rational methods.

Ultimately, new goals and methods would be needed to express the far-reaching needs of the people being served and the full potential of their combined strengths. In Peru, for example, the targets would be structural changes going beyond the benefits made available by the incremental enlargement of the system of interests. One target that is frequently proposed is the relationship of domestic manufacturing and foreign trade.

This kind of goal has long been a part of Aprista programs. It rests on the theory that the proceeds of principal Peruvian products for export are squandered on the importation of consumer goods for the use of the relatively small upper- and upper-middle-class holders of financial power. Instead, it is said, imports should be controlled in order to put foreign exchange to more productive use. This would necessarily include accelerated industrialization for purposes of import substitution and providing fuller employment for the hoards of city-dwellers now inadequately absorbed by the tertiary sector.[27]

The new methods that would be needed to pursue a broader goal such as industrialization would bring into play the full potential of the mass reform party. Interest articulation by tenant councils and presentation through intermediaries are methods which necessarily atomize the demands of organized groups. The party as an instrument of interest aggregation would need to find higher levels of commonality (such as industrialization) among the expressed demands of organized groups and to chart new paths of communication between the community and the state.

No guarantee could be offered that the political system would adjust to new strains of this kind. But at least it would begin to approach a working system, and the party probably would prosper (under conditions of free political competition) from a broadening of its base of popular support. In place of this bold approach, however, APRA appears to have played the game more cautiously.

An Indian Party?

APRA is widely known as the party of the Indian. The reputation is in no sense based on success in organizing the rural, sierra Indians as a political force or even in large numbers as interest groups. Instead, Aprista doctrine and publicity in favor of "redemption of the Indian" expresses a concern which is largely paternalistic.

[27] Bourricaud, *Poder y Sociedad*, pp. 202ff.; Astiz, *Pressure Groups*, pp. 61ff.; Larson and Bergman, *Social Stratification in Peru*, pp. 191ff.

There are several good reasons for the continued isolation of the Indian from political life. By social position and cultural outlook, the typical rural Indian is outside the Peruvian society. He is neither socially nor psychologically prepared for political participation. In addition, he is barred by language from easy communication with the dominant society and by the literacy test from even the formality of voting.

Even among transitional Indians, the sturdy peasant type that is implied in the term *campesino* is not often encountered in Peru. He is certainly not the dominant rural type. If he exists as an independent farmer relying primarily on his own land and labor, he is to be found mainly on the coast. Increases in commercial plantation agriculture on the northern coastal plain, however, mean that small semi-independent plots increase toward the South.

In the sierra, especially in the North and increasingly in central Peru, the small tenant, worker, or near-serf generally associated with haciendas has often been liberated by the advance of transitional estates or commercial grazing. He may work for wages or move closer to the money economy by becoming a rent-paying tenant. Southward, the degree of dependence on sharecropping and Indian communities increases (along with semifeudal or communal ties to the land) to the extreme conditions of the southernmost department, Puno.

A variety of more independent forms of work and land tenure can be seen in the montaña that fringes the jungle, and in the selva itself. They range from the wage-earners of certain commercial plantations to a special kind of semifeudal *colono*, one who improves someone else's land in the hope of someday owning it.[28]

APRA thus has been torn between its sentimental and intellectual commitment to improve the lot of the Indian and the difficulty and political unprofitability of undertaking the task. No real penetration of the sierra was begun before 1956. In 1959 concrete steps were taken to organize the Aprista-led Federación Nacional de Campesinos del Perú (FENCAP) for the gigantic task of political organization of the agricultural masses.[29]

[28] Charles Wagley, "The Peasant," in *Continuity and Change in Latin America*, ed. John J. Johnson (Stanford, Calif.: Stanford University Press, 1964); Wagley distinguishes between Indian and mestizo cultures; see pp. 25–27. This section draws principally on Ford, *Man and Land in Peru*, esp. chap. 4; CIDA, *Tierra y Desarrollo*; and J. Payne, *Labor and Politics in Peru*, pp. 224–33.

[29] Ford, *Man and Land in Peru*, p. 124. In 1948 the party literature claimed that "more than 50 percent of the Aprista militants live from the land, through the land, and for the land" (PAP, *Plan Agrario: Documentos del II Congreso Nacional* [Lima, 1948], p. 5). A FENCAP statement prepared for the U.S. National Farmers' Union recounts the history of the years 1922–48 under the Federación General de Yanaconas y Campesinos del Perú, which it describes as being run by "factions of socialist and communist extraction." Local *campesino* organizations emerged between 1948 and 1956, while APRA was outlawed. Reorganization of the old federation led to the formal creation of FENCAP in January, 1960. See FENCAP, *Boletin Extraordinario No. 4* (Lima), April 19, 1965.

The situation is reflected in the current state of *campesino* organization in Peru. The strongest and best-organized rural workers' unions—notably the Sugar Workers' Federation with from 35,000 to 40,000 members—are not part of FENCAP but affiliate directly with CTP, as does FENCAP itself. They are more like wage-earners than farmers.

The membership claimed by FENCAP—between one and two million—is about the same as the economically active rural population and is therefore meaningless. One writer lists it among unions "of very low cohesion" and estimates that it could mobilize only about 5,000 members on strike.

Before the intensified land invasions of the early 1960s, FENCAP was called a "combination of politics, altruism, and chaos" which tries to coordinate a heterogeneous collection of basic organizations using "10 or 12 active leaders." Logically enough, it tries to concentrate on political aspects, but the nature of the problems and the size of the task means that "the positive role which FENCAP can play is clearly limited." As some specific cases show, however, it "has at least begun to serve as a productive national lobby for agricultural workers."[30]

A later characterization calls FENCAP "the organization most representative of the small producers . . . which frequently looses serious campaigns on behalf of its members, organizes congresses, and tries to influence governmental decisions, including those relating to agrarian reform." But its limitations are recognized in that it "performs only work of a general character and is not able in each specific case to demand better treatment" for those it represents.[31]

The complexity of the task and its limited resources notwithstanding, FENCAP has sought to simplify it by classifying affiliates (actual and potential) in five groups. Since each form of tenure tends to prevail in one zone of the country more than in others, the following classification identifies areas of concentration for each type of organizing activity:[32]

[30] J. Payne, *Labor and Politics in Peru*, pp. 175, 231–32. This appraisal was based on observations pre-dating the intensification of peasant land invasions and related activities of 1963; see U.S. Department of Labor, *Labor in Peru*, pp. 26 and 55.

[31] CIDA, *Tierra y Desarrollo*, p. 262. The situation was met in an interesting way by a FENCAP leader on successive visits to two villages that were asking for government help. In the one that obviously needed help he agreed to take up the villagers' case in Lima, while in the second, where the need was less severe, he advised the leaders to work directly with the government. These statements are based on information supplied by Neale J. Pearson in an interview in December, 1965; the interpretation is mine.

[32] While these conclusions are primarily mine, they were suggested by the comments of César Aldea Cancino of FENCAP during interviews on March 14 and 16, 1966. The categories were found in "This is FENCAP," mimeographed press release (n.p., n.d.), which was issued in English and Spanish.

	Coast	Sierra	Selva
Indian communities		xx	
Rural workers (for wages)	xx	—	—
Sharecroppers, etc.	—	xx	—
Jungle settlers			xx
Small farmers (cooperatives)	xx	—	—

Note: xx indicates greatest frequency, — less frequency.

Each group presents different organizing problems. The small sharecroppers (generally those who pay any kind of rent in kind, money or work, and who may be indebted to the owner) usually do not organize, for they have little choice but to quit the land, resort to the law in an effort to obtain larger parcels, or renew their contracts.

"Committees of small producers" are formed, however, which may include small owners and sharecroppers; they are organized not to make demands on the landlord but to present their case to the government. Because they do not meet the test of employer-employee relations, the government has long declined to recognize such farmers' associations as trade unions, with the legal benefits that such recognition carries. The associations nevertheless operate, and, at least on the coast, they take advantage of the "Law of *Yanaconaje*" of 1967, which regulates sharecropping. Some peasant organizations have been effective, particularly in parts of the southern sierra, in extracting concessions from landowners.[33]

The 1960 organizing congress of FENCAP was attended by representatives of fifty-nine *campesino* organizations, comprising twenty-nine Indian communities, eleven of workers, eight of renters, six of sharecroppers, and five of small farmers.[34] Five years later the National Plenary of *Campesino* Unions (attended by all types of organizations) was held. Resolutions were presented by sixty-nine affiliated organizations which, if they did not represent the total number attending, certainly were the most active. This seems a small increase. FENCAP "has contact" with a much larger number of groups, but most probably prefer political neutrality or see no advantage in formal affiliation.

As might be expected from its organizing problems, FENCAP has been most successful on the coast, for that is where the greater degrees of *campesino* independence are found. Of those 1965 affiliates of FENCAP

[33] See CIDA, *Tierra y Desarrollo*, pp. 262–63, 373ff., concerning the 1947 law, as well as Ford, *Man and Land in Peru*, pp. 87–88.

[34] J. Payne, *Labor and Politics in Peru*, p. 232.

that were readily identifiable as to place of origin, almost 40 percent came from the Department of Lima, and a total of two-thirds came from there and three neighboring, mainly coastal, departments. Only two could be identified as coming from departments (Cuzco and Puno) outside the area of the Aprista Solid North. The pattern of membership types reinforces the picture of an organization composed heavily (more than half, judging from organizational titles) of affiliates representing landless workers, a category found mainly on the coast.

The second largest group was small farmers (often organized as co-operatives) and sharecroppers, which in this example cannot be segregated and are probably intermixed in the basic organizations. Finally, a number of Indian communities were represented, which may or may not be operating on a communal basis, for traditional units often register as communities even though they no longer own any land in common. The summary data in Table IV–2 seeks to provide a faithful picture of FENCAP membership as of the beginning of 1965.[35]

TABLE IV–2: FENCAP MEMBER ORGANIZATIONS, BY DEPARTMENT AND TYPE, 1965

Department	Totals	Communities	Workers	Sharecroppers and Small Farmers
Lima (and Callao)	27	6	19	2
La Libertad	7	1	2	4
Ica	6		6	
Ancash	6	1	2	3
Amazonas	3	2	1	
Cajamarca	2	1		1
Huánuco	2	1	1	
Regional Federations				
North	1		1	
Center	1		1	
Rice Workers' Federation	1		1	
Other (or unknown)	13	1	1	11
Totals	69	13	35	21

Source: The groups listed were those presenting resolutions at the national meeting (FENCAP, *Conclusiones del II° Plenario Nacional Sindical Campesino, 26–27 de Feb., 1965* [Lima, n.d.]).

Although FENCAP strength originates mainly in the North, the organization obviously is seeking to expand elsewhere. Haya de la Torre was reportedly planning a speaking tour in the South early in 1966. New

[35] FENCAP, *Conclusiones del II° Plenario Nacional Sindical Campesino, 26–27 de Feb., 1965* (Lima, n.d.). Neale J. Pearson, who visited Cuzco in September, 1964, was told by local authorities that there were no FENCAP offices in the neighboring Department of Apurímac or in the jungle department Madre de Dios (interview with Pearson, December, 1965).

affiliates accepted at the 1965 plenary of FENCAP totaled forty-five in eleven different departments. Of these, eighteen were in the five southern departments of Huancavelica, Arequipa, Apurímac, Puno, and Cuzco, all of which APRA lost in the 1963 election.[36]

Other events held by FENCAP during 1965 support similar inferences. The twenty-two trainees in a class for *campesino* union leaders came from eight different departments, ten of them from Lima (the rural parts of which are traditionally pro-Aprista), but five from Cuzco and an equal number from other non-Aprista departments.[37]

FENCAP also sponsored a convention of communities and *campesinos* for the Department of Cuzco in 1965. It was attended by eighty delegates from twenty-seven organizations, mostly communities, but including cooperatives and *sindicatos* (literally, trade unions, but in Cuzco also the term for organized communities). Since several localities sent between five and ten representatives, these organizations probably represent the approximate total of active FENCAP strength in Cuzco.[38] These may be taken as rough indications of the status of FENCAP efforts to penetrate this area, the domination of which by extremist-led *campesino* organizations was fully evident in the agitation centering in the Cuzco area in those years. They are no basis for gauging results, however, in terms of the size and loyalty of memberships, or for judging how many of the organizations were mere paper affiliates.

Whatever success FENCAP has enjoyed in the sierra, particularly in the southern parts, has been achieved against formidable odds. The obstacles may not have been sufficiently appreciated initially in political quarters; or the importance of the task may have been underestimated prior to the land invasions of the early 1960s. But this has changed to some degree. For what it is worth, CTP in the sixties gave FENCAP three ranking positions on its National Executive Council, plus four subordinate places.[39]

[36] FENCAP, "Conclusiones del Plenario," *Comunicado de Prensa No. 2* (n.p., n.d.); *Expreso*, February 24, 1966, and March 3, 1966, p. 2.

[37] FENCAP, with Centro de Estudios Laborales del Perú (CELP), *Los Alumnos del IX⁰ Ciclo de Capacitación Sindical Campesina Grupo "A", Mayo-Junio, 1965* (Lima, 1965).

[38] FENCAP, *Conclusiones: II Convención Departmental del Comunidades y Campesinos del Cuzco, Julio 3–4, 1965* (Lima, n.d.). Still less organized, it would appear, are the "jungle settlers" for whom FENCAP held a convention at Tingo María, Huánuco, in November, 1965. Participation was not indicated in the brochure, which consisted largely of quotations from pertinent laws and instructions on the formation of cooperatives on Rochdale principles (including political neutrality); FENCAP, *Tercera Convención de Campesinos Colonos de Selva, Noviembre 27–28–29, 1965* (n.p., n.d.).

[39] CTP, *Consejo Nacional Ejecutivo, Período 1964–1967* (Lima, 1964). The three are the associate secretary for central Peru and the secretaries of the press and of peasant affairs. In 1961 J. Payne thought that one FENCAP place on CTP's board of officers was excessive (*Labor and Politics in Peru*, p. 175).

In practical terms, however, the southern sierra region where FENCAP is weakest is still both the seat of Peru's most stubborn peasant problems and the area where any Aprista-affiliated organization suffers from the greatest disadvantages. For FENCAP it has been a region of particularly intensive rivalry with its major competitors.

The main rival is the extremist-sponsored Confederación de Campesinos del Perú (CCP), although it has been characterized merely as "a group of agitators in Lima." Its local affiliates in Cuzco were organized actively by the Trotskyites and former Apristas (later the guerrilla-supporting MIR—Movimiento de la Izquierda Revolucionaria) and passively by other extremists and parties in opposition to Prado. Since the Peruvian Army's anti-guerrilla campaign of 1965 the effectiveness of CCP and related elements in building a loyal following has been open to question.[40]

In the neighboring Department of Puno, FENCAP faced competition which, while avoiding violence, was nonetheless popular and dynamic. Originally associated with the Christian Democratic trade-union movement, the *campesino* organization in Puno was created mainly by the Cáceres brothers, two of whom were deputies in Congress. Later it declared its independence of party ties.[41]

Some of the competitive organizing activity was tested in the land invasions that began between about 1954 and 1960 in a series of isolated incidents scattered throughout rural Peru. At an increasing pace, the period 1960–63 saw the invasions concentrated in the central sierra and in the southeastern valleys of La Convención and Lares in the Department of Cuzco. In this second stage the organization of peasant syndicates, in which APRA had not been highly successful, became an important element.[42]

At the height of the action in Cuzco early in 1964, reports pictured the invasions as massive, yet peaceful and well-organized assertions of Indian rights. Overpopulation, which put an unbearable burden on the land available to Indians, was the ostensible cause. Although sponsored by the extremist-led Cuzco *campesino* federation, the actions apparently reflected the resolve, especially among Indian women, to "regain lost lands

[40] J. Payne, *Labor and Politics in Peru*, pp. 229–31. According to a U.S. journalist, *sindicato* organization in the highlands began in 1952, and older-generation Communists had little part in it; see Norman Gall, "Letter from Peru," *Commentary* 37, no. 6 (June, 1964): 66; see also "Atlantic Report," *The Atlantic* 217, no. 4 (April, 1966): 40.

[41] CIDA, *Tierra y Desarrollo*, p. 398; U.S. Department of Labor, *Labor in Peru*, pp. 53–54; and interviews in Lima, February–March, 1966. This union is the Frente Sindical de Campesinos y Trabajadores de Puno.

[42] CIDA, *Tierra y Desarrollo*, pp. 394–98.

and rights" and not to allow any political party to capture the movement for other purposes.[43]

Violence associated with *campesino* land invasions seems to have been either initiated by the authorities or related to guerrilla activity. It was not started by Indians, but by students and intellectuals from outside the sierra who were frankly imitating Fidel Castro. Guerrilla bands were easily eliminated by the police or, when they intensified their activities in 1965, by the armed forces. The fact that none of them attracted any significant support from *campesinos* was attributed to basic differences of outlook between student leaders and the habitually passive Indian.[44]

The experience suggests two hypotheses. First, despite all the Aprista rhetoric, the party has never really come to terms with, or understood, the Indian problem. APRA's problem is somewhat like that of the guerrillas from the universities (some of whom were former Apristas). Moreover, the land invasions came at a time when APRA was trying to assert its leadership in Congress and appease the armed forces. Its response was to brand the guerrillas as Castro Communists and to call for repression.

In a more fundamental sense, the failure of APRA to face the Indian problem is apparent in its sources of electoral support. The hard-core areas of Indianism as shown in Table II–1, especially the departments of Cuzco and Puno, are also the places where APRA got fewer votes in 1962 and 1963 than it did in almost any other departments in the country (see Figure IV–1).

What is true at the extremes of Indianism in Cuzco and Puno is also valid for a larger number of the Hispanicized departments. Leaving aside both Indian and mestizo departments and the Lima-Callao area, the remaining eleven departments can be ranked according to a factor combining proportions of Indian monolingualism, bilingualism (reduced by half), Indian race, and adult illiteracy. Except for three of the eleven departments, the results are precisely the inverse of a ranking according to the Aprista share of the 1963 presidential vote.

The second hypothesis suggested by the outcome of the land invasions is that the sierra, particularly in the South, is an arena for unconventional politics. The Indians in the most remote departments have not undergone social mobilization, nor are most of them prepared to change either their behavior or their attitudes. Those few who are ready will be likely to migrate toward the coast or the jungle.

[43] Hugo Neira, *Cuzco: Tierra y Muerte* (Lima: Problemes de Hoy, 1964), esp. pp. 80–100. Two interesting comments appear in this collection of newspaper stories: that most of the young members of the peasant syndicates who attended meetings were army veterans, and that the "traditional communism of Cuzco and Arequipa" was too urban to inspire the peasants to action (pp. 81–82).

[44] Astiz, *Pressure Groups*, pp. 156–57, 254.

By suggesting unconventional politics, I do not in this case mean new attempts at violence. If the Indians were ready to become guerrillas, they might also be ready to join political parties and qualify to vote. By unconventional politics I mean exactly what the young proto-Apristas tried to do in the early 1920s in forming adult evening schools for workers. In organizational terms, the opportunity for APRA has been not to try directly to enlist the *campesinos* in all parts of the country in a battle for their rights, but rather to prepare them for someday taking advantage of those rights.

The task was to try to begin the process of acculturation, especially in the period 1956–62, so that the Indians might have some chance of employing improved agricultural methods, protecting their legal rights, and getting more out of their preferred existence in the sierra without (or before) migrating elsewhere.

This would have been a long-lead strategy, requiring investment of human and physical resources in an enterprise with no visible or immediate returns. On the other hand, it would be low in risks, unlikely to excite the suspicions of the armed forces or more than a few landowners directly acquainted with the efforts. Over time it would help immeasurably to increase the capabilities and cohesion of the Indian population of the sierra. Eventually, the flexibility thereby given to the Indians to marshal their political power would be immense.

Summary

Aprista organization has followed the general lines of a mass reform party, but without the degree of success which would keep it from remaining predominantly a regional and a labor party with moderate amounts of middle-class support and only a small truly rural following.The remedies in the latter two sectors might best have been applied during the 1956–62 period. The middle-class approach would have concentrated on Lima-Callao, using conventional politics to achieve fairly short-range goals. The attack on the Indian problem, which is synonymous with the rural problem, would have spread over the whole sierra a long-range effort to use the political party for ostensibly non-political purposes.

V

THE METHODS OF APRA

Besides being in large degree a regional and labor party, APRA has other characteristics and tendencies which require examination. Methods used by the party, or available to it, are sufficiently elusive to require a broadening of the inquiry into the concept of style. The aim is to discover why, with small but solid bases of strength outside the labor movement and the Solid North, APRA has not succeeded since 1956 in expanding them into something more than beachheads.

Party Style

The kind of party that APRA had become by 1956 is revealed through a number of indicators. Although intangible and difficult to assess with precision, they were nevertheless decisive. These influences include the continuing place of Haya de la Torre and his personally compounded ideology, the effects of long periods of repression and defeat, the tendencies to resort to violence, and the party's response to changing circumstances.

Personalism of Haya

It is inevitable that some of the traits and experiences of APRA should be attributed to the *personalismo* of its unquestioned leader. In fact, it is surprising that this is not the *only* party view expressed, especially since Haya is accorded the title and station of "founder" and *jefe máximo*, one not subject to removal or in need of re-election.

Almost without exception, analysts have avoided the temptation to compare Haya with Perón or Vargas, much less with the petty *caudillos* who are more numerous in Latin America. Clearly, there are valid distinctions between the role occupied by Haya and that of the typical personalist party leader.

The differences must first be sought in Haya's personality. Without attempting long-range psychoanalysis, one can quote with assurance the view of a non-Peruvian political leader. He characterizes the Aprista leader as more philosopher than administrator, more intellectual than manipulator. In this, Haya is contrasted with Víctor Paz Estenssoro, the Bolivian president of 1952–56 and 1960–64, who excelled in the pragmatic side of politics.[1] The main influence of Haya in APRA was originally, and still is, represented by its ideology and doctrine.

Personalist parties, at least in Latin America, are typically lacking in stable and elaborate ideologies, although they may advance pseudo-ideologies. (Who can define—without reference to inventors—the doctrine of *Justicialismo* or *O Estada Novo*?)[2] Haya's greatest contribution being ideological, this is the aspect of *Aprismo* which has remained most "untouchable." Precise words from the early speeches of the founder are repeated a third of a century later; a party youth asking a question of Haya is called a "disciple"; debating points are made in Congress with lengthy quotations from his writings and reprints of his statements. The result is a rigid and obsolescent quality; but it has a stabilizing influence which tends to place party ideology above, and out of the reach of, the party. In some ways, even Haya is subject to the discipline of Aprista ideology.

Whether such a discipline has effectively limited opportunism is debatable. It is said that in a transitional situation ideology satisfies a psychological need for symbolic reassurance, but that citizens respond to concrete acts. The tendency, then, will be for politicans to speak ideologically but to act pragmatically.[3] This is descriptive of the present APRA.

If Haya can be called an opportunist, his hardly seems to have been the opportunism of a power-hungry personalistic leader. Instead, Aprista opportunism has been a response to changing circumstances. One interpretation of the party style carries it through three phases: (1) the "heroic

[1] Interview C, March, 1966.

[2] Germani, *Política y Sociedad*, p. 138; Blanksten, "Politics of Latin America," p. 495.

[3] Scott, "Political Elites," p. 129. See, for example, Véliz Lizarraca, *Principios*, and the debates by Armando Villanueva in *Presente*, September–October, 1965, pp. 42–46. PAP, *El Pueblo* (Province of Bolognesi, Ancash), November 30, 1965, devoted more than half of eight mimeographed pages to this kind of material. Apter states that most ideologies in societies undergoing modernization are highly perishable as bases for building consensus; see *Politics of Modernization*, p. 327.

style of movement" in the years 1930–33, when APRA sought to take the country by storm and remake Peruvian society; (2) the "stoic style of resistance" during the underground periods of 1933–45 and 1948–56, which called for a war of siege and position; and (3) the "style of maneuver" of the period after 1956, which required a great deal in the way of compromises.[4]

The opportunism of the latest phase has yielded little or nothing of the fruits of power to Haya personally. On the contrary, personal gain has seemingly, sometimes inexplicably, been subordinated to other considerations. In 1945, for example, the goals of program application were pressed at the expense of a stabilization of party and personal position. During the *convivencia* of 1956–62, participation in the exercise of power was deferred in the interest of political-system evolution. And the decision to step aside in favor of Odría in July, 1962, whatever else might be said of it, represented for Haya a real personal sacrifice.[5]

Power can also be turned inward, however, through the exercise of authority within a party. It is generally agreed that intraparty discipline has been strict in APRA and that Haya passes on all major policy decisions. One view relates this to the demands of past periods of illegality and suggests that it has relaxed. Another maintains that centralization and discipline have tightened since the appearance of party factions in the fifties.[6]

Although Haya occupies a unique position in Aprista decision-making, he does not seem to inhibit the development of leadership at other levels. In contrast to the typical personalist party, APRA is not without subordinates of stature and individuality. Until his death in 1963, for example, Manuel Seoane was the best example of an Aprista with a standing of his own and the freedom to debate decisions when he differed.

This statement may not be convincing if it is limited to the "original" Apristas of the 1920s. New leaders also have been developed to positions of personal prominence, among them Ramiro Prialé, Andrés Townsend, and Armando Villanueva. Still others have been expelled from the party or have resigned out of frustration over differences they considered basic.

[4] Bourricaud, *Poder y Sociedad*, pp. 139, 184–85.

[5] German Arciniegas calls Haya an idealist lacking in malice who repeatedly has had to choose between violence and peace and has chosen peace (*Entre la Libertad y el Miedo*, rev. ed. [Mexico, D.F.: Editora "Zarco," 1955] p. 101). Alba has elevated this to the principle of a political death wish; see *Alliance Without Allies*, pp. 88–92. An American diplomat outside of Peru applies it to Haya de la Torre because of the number of times he has come close to political victory without, it is claimed, making the relatively small added effort that would have ensured success (Interview A, March, 1966). See also Hubert Herring as quoted in Kantor, *Peruvian Aprista Movement*, p. 57.

[6] McCoy, "Aprista Party, 1948–63," pp. 91–101, and *idem*, "Aprista Party, 1965," pp. 6–9; Bourricaud, *Poder y Sociedad*, pp. 161–63; Astiz, *Pressure Groups*, p. 109.

But the general relationship among Aprista leaders seems to be somewhat as follows: Haya deals with APRA as if it were a Heidelberg seminar, seeming to enjoy most the role of classic professor, and heading a "school of thought" which is the mass following of Apristas. His position leaves most other party tasks in an open field for second-rank Apristas. If Haya lacks organizing talent, for example, he has been fortunate to have others—notably Prialé during the 1956 rebuilding—with the ability and the will to move ahead independently.[7]

Aprismo as a Cult

The ideology of APRA also has the effect of giving the party the quality of a religion. This is something more than an analogy between political movements and certain religions. *Aprismo* shows such similarities, but it goes beyond (or departs from) the levels of symbolism and conformism of those analogies. It extends to the participation, by an in-group, in a variety of activities unrelated to politics. The Aprista *Casas del Pueblo* are, or seek to become, all things for the initiated—restaurant, barbershop, drugstore, pool hall, in short, the social center of the community.[8]

This side of *Aprismo* has been discussed in connection with the Apristas' ability to turn out thousands for public demonstrations without necessarily getting the same response at the polls. Townsend wrote, following the February, 1966, rally in Lima, that "the strictly political, partisan *Aprismo* is only the visible peak of a wave which bespeaks an enormous displacement in the farthest depths of popular sentiment." If APRA had been nothing but another political party, it could not have withstood the long years of adversity and proscription. It is no accident, Townsend says, that the vocabulary of religion was used by APRA, or that the party "hymn" calls it "the new religion." It is this "emotional factor" which gives the party its longevity as "a spiritual movement." Townsend suggests a dichotomy:

> . . . The party as a political body, subject to contingencies, errors, chance, and fortune of any group of this kind. And the party as an emotional movement, deep, charismatic, and mystical, which overcomes crises and feeds, not on external stimulation or gratification, but on an essential revolutionary devotion. . . .
> . . . It matters not that APRA might err or that some of its men might turn out to be inconsequential or not up to their responsibilities. Bad priests do not deprive the Church of its divine origin or its supernatural character.[9]

[7] McCoy, "Aprista Party, 1948–63," p. 102; Alexander, *Prophets*, pp. 103–5.

[8] McCoy, "Aprista Party, 1965," pp. 4–5; J. Payne, "Politics of Structured Violence," p. 368.

[9] *Correo* (Lima), March 14, 1966, p. 20.

All of this welds APRA together as a unit, re-inforcing individual identity with the party, and therefore party solidarity and cohesion. It also has negative effects, however, in efforts to expand the party outside its traditional bases or, in a changing society, even to maintain its strength in the emerging sectors of youth, women, middle class, and, in the future, the militant *campesino*. The same characteristics that bind together "the communion of true believers" tend to exclude and repel those who hold different attitudes and subscribe to other values. This is especially true of the middle class, and it is part of the general phenomenon of middle-class estrangement from the parties of the democratic Left. For APRA the problem is intensified for several reasons, among them the inconsistencies between the newly found needs and values of the middle class and that which APRA typically offers.

For the recent migrant from the integrated society of the highland Indian community and hacienda, the *Casas del Pueblo* may substitute another kind of (superficially) integrated life and a set of values which appeals to the socially insecure. But for those attracted by, and unafraid of, the secularism of the cities, including the pluralism and cosmopolitan veneer, APRA has less to offer. To either kind, it may be repellent simply because it is so completely a closed group which has more meaning for members than for newcomers.

The Image of Violence

Still more repellent to some outsiders is the role that violence is believed to have played in party activities and policy. The question is solely one of party image. Many Peruvians are convinced that APRA used violent methods in the past. The truth has not been clearly established, but statements of denial and the ineptness of apparent attempts to use it on a large scale are evidence that it was not deliberate party policy. Outbreaks of violence ranging from street fighting through political murders to armed insurrections did occur, however, and were laid at the door of APRA. Aprista involvement, circumstantial or emotional, was equated in the minds of many with conspiracy, and the impression persists.

The Apristas' image as a party of violence originated with the Trujillo insurrection of 1932, which is also blamed for the army's long-standing antipathy for APRA. It culminated in the 1948 naval insurrection at Callao, which is reported to have surprised the party leaders and to have been the work, if not of provocateurs, of a minority group of Aprista hotheads. During that period, as well as before 1932, party plans were considered and prepared from time to time which contemplated the forcible seizure of power.[10] If any of these were deliberately put into effect, however, none succeeded as planned.

Renunciations of force are contained in a number of Aprista statements over the years. Notable was that of Haya immediately after the mass executions that ended the Trujillo uprising. He said that the road to the presidential palace could be bought with gold or captured with guns, but that APRA had the mission of first reaching "the conscience of the people." In the same speech, however, he said: "We want no cowards. We want no traitors." He warned of new repression and said that "more Aprista blood will flow," but that the party would persevere in "revolutionary spirit" to build the new Peru.[11]

The defect in Aprista renunciations of violence, which may have been crucial in Callao in 1948, was that the statements themselves were generously sprinkled with a vocabulary of violence. Although they were used figuratively, the words were easily subject to misinterpretation by the rank and file. More serious is the charge by the perpetrator of the Callao revolt that Haya and the party engaged him to plan the event, but failed to support him when he went ahead on his own initiative.[12] Since 1948, however, there has been no question of APRA's renunciation of violence.

Apristas today are reluctant to discuss the question of violence in their image. If they do, it is explained as self-defense. One leader pointed out the contrast between the first and second terms of President Prado (1939–45 and 1956–62). "In the first, we were persecuted," he said, "and we threw bombs. In the second, we were not, so we threw no bombs."[13]

Yet there remains the question of street violence as a by-product of politics. Other parties and the press still accuse APRA of using "goon squads," called *búfalos*, during election campaigns as recent as 1962 and

[10] Sánchez recounts two such cases. First, in 1927 the Aprista exiles prepared the "plan of Mexico" by which Haya de la Torre, as a young presidential candidate, "would serve as figurehead for the uprising" in the "oil region" of northern, coastal Peru (*Haya de la Torre*, pp. 204–8). Much later, frustrations of trying to work with President Bustamante (1945–48) led to a discussion of alternatives open to APRA. Although Haya was inclined toward counsels of caution, "from February, 1948, permission was given to investigate . . . the idea of a *coup d'état*." APRA later agreed, writes Sánchez, to the armed forces' request for Aprista neutrality in a coup to remove Bustamante and call elections (*ibid.*, pp. 411, 451–52). The abortive Callao uprising intervened; see Villanueva, *Tragedia*.

[11] PAP, *Aprismo*, pp. 14–15, 42–43. As early as February, 1932 (before the Trujillo insurrection), Haya felt the need to explain that "one can be a revolutionist and make a revolution, without resort to violence"; he referred to the event in Marxian terms as an accelerated stage of evolution. See also Kantor, *Peruvian Aprista Movement*, pp. 55–57.

[12] Villanueva, *Tragedia*, esp. pp. 16 and 89ff. Pike (*History of Peru*, p. 288) accepts the version that APRA, although conspiring for a bloodless coup, was surprised by the revolt.

[13] Interview B, March, 1966.

1963 to intimidate opponents.[14] Violence can also easily grow out of political or labor demonstrations, which are an essential method of the mass reform party, but APRA made much less use of these weapons in the 1960s.

One of the results of violence, and of long years of proscription, is the conspiratorial connotation still carried by the name Aprista. In some it invokes fear. One prominent party member who lives in an upper-class suburb of Lima and is utterly respectable in appearance tells of the horror registered in the face of a middle-aged matron living nearby upon learning his name. At other levels of society the attitude is reported to be one of extreme hostility, even in the trade unions, where the Apristas should be best known. The result is a tendency among some Apristas to conceal their membership, with obvious consequences for proselytization.[15]

Aprista Techniques

Having the styles that it does, APRA displays some of the features of devotee parties: it is "more open than cadre parties, but more closed than mass parties."[16] It turns a different face to the world than it shows to its membership. This means that the methods it uses are designed, perhaps unconsciously, to appeal to Apristas more than to attract new members.

APRA has long stressed mass membership, and in the 1930s it set extravagant goals in keeping with its claim to be the party of the national majority. In fact, it follows the practice of registering all members anew after every election or emergence from illegal status. In the mid-sixties, enrollment was reported at around 700,000, or well above the 623,000 votes received by Haya in 1963. Supposedly the increase resulted from a subsequent membership drive.[17] If accurate, this close correspondence between membership and votes demonstrates the scant degree to which APRA appeals to, or relies upon, the independent voter.

The inward-looking emphasis of Aprista methods is evident in both conventional and innovative activities of the party. The difficulty with the former is that the party labors at a severe disadvantage in competing with the conventional proselytizing of other parties.

The principal newspaper of APRA is the daily *La Tribuna* in Lima. It is estimated to have a circulation of about 20,000, and competes with the much more prosperous group of non-party papers, which sell 65,000–

[14] McCoy, "Aprista Party, 1948–63," p. 82. The incidents seemed to arise frequently out of competitive wall-painting and the posting of placards.

[15] Interview F, March, 1966; J. Payne, *Labor and Politics in Peru*, pp. 105, 117–18.

[16] Duverger, *Political Parties*, p. 70.

[17] Interview with Ramiro Prialé, March 18, 1966; McCoy, "Aprista Party, 1965," p. 3.

100,000 copies each.[18] Heavy with polemical content and without much entertainment or feature material, *La Tribuna* is not the kind of paper that would attract new members, or even the casual reader. Instead, it seems to be used mainly as a medium of party communication downward. By including quotations from major party statements, summaries of positions on certain issues, and "success stories" of party activities, the paper serves the combined purpose of disseminating the party line and maintaining the morale of key party leaders.

APRA has been highly innovative in the development of new political methods. Undoubtedly these were originally aimed at attracting new adherents, but they have become so ritualistic that they now serve to maintain the exclusiveness and solidarity of the party itself.

Haya de la Torre and others have often spoken of the educational task in Peru. In his *coloquios* he has asserted the role of the political party as "a new agent" of *actividades formativas* (which might be translated as education, or socialization) supplementing the home and the school. Haya is paraphrased thus: "To vote is a technique. To know how to vote supports the base of a mature democracy." The *coloquios* themselves, impromptu question-and-answer sessions intended primarily for the youth, present Haya in his favorite role of professor. The publication of these discussions was designed to train the Peruvian youth "in order that they might assume fully their role of changing and perfecting the structures of our society."[19]

The difficulty in achieving this ambitious goal lies in the channels through which the effort is launched. The *coloquios* are held in the "great hall" of the *Casa del Pueblo* in Lima. This is not a place the political independent enters casually. More likely he will go there, if at all, only *after* he has decided to become a member of APRA. Even as reported secondhand, the *coloquios* are handled as messianic utterances rather than as educational lectures, which they are, with flashes of humor. Therefore, the potential of Haya's discussion as a vehicle for proselytizing is largely lost.

The same is true of many other party activities. The "popular universities" (adult evening schools) should be a valuable force for both raising the educational level of the lower classes and bringing them into participation in the political system. Because they are typically held only in the party establishments, however, a whole category of non-party members is almost automatically excluded by inhibition.[20]

[18] U.S. Information Agency, *Basic Data Book for Latin America*, R–139–65 (Washington, D.C., 1965), p. 84; the figures are for August, 1964.

[19] Ignacio Campos, *Coloquios de Haya de la Torre*, vol. 2 (n.p.: Universidad Popular González Prada, n.d., probably 1965), pp. 5 and 238.

[20] Interview H, March, 1966.

APRA is forted up in its *Casas del Pueblo* and thereby, like the French in Indo-China, is reduced to fighting unprofitable wars of position in competition with other parties. Or, like some middle-class churches in the United States, it has reached a stagnation of togetherness, because its centers are not attractive to outsiders and because it has not found novel ways of going where the prospects are.

Some of the limitations of Aprista methods can be attributed to the problem of transition from one phase of its existence to another. Others are perhaps inherent in the conflict between APRA's "scientific" doctrinal base and the characteristic "politics of improvisation" (à la *criolla*) which marked its earliest days.[21] Less well-recognized are the implications that social change might have for the techniques used by the party.

Default of Innovation

The mass party in developing countries is potentially a powerful tool, an independent variable, by which the mobilization and integration of its members and prospective members can be promoted. The basic questions of method and organization pose a choice between an open and a closed party. Even parties that are ostensibly and formally open can in reality be closed.

To have altered the historic methods of APRA in 1956 might have changed its fundamental unity and strength, possibly sacrificing as many old members as it would have gained. The impulse and desire to do so were present, as can be seen from the party's organizational initiatives. Inter-party negotiations may have had similar goals of broadening the Aprista appeal. The actual efforts, however, were caricatured by such combinations as the "Coalition of the People" with the party of former President Odría after 1963.

Less threatening to the integrity of the party would have been the extension of its educational institutions deeper into the sierra. As a minimum, APRA might have begun a literacy campaign, for example, in the region of its existing strength. The "Solid North" is not the most illiterate part of Peru, but it is highly illiterate when one considers the limited use of Indian languages there. In most of the nine departments which gave the Apristas pluralities or better in 1963, the illiteracy rate far exceeded the percentage of non-Spanish-speaking inhabitants. In the three departments of greatest

[21] Bourricaud, *Poder y Sociedad*, p. 176. Prialé recognized the need for adjustment as one of his first priorities in reorganizing the party in 1956 (interview, March 18, 1966). Little is publicly known, however, about how APRA operated when it was proscribed. As Arciniegas wrote in 1951: "If it were possible to make an academic study of how the proscribed parties of Latin America operate underground, one would encounter an inexhaustible source of surprises. There are hundreds of periodicals, radio transmitters, working cells which operate Lord knows how" (*Libertad y Miedo*, p. 345).

Aprista strength (La Libertad, Lambayeque, and Cajamarca) illiteracy exceeds by multiples of from eight to one hundred the proportion of those with any ability to speak the indigenous language.[22]

A program of this kind would have been the party's direct contribution to development. To be successful, it would have had to go "to the people," where they live. This would have reversed the conventional sequence of development programs that seek by massive investment of resources to "pull" the productive capacity upward from the crisis points of urban settlement. It would mean going to the villages of the sierra rather than only as far as the provincial capitals, which are now the most remote locations of the *Casas del Pueblo*. APRA, known as the most "Indian" of the Peruvian parties, would have had great psychological advantages in initiating such a program. It was left to Belaúnde, however, to start something similar, along with technical and material aid, in *Cooperación Popular*. Although it later withered for "lack of budgetary support," the response of the villagers to the program demonstrated that constructive, as well as violent, action can be organized among the Indians of the sierra.[23]

A further stage would be the organization of "clientele groups," such as associations of irrigation-water users, cooperatives "without manifest political intent," and peasant syndicates—all in "the rural, pre-modern sector." It is argued that achievements at the policy level can best be guaranteed by the existence of a "political infrastructure" supporting and advising on policy formulation.[24]

In contrast to the methods of APRA and most other parties, such efforts need not, and perhaps should not, be directly linked to the party. It is more important that they be appropriate to the functional purposes

[22] Ciro Alegría and John Gillin have attested to the disappearance of Indian languages in the North. Alegría noted it in *Broad and Alien is the World*. Gillin reported that in Moche no one knew the ancient Mochica language. "Only Spanish is spoken [in 1944]," although about half of the district declared itself to be Indian in the 1940 census (the other half mestizo). See John Gillin, *Moche: A Peruvian Coastal Community*, Institute of Social Anthropology, Publication no. 3 (Washington, D.C.: Smithsonian Institution, 1945), pp. 7–8; see also Larson and Bergman, *Social Stratification in Peru*, pp. 363–64.

[23] *The Atlantic*, April, 1966, p. 40. This report blames the failure on Belaúnde's promising more than he could deliver with limited "technical advisers and administrators." It seems more accurate to accept the observation of a junior faculty member of one of the provincial universities that *Cooperación Popular* was too closely identified, not only in name but in personnel, with Acción Popular for the APRA/UNO coalition controlling Congress to continue voting it adequate funds (Interview J, March, 1966). It was no help that the first secretary general of *Cooperación Popular*, after losing this job and being expelled from AP, was arrested with guerrillas rounded up in 1965 (*Presente*, September–October, 1965, p. 50). Alba also proposed a kind of domestic peace corps of this kind; see *Alliance Without Allies*, pp. 183ff.

[24] Charles W. Anderson, "'Reformongering' and the Uses of Political Power," *Inter-American Economic Affairs* 19, no. 2 (Autumn, 1965): 39–40; Anderson's reference is to Albert O. Hirschman, *Journeys Toward Progress* (New York: Twentieth Century Fund, 1963), esp. pp. 2–5.

they serve. The party's contribution would be amply rewarded, directly through interpersonal relationships identified with APRA and indirectly through the promotion of development.

Although seemingly very remote in their promise of returns, non-political initiatives such as these have yielded political results. It is probably no accident that the Urubamba River region of Peru, where numerous "scholastic centers" were formed beginning in 1946, was later the site of flourishing *campesino* syndicates.[25] A similar coincidence of early educational activity and later political activism has been noted in Bolivia.

The use of non-political means to seek political ends is also another European idea adapted to the conditions of Latin America. The popular universities of pre-APRA and later years were comparable (in a different setting) to adult extension services operated in Britain and other countries through organizations such as the Workers' Educational Association. These ostensibly non-political programs seeking political ends had counterparts in the nationalist movements of the nineteenth century in countries as far apart as Italy and Finland.

Whether through conventional activities to gain quick results in the cities, or through more unconventional ways of promoting cultural change in the sierra, APRA has not succeeded in using organization and method to maximum advantage in expanding its bases of popular support. The paradox is that the party that was historically the most innovative and expansive was unable to apply its genius to the opportunities created by accelerated social change.

There is no such thing as the inexorable aging of institutions, but there may be an approximation of it resulting from the aging of leadership, doctrine, and methods. Although APRA has gone through more than one transformation in its relations with the state and with other parties, it has not shown the same flexibility in adjusting to the demands of change in its relationship with the community.

[25] Ford, *Man and Land in Peru*, p. 138. Ford also argues against leaving the future to the mercy of purely economic forces (*ibid.*, p. 143). The question of whether the party or the trade unions should undertake educational activity is discussed by Bruce H. Millen in *The Political Role of Labor in Developing Countries* (Washington, D.C.: The Brookings Institution, 1963), pp. 110 and 118.

VI

PROGRAM APPLICATION AND TACTICS

WHEN ACCESS TO EXECUTIVE POWER was once again blocked, as it was for APRA in 1963, the party had the opportunity to consider alternative means of making its influence felt. It had never before been in precisely the same situation. With a plurality of the seats in Congress, it was faced with the immediate question of the exercise of legislative power. Considerations of partisan advantage had to be weighed against opportunities for the enactment of Aprista proposals bearing on reform. Of longer-range importance was the strategic choice between strong and weak approaches to the presidential election of 1969.

The decision that was made tended to merge the short- and long-term factors into a kind of legislative alternative. Without relinquishing its future claim to the presidency, APRA sought to modify the nature of the political system by enhancing the power of Congress. This almost dictated that the Aprista delegation would be used more for partisan maneuver than for program application.

On its face, the Aprista choice seemed to be an abandonment of principle in favor of partisan advantage. It is true that APRA might have served Peru better between 1963 and 1968 by supporting and promoting the plans of President Belaúnde. On the other hand, there were grounds for asserting that what the country needed was not more legislation but implementation of programs already approved. In the process, a loyal opposition in Congress could play the vigorous role of watchdog. Moreover, if program application is the real aim of a mass reform party such as APRA, the objective can often be reached indirectly. In the thirty-odd years before 1963, much of what APRA stood for in 1931 had been achieved. A summary will help to place this aspect of Aprista success in better perspective as background for the party's congressional behavior in the years 1963–68.

ACHIEVEMENTS OF APRA

Several writers have observed that reform parties do not always need to take power directly in order to make their influence felt. The parties of mass reform have "played a role in Latin American politics similar to that of the socialist and anarchosyndicalist movements in Europe before World War I. . . . These populist movements have exercised a great influence—perhaps more when in opposition to dictatorship than when in power themselves—as much in the political evolution of Latin America as in reform theory."[1]

The effects are evident in several forms. In most general terms, Peru attained political freedom and the whole attitude and atmosphere of politics changed to make reform respectable. This situation prevails despite the intervention of the 1968 coup. Commenting on APRA's missed chances to rule, Kantor wrote in 1963:

> . . . Perhaps a country needs an organized and responsible opposition more than, or as much as, a good government. . . .
> . . . The Apristas have always been an educational force; an opposition dedicated to improvement of the nation. . . . They have always been a responsible opposition. Now, without the firing of a single shot, Peru has a constitutional government. Constitutional liberties are respected, and all political groups can strive for power in the free market of ideas. Perhaps the Apristas, in helping to reach this end, have achieved more than any other political party. . . .[2]

APRA cannot take sole credit for the appearance of an atmosphere favorable to internal reform. In various forms it had earlier roots in Peru, and it has flowered much more widely, in combination with nationalism and anticolonialism, since World War II. The Apristas have certainly had a large part, however, in bringing the favorable climate to Peru.

In operational terms, this can be seen in the practical political choices open to conservative forces in Peru, once they began to divide internally over a combination of institutional and personal differences. As the gulf

[1] Alba, *Alliance Without Allies*, p. 88.

[2] Kantor, *Movimiento Aprista Peruano*, pp. 18–19. See also Patch ("New Techniques and Old Ideas," pp. 14–15), who observed this at the psychological as well as the political level: "It is now socially necessary for decent people to express at least formal concern for those persons beyond and below their own web of interrelationships; and it has become politically necessary for even the most reactionary of parties to promise agrarian reform, housing programs, and expanded educational facilities."

within the "oligarchy" began to open up, APRA was the third element which could not be ignored.

In another context it has been written: "The Aprista party is a constant of Peruvian politics. It is a factor which must be reckoned with inevitably, for or against, for good or for bad. It is like the factor *pi* in mathematical formulas."[3] It was this equation which forced other interests to come to APRA for support, especially at times when free elections seemed required, and in turn brought APRA to the point of recognizing the possibility of alternative strategies.

The mass reform parties of opposition, then, find themselves in a spot somewhat like that of the European socialists. "One part of their programs (the nationalist part) is being applied (at least in speeches) by the oligarchies, who use nationalism to disguise their real motives and to divert the attention of public opinion. The part that is not applied has been overtaken by events. . . ."[4]

One of the cautions with which this situation must be viewed is that the enactment of reform does not mean implementation:

> A major reason why radical reform movements have never achieved predicted proportions in Peru is that few national administrations have been totally unresponsive. . . . Nearly every government has accorded some recognition to agrarian problems, and has pledged alleviation. Almost as frequently the promises have remained unfulfilled. Even the reform measures actually promulgated have often been merely paper laws issued more for the pacification of an aroused group than with the sincere intention of application.[5]

Against this background, the reform measures which have been adopted over some thirty years and which bear a direct relationship to Aprista programs can be reviewed. Wherever possible, the extent to which they resulted from direct efforts of APRA and the vigor with which they have been implemented will be indicated.

It bears repeating that APRA has never had sole authority or responsibility for either branch of government. Its control of the executive has never been direct, much less undisputed; it shared cabinet representation (as a small minority) for only about one year (1946–47) under Bustamante. Its congressional delegations have always had to work by compromise, even when—as in 1945–48 and 1963–68—they have dominated a majority coalition.

[3] Enrique Chirinos Soto, "La calle de los Panuelos Blancos," Sunday magazine *7 Dias . . .* , *La Prensa*, February 27, 1966, p. 10.

[4] Alba, *Alliance Without Allies*, p. 88.

[5] Ford, *Man and Land in Peru*, p. 125.

Labor

Organized workers outside the traditional agricultural sector have probably benefitted more during the thirty-odd years of *Aprismo* than any other element of the population. Paradoxically, however, most of the advance has not come from legislative enactment traceable directly to Aprista initiatives. This results from the special circumstances of labor in Peru.

Although APRA is closely identified with organized labor and bases its political power largely on the loyalty of Aprista-led trade unions, labor reform pre-dates the party. As early as 1911, Peru enacted a Work Accidents Law, and in the next two decades, before APRA was formally organized, it added laws benefitting women, children, and white-collar employees, and legislation on wages, hours and, safety.

The constitution of 1933 (still in effect) includes a number of broad statements of policy and concessions of power to Congress which incorporate these advances and presage others. The document was prepared by several drafting bodies, but formally by the Constituent Congress sitting during 1931–32. Congress was purged of its twenty-two Apristas before the discussion of the constitution was well under way, but they had defined positions on its content, including guarantees of trade-union rights, the development of industry, and social attitudes toward education.[6]

Since the early 1930s, two other factors have affected the number and variety of advances won by organized labor. Both are more or less directly related to the strength that organized labor showed beginning in the twenties. Direct bargaining is responsible for many of the significant advances. The changes depend in large part on the degree of unionization and militancy in each industry or firm, and they often take the form of executive decrees. Gains won by direct action thus have made for unevenness because they have not been generalized. These factors, plus the difficulty of enforcing laws once they are enacted, reduce the importance of labor legislation as a means of reform.

Second, organized labor has been a special and continuing target of the rivals of APRA. Whether political parties or regimes in power, they have attempted to eliminate Aprista influences in the trade unions by offering labor special favors. Even in the thirties this tactic began to take the form of official tolerance for Communists, who in return were expected to

[6] U.S. Department of Labor, *Labor in Peru*, p. 33; Sánchez, *Haya de la Torre*, pp. 283–86. Sources differ as to the number in the Aprista delegation. Kantor, *Peruvian Aprista Movement* (and at another point Sánchez), says there were twenty-seven, a number reached perhaps by adding independents or the five Apristas identified as "workers." See also Pike, *History*, pp. 220ff., regarding the liberal nature of the constitution of 1920.

supplant Apristas in positions of trade-union leadership. It went so far under the first Prado regime that the Communist labor boss, Juan P. Luna, was elected to Congress and in 1944 was allowed to re-establish CTP. In 1945 CTP returned to Aprista control, only to be suppressed again in 1948. The cycle was repeated, with Luna being elected to the Senate in 1951 and the Apristas returning to take over the re-established CTP in 1956.[7]

Under Prado's second administration Aprista leaders consolidated their control in CTP until 1962, when, at least initially, the military junta seemed to return to the tactics of Odría and his predecessors. Even under the presidency of Belaúnde there were some reports of efforts to use the Communists to eliminate Apristas from certain unions.[8]

The combination of these factors has meant that very few notable laws or decrees in the labor field can be identified closely with APRA, except perhaps through original advocacy. In a search of party and other sources for laws and decrees benefitting labor during the 1945–48 period of maximum Aprista power in the executive and Congress, only two could be specifically identified, and both concern white-collar workers. Under the *convivencia* with Prado in 1956–62, a somewhat better record appeared. But it was no stronger, if one counts only the number of significant actions, than the record under Odría or, considering its brief duration, that of the 1962–63 military junta.[9] The significant measures, in terms of the periods of enactment, were:

Dictatorial or Anti-Aprista Regimes		Periods of Aprista Influence	
1932	Holiday pay		
1936	Severance pay		
1938	Survivors benefits		
1939	Severance pay		
1940	Paid vacations		
		1945	Severance pay (white collar)
		1946	Social security (white collar)

[7] U.S. Department of Labor, *Labor in Peru*, pp. 33–36; Crowley, "Labor and Political Parties," pp. 47–51; Alexander, *Organized Labor*, pp. 116–22.

[8] U.S. Department of Labor, *Labor in Peru*, p. 49; Delmas, "Peru's New Politics," p. 38. Chaplin cites these and other reasons for the passage of Peruvian labor laws in "generous and progressive form," and for their enforcement "only in urban areas and/or where unions are strongly organized" ("Major Issues," pp. 8–9).

[9] U.S. Department of Labor, *Labor in Peru*, pp. 33–47; Manuel Seoane, *Obras Apristas de 1931 a 1948* (Lima: Empressa Periodistic, n.d.), pp. 58–60.

Dictatorial or Anti-Aprista Regimes		Periods of Aprista Influence	
1948	Sunday pay		
1949–51	Labor Ministry		
1950–51	Mine safety		
1951	Profit sharing		
1953	Employment service		
		1957	National Labor Council
		1960	Profit sharing
		1961	Paid vacations
		1962	Severance pay
1962	Severance pay		
1962	Minimum wages		
1962	Employment service		

Despite recurrent efforts, Apristas have not been eliminated from the leadership of CTP nor, would it therefore seem, does the lack of identifiable Aprista legislative benefits carry much weight with rank-and-file workers. Odría, who had the longest and economically most favorable recent period in which to work for labor support, probably succeeded in winning for his party many who were attracted more by paternalism than by the freedom to organize. It is said that he, like Benavides in the 1930s, "was anti-union but not antiworker."[10] Nevertheless, it is APRA which gets most of the credit for achievements in this field.

Agriculture

For the *campesino* or Indian *comunero*, whom APRA includes among its principal constituents, the situation is the reverse of that of labor. Organization has not proceeded very far, and bargaining has not proved effective. Consciousness of the problem has not been lacking, however; for some fifty years it has been widely discussed in Peruvian intellectual circles. Only action has been delayed.

[10] J. Payne, *Labor and Politics in Peru*, p. 51. The survey reported in Briones and Mejía Valera, *El Obrero* (pp. 82–89), shows that almost as many factory workers regarded themselves as either rightist, centrist, or independent as leftist, but that the "rightist" group diminished sharply among those who had migrated to the city more than five or ten years earlier.

Tangible reforms benefitting the Indian are peculiarly dependent upon official legislation, regulation, public works, and assistance. Nevertheless, as of 1955 it was estimated that "about half of the agrarian platform of the 1931 National Aprista Congress . . . has been approved by various national legislatures. . . ." This has by no means ensured the implementation of laws on the books, for a coordinated "frontal attack" on the land problem has been lacking.[11] Such a comprehensive approach was studied under Prado and enacted into law under Belaúnde in May, 1964.

In these circumstances, Aprista efforts to apply its agricultural program were for many years highly fragmented. APRA influence on the constitution of 1933 succeeded in establishing certain principles which much later were the bases for executive and congressional actions. The constitution stated that "property must be used in harmony with social interests" and authorized the enactment of laws subjecting property to taxation, regardless of ownership, restricting its transfer, and regulating the use of natural resources, including mines, land, forests, and water (Articles 31, 34, 35, and 37).

The constitution gave special mention to two groups in the rural population. It said that (1) "the state shall favor the preservation and extension of medium and small rural property" and (2) "the state guarantees the integrity of the property of the communities" of Indians, the latter being surrounded with additional protections, some of them brought forward from previous documents that had not proved effective (Articles 47 and 207–12).

These same articles authorized the expropriation of private land for transfer to small or medium-sized farms and communities, but only against "prior compensation." Because this meant cash payment, land redistribution was entirely dependent upon state resources until 1963–64, when the constitution was amended to permit the issuance of bonds, but only for expropriated land. (Improvement costs were not covered until the Velasco regime acted on land reform.)

The land problem had been acted on by the state in the twenties and thirties. Even then, the points of attack were limited to colonization of the jungle and to irrigation, mainly on the coast, both of which were easily turned to the advantage of large landholders or speculators. During World War II the first Prado regime extended irrigation projects to the sierra and established the Ministry of Agriculture and what became an agricultural extension and experiment service.

APRA saw the Bustamante election in 1945 as the first real opportunity to apply its program in agriculture, as elsewhere. The surprises of that

[11] Ford, *Man and Land in Peru*, pp. 125, 142–43.

interrupted term prevented the realization of this goal, but they permitted some advance toward it. During 1945–48 the administration "began to interest itself deeply in the agrarian problem." In Congress it was the subject of "long and heated debates . . . culminating in various, even though still timid, reform measures."[12] The Apristas succeeded in enacting several laws, mostly individual irrigation projects but also including expropriations in favor of Indian communities. Many more projects were approved by only one chamber or otherwise failed to be implemented.[13]

On the other hand, comprehensive studies of the land problem were launched within the party. They appeared in publication form and in a long list of proposals to the Second National Congress of the party in May–June, 1948. Two measures of some significance, in law if not in practice, were nevertheless enacted in 1947 and largely carried over without change in the Agrarian Reform Act of 1964. They sought to regulate contracts between landowners and feudal tenants (*yanaconaje*, no. 10,885, March 15, 1947) and share tenants (*arrendamiento*, no. 10,841, May 20, 1947). Neither was enforced or perhaps enforceable.[14]

For the eight years of Odría's rule (1948–56), APRA was outlawed and unable to influence the government on agricultural or any other policies. Measures taken by Odría reflected a willingness to "tidy up" some aspects of tenancy arrangements (no. 10,922, December 3, 1948, and no. 11,042, June 27, 1949) without removing the "paralysis" of state action that had begun in 1948.[15]

With Prado's election in 1956, the clock seemed to begin turning again, with emphasis on the study of comprehensive approaches. Agrarian reform had become a subject for active discussion, and in August, 1956, the new president appointed the Commission on Agrarian Reform and Housing (CRAV). Giving its attention first to housing, however, CRAV did not present recommendations on agrarian reform until four years later.

Establishment of the Agrarian Reform and Colonization Institute (IRAC) in June, 1960, was the main tangible result of the commission's

[12] *Ibid.*, pp. 139–41; Chapter 10 of CIDA, *Tierra y Desarrollo*, on which the foregoing paragraphs are mainly based, has the best discussion of the legal bases of land reform through 1965. It is pointed out there, however, that these constitutional articles long had "scant application" and "could almost be said to have remained forgotten" (p. 358); see also pp. 393–94.

[13] Andrés Townsend Ezcurra, *El APRA y la Reforma Agraria* (Lima: Ediciones Pueblo, 1963), p. 14. Establishment of the National Irrigation Service is also mentioned in Seoane, *Obras Apristas*, pp. 54–55. Neither of these sources, in enumerating expropriations during the period, mentioned those affecting a monastery and the Beneficencia Pública of Lima.

[14] Ford, *Man and Land in Peru*, pp. 85–88, 94–95. The studies were Alfredo Saco, *Programa Agrario del Aprismo* (Lima: Ediciones Populares, 1946), and PAP, *Plan Agrario.*

[15] CIDA, *Tierra y Desarrollo*, pp. 373–77, 393–94.

studies, for the reform bill later presented to Congress was not approved. "IRAC was limited to laying the administrative and technical bases for future reform, and to undertaking land settlement programs."[16] Other than the continuation of irrigation projects, minor rectifications in imperfect regulations, and participation in pilot projects of a local nature which enjoyed international support, the Prado period did not achieve anything substantial enough to reflect credit on APRA.

Aprista impatience over delays in the completion of the CRAV report is evident in the party's public statements around the middle years of Prado's term. These were not dissident statements but authoritative protests, and they included a speech by Aprista Secretary General Prialé and an editorial in the party newspaper.[17] In the end, however, APRA supported the results of Prado's efforts in the agricultural field. Or, put into the context of the party's general attitude toward the regime, it evidently concluded that the less said about it, the better things would be for the party.[18] Subsequent events showed that land invasions and guerrilla activities were building to a climax during the Prado presidency.

The military junta of 1962–63 took actions in the agrarian field which were resolute and, by comparison with the past, even radical. These included a decree seeking to annex as state property all unexploited lands other than those of Indian communities (no. 14,197, August 31, 1962), which was frustrated by the landowners; a basic law establishing criteria for agrarian reform, but without actually effecting it (no. 14,238, November 16, 1962); and a measure ordering redistribution of haciendas to dispossessed *campesinos* in the Cuzco valleys of La Convención and Lares (no. 14,444, March 28, 1962). The last was unique and came to be

[16] IDB, *Social Progress Trust Fund: Fourth Annual Report, 1964* (Washington, D.C., 1965), p. 538. See also Alvin Cohen, "Societal Structure, Agrarian Reform and Economic Development in Peru," *Inter-American Economic Affairs* 18, no. 1 (Summer, 1964): 46, and Richard W. Patch, "A Note on Bolivia and Peru," *AUFS*, RWP–4–'62, April, 1962, pp. 15–16. Both maintain that the conservative makeup of CRAV foreclosed any prospect that real reform would be proposed by the commission.

[17] *La Tribuna*, May 24, 1958, p. 6, reported a speech by Aprista Secretary General Prialé reminding Prado's party that the president "had declared the elimination of the *latifundio* to be one of the aims of his political group" and asking it to join in the fight to that end. An editorial of August 23, 1958, p. 4, endorsed a bill (evidently abortive) for the distribution of irrigated coastal lands, with changes that could be promoted by those (the Apristas) "who believe that the *convivencia* is more than a political climate. . . ." A signed article of September 10, 1960, p. 4, criticized the CRAV report and asked questions such as "How soon is the imminent transformation?"

[18] *Expreso*, December 5, 1961, p. 1. In his comprehensive recitation of the history and achievements of APRA in agrarian policy, Townsend ignored developments under Prado; see Townsend, *El APRA*. Three laws benefitting the Indian communities were passed in the second Prado administration, but they were not promulgated by the president. The new Congress made them effective in August, 1963.

known as a "pilot plan" on which later action elsewhere might be patterned.[19]

Less direct credit is claimed by APRA in related fields. One reason is that housing was long the concern of the architect, later president, Fernando Belaúnde. Early in the 1945–48 period he introduced the bill (adopted with support from his Aprista allies) for creation of the Housing Corporation (Corporación de la Vivienda), which was to build homes for a million people "of the working and middle class in the principal cities."[20]

Such efforts lagged, however, and in any case could not have kept pace with the deficit of adequate housing resulting from rapid urbanization. The housing report submitted by CRAV in December, 1957, had no spectacular results, and it remained for the military junta early in 1963 to centralize housing activities under the National Housing Board. Another action by the junta was formation of the National Planning Institute in October, 1962. Being straight out of Aprista doctrine, this could be viewed with some satisfaction by the party as vindication of long-standing proposals. Later, in 1964, the General Law on Cooperatives (no. 15,260) was adopted and the National Office of Cooperative Development was established, both with Aprista support.[21]

General

In various other areas of government, a number of Aprista proposals have been adopted, with or without the direct help of the party. Having urged since 1931 the broadening of participation in elections, the Apristas in 1945 promptly sought to have municipal elections held for the first time since 1923. In 1946 they succeeded in passing an interim election reform law and in having female suffrage included in it. The law provided for elections within two years. The appointive *Juntas de Notables* were replaced with transitional councils chosen locally by assemblies composed of functional representatives (employers, workers, teachers, judges, priests, etc.). Elections were repeatedly postponed, however, in an atmosphere of worsening relations between APRA and President Bustamante until, in March, 1948, he discharged the transitional councils by decree.[22]

One of the first acts of Belaúnde upon being inaugurated in 1963 was to propose municipal elections, and they were held in December. Mean-

[19] CIDA, *Tierra y Desarrollo*, pp. 398–400. The actual distribution of land titles began in July, 1963; see *HAR* 16, no. 7 (1963) : 707.

[20] Sánchez, *Haya de la Torre*, p. 436; Seoane, *Obras Apristas*, pp. 66–67.

[21] IDB, *Social Progress Trust Fund, 1964*, pp. 450 and 457, and Unión Panamericana, *Estudio Social de América Latina, 1963–64* (Washington, D.C., 1964), pp. 114–115. See also CIDA, *Tierra y Desarrollo*, p. 436, and *Presente*, May–June, 1965, p. 39.

[22] Sánchez, *Haya de la Torre*, pp. 401–2.

while, a constitutional amendment of 1955 (no. 12,391) had granted voting rights in national elections to women on the same terms with men.[23]

In the general field of public administration, APRA claims credit for the establishment of several new ministries because it proposed them, even though they were created while the party was outlawed. The party was also outlawed when the first national census since 1876 was taken, under Prado, in 1940. The second census was held in 1961, when Prado again was president. APRA had complained in 1956 that Peru continued to have its taxes collected by a private firm organized by one of the large banks. Belaúnde corrected this in his first months in office in 1963.[24]

Education was another of the many subjects the Apristas wanted improved. They claimed credit for proposing Article 75 of the 1933 constitution, which states that free secondary and higher education should be promoted by the state. An Aprista bill for approaching that goal over a five-year period was enacted early in the Bustamante period (no. 10,263), but "the dictator" (Odría), according to Seoane, later put an end to it. APRA asserted that in the 1945–48 period it initiated numerous projects for the construction of schools.[25] In the following years of Odría's rule the number of schools increased from 11,150 in 1950 to 16,000 in 1961, while the number of teachers (primary and secondary) more than doubled. Nevertheless, a substantial proportion of primary school children still were not enrolled.[26]

Some miscellaneous areas in which APRA believes that it achieved some of its goals, at least temporarily, are economic stabilization, public works, and the armed forces. In 1946, when an Aprista was minister of finance, the stabilization issue was formulated mainly in terms of the control of foreign-exchange earnings, with social welfare as a side objective. The Apristas succeeded in requiring exporters to surrender dollar earnings to the government at a fixed rate. This permitted the state to restrict imports to essentials and also to subsidize the importing of basic foodstuffs out of the gain from sale of exchange. In reviewing this episode in 1956, Seoane

[23] Pan American Union, *Constitution of the Republic of Peru: 1933* (Washington, D.C., 1962), p. 8.

[24] Seoane, *Obras Apristas*, p. 19; PAP, *El Plan*, p. 4. APRA had always viewed the census as a prerequisite to national economic planning, and the 1961 enumeration proved useful in the CIDA study of land tenancy and development, *Tierra y Desarrollo*. See also Delmas, "Peru's New Politics," p. 36.

[25] Seoane, *Obras Apristas*, pp. 63–64.

[26] IDB, *Social Progress Trust Fund, 1964*, pp. 449–50. Sources vary as to the last figure. IDB gives 46 percent in 1961. Unión Panamericana (*Estudio Social*, p. 328) lists a percentage of only 21.8. The more than 85 percent not enrolled in secondary school is a measure of the problem APRA attacked in proposing free education at that level.

was careful to explain that such controls were not preferred per se, but were used as a crutch when necessary.[27]

Public works came into Aprista efforts to revive local self-government in 1945–48. At the suggestion of Haya, departments, provinces, and districts were given grants (and loan authority) as a kind of "seed money" with which to undertake local improvement projects of their own choosing—an idea similar to the one later elaborated by Belaúnde under the name *Cooperación Popular*. The executive soon cut off the grants, however, which came to be viewed, in Seoane's words, as coming "from the party which had from the beginning promoted effective help through a program of decentralization," that is, APRA.

Finally, APRA was also able to claim credit for a series of laws in 1946 concerned with fringe benefits and training for the armed forces, including the Civil Guard and police.[28] Today it could say that its early proposals for civic action by the army have been adopted in Peru and many other countries.

Significance

This summary of certain Aprista achievements is sufficient to indicate that there was something besides opportunism in the way APRA viewed the political situation beginning in 1956. Not only was it mainly concerned with re-establishing a system in which the party could operate freely, but it also recognized that such freedom would make possible a new mode of behavior.

One of the lessons of APRA's 1945–48 trial period was that the revolutionary themes of the past were now much less saleable. In a free political system it would be implausible to seek votes on a platform of "overturning the system," especially if the reforms for which that overturn would be sought had already, to all appearances, been accepted gradually by the surviving parties competing with APRA, and, still more, if the few who could take advantage of the reforms were the most reliable elements of organized party strength. Hence, an Aprista policy of compromise, of working within the system instead of overturning it, could easily be rationalized.

[27] Sánchez, *Haya de la Torre*, pp. 444–45; Seoane, *Obras Apristas*, pp. 46–51. An otherwise friendly observer says, however, that neither the Apristas nor AP has any understanding of modern economics (Interview K, March, 1966).

[28] Seoane, *Obras Apristas*, pp. 32 and 72.

The Role of Congress

It was not only the debates on substantive issues of reform which gave APRA problems following the 1963 election. The strategic situation of the party also required review. For the first time the party had suffered an unequivocal defeat of its presidential aspirations in free elections. Nevertheless, the Aprista delegation would be the largest group in the new Congress, and this was presented as a major achievement. What was to be done with the congressional strength was not immediately clear, except that the Apristas seemed determined to make the most of it.[29]

In succeeding years the new situation was strongly reflected in strategy and tactics. While still viewing the presidency as a principal goal, the Apristas took steps to bypass it as a *necessary* element in getting their program adopted and executed. They did this by deliberately trying to shift the government away from an exclusively presidential emphasis and toward a parliamentary form. At the same time, the coalition with Odría took on signs of greater permanency. Both features were readily apparent in the speech by Haya on February 21, 1966, at the annual party rally in Lima.

Proposing that Congress be made the "first power of the state," Haya said: "In countries where democracy reaches its highest degree of perfection, the chief of state is a legal fiction and Parliament is the ruling element of the state." Such a "de-presidentialization" of the executive would bring Peru that much closer to "truly representative democracy." Haya recalled having promised, when he was a presidential candidate, to take this step if elected. The other subject stressed in Haya's speech, the coalition with Odría's party, presaged continued cooperation, including a formal campaign alliance for the municipal and by-elections of November, 1966. He said that *Aprismo* had "never had better allies than now." As had others, he referred to the combination as the Coalición del Pueblo, an obvious analogy to Partido del Pueblo (Party of the People), the formal name for APRA in Peru.[30] Remembering that it was Odría who as president persecuted Apristas and kept Haya imprisoned in the Colombian Embassy for most of his eight-year rule, Peruvians and foreigners were bewildered.

[29] *La Tribuna*, July 15, 1963, p. 1. The paper asserted that the legislative branch should have the autonomy and prestige to make an equal contribution to "official action for the public good." See also *La Tribuna*, March 3, 1966; Campos, *Coloquios*, 2: 193–95; and Leonidas Castro Bastos, *Golpismo* (Lima: Libreria e Emprenta D. Miranda, 1964), pp. 65–66. APRA also initiated a constitutional amendment to require Senate confirmation of ambassadorial appointments; see McCoy, "Aprista Party, 1965," p. 29.

[30] *La Tribuna*, February 27, 1966, p. 9; see also *ibid.*, February 28, 1966, p. 4, and *Presente*, March, 1965, p. 47.

The Coalition

The purely tactical calculations which brought APRA and UNO together in the congressional coalition of July, 1963, are easy to follow. First, Odría's party had qualified for respectability in Aprista eyes—despite his persecution of the party from 1948 to 1956—by accepting free party competition as his term came to an end. (Whether weakening army support for him forced the decision is a separate question.) Odría had shown some inclination to perpetuate his term beyond 1956 but finally held the elections which brought Prado to power. He had also submitted to election defeats in 1962 and 1963 and, in the negotiations just prior to the 1962 coup, "revealed a gentlemanliness and sense of civility that surprised me favorably," according to Seoane, an Aprista not inclined to cooperate with Odría.[31]

In the circumstances of July, 1963, moreover, APRA had no choice but to cooperate with some other party or be left isolated and impotent. The first opportunity came from Belaúnde in the early days of the month. Conscious of the difficulty of governing without a majority in Congress, he invited APRA and UNO to agree to his calling upon members of any party to serve in the cabinet, "without committing them [the parties] and letting all responsibility fall on my shoulders." Both parties rejected the idea, evidently finding it both disadvantageous and inconsistent with the idea of cabinet responsibility to Congress.[32]

Negotiations on the organization of Congress nevertheless continued among the AP/DC alliance, APRA, and UNO, and included meetings between Belaúnde and Haya de la Torre. When the negotiations failed only a few days before the inauguration, it was revealed that the government parties had proposed dividing the positions of presiding officers in Congress three ways: three for AP/DC, two for APRA, and two for UNO. APRA was reported to have agreed, provided consensus could be reached on a statement of program. This was done, *ad referendum* and apparently with only minor differences, and it was published July 23. Each of the three main parties insisted, however, on having the presidency of either the Senate or Chamber of Deputies the first year. At this impasse APRA saw its only course in combining with the Odriístas, dividing

[31] Chirinos, *El Perú*, pp. 111ff. See also Manuel Seoane interview quoted in Martín, *Política Peruana*, p. 117. When asked in 1961 to comment on the Odriísta movement, Seoane had replied, "Of the penitent is the Kingdom of Heaven" (*ibid.*, p. 113). It is not suggested that UNO was transfigured between 1956 and 1962–63; for example, in 1963, UNO leader de la Piedra told the press that he was completely opposed to progressive taxation (*ibid.*, p. 97).

[32] *La Tribuna*, July 7, 1963, p. 1; see also McCoy, "Aprista Party, 1965," p. 25.

equally the positions in Congress, and rotating them annually.[33] Thus the choice that arose immediately between program application and partisan advantage was decided in favor of the latter.

The nature of the APRA/UNO coalition has been the subject of speculation even among those who study it disinterestedly. Spokesmen of both parties have said that the coalition covers only the basic organization of Congress. APRA and UNO have acted in concert on some issues (notably, censure of cabinet ministers) and disagreed on others (such as some aspects of agrarian reform). Cooperation has included joint lists of candidates in the municipal elections of December, 1963, and November, 1966.

The government parties publicly condemned APRA for allying itself with the oligarchy, while APRA charged that they were infiltrated with Communists. Actually, the coalition had its origin in the new attitude which had been evolving in APRA for several years, but which was not plainly evident until after 1963.

As early as 1956, top Aprista leaders publicly broached the idea of an alliance with the industrial interests, against the traditional element, in the Peruvian economy:

> The growth of national capitalism and its final triumph over imperialism and feudalism depends on the strength at its disposal, and this, as is well known, [depends] on the markets which nourish the national industries. The growth of the market for national capitalism is therefore a factor *sine qua non* in the triumph of nationalist forces over imperialism, on the one hand, and over its ally, feudalism, on the other. . . . Supporting the interests of national capitalism and orienting them toward international Indo-American integration is to promote the original Aprista ideal of Indo-American integration, to rid the region of feudalism. . . .[34]

The outcome of ideas such as this, along with other initiatives outside Aprista control, such as the entry of new reform-minded parties into Peruvian politics, has been a political style of maneuver in which gradualism is favored as an approach to reform by the once-revolutionary APRA. Whether or not it is an illusion can be seen only in performance.

The key word in this new Aprista approach to politics was "maturity"; with it the leadership sought to reassure old enemies of its new reasonableness and attachment to the free political system and to re-educate its own

[33] *La Tribuna*, July 14, 23, 25, 26, and 28, 1963, all on p. 1, and July 25, 1963, p. 2. The pro-government *Expresso* said that Belaúnde wanted to trade cabinet places for a minimal program commitment (*HAR* 16, no. 7 (1963) : 705).

[34] Seoane, *Obras Apristas*, pp. 79–80; he was quoting and endorsing a memorandum prepared by Manuel Vásquez Díaz, Aprista finance minister in 1946–47. It is of interest that Seoane is later reported to have opposed strongly the idea of a campaign alliance with Odría for the 1963 election; see McCoy, "Aprista Party, 1948–63," p. 91. It appears that Seoane's 1956 remarks were aimed at a rapprochement with Belaúnde, whose following included some "national capitalists."

membership, which was unaccustomed to thinking in flexible terms. Events late in 1957 provided occasions for educational editorials. One concerned the peaceful solution of the strike of Post and Telecommunications workers and the suspension of a supreme decree on the re-election of union officers; the other called the new Industries Law a "victory for democracy."

> . . . The positive element of this lesson is that the forces of organized capitalism and those of labor, also organized, have come to a point of equilibrium in the state. By its nature, democracy acts more slowly than a dictator. But this maturation makes it more positive and more permanent.
>
> . . . And liberty can be understood only as a process which is creative, efficacious, and dynamic. . . . The administration can count on a law for the actual development of industry. . . . For now, we must await the results. The country, no doubt, will soon assess the results, which are nothing but the benefits of democracy.[35]

The criticism which earlier had been directed at APRA because of the *convivencia* with Prado, and party efforts to point out that it was not a partnership, obscured the early debate within APRA over the possible need for alliances with other parties. Campaign pacts were not automatically ruled out in the preparations for the 1962 election, except in the practical sense that no candidate was willing to stand aside for another.[36] Finally, concentration on the 1962 and 1963 campaigns to elect Haya diverted the party's thinking from the probable need for post-election alliances until it was forcefully reminded by the election results.

Just after the 1962 coup and the abortive agreement to support Odría's election in Congress, the debate was renewed on possible alliances for 1963. Other Apristas wanted to continue with Odría. Manuel Seoane was strongly in favor of an "understanding" with AP/DC, he explained afterward, as "the most reliable and productive solution by which to advance victoriously stimulating radical and profound changes in the anachronistic structure of Peruvian society."[37] These opposing views were irreconcilable except through the renomination of Haya.

Renewal of the disagreement after the 1963 election, and the pact with UNO to organize Congress, almost drove Manuel Seoane out of APRA, but he returned before his death later that year. The need to justify, after the fact, the strategy of going it alone in the 1963 election was evident in a

[35] *La Tribuna*, October 19, 1957, p. 4, and November 1, 1957, p. 4.

[36] Rumored combinations were reported in Martín, *Política Peruana*, pp. 121–22; *HAR* 16, no. 4 (1963): 381; Héctor Cornejo Chávez, *Qué se Propone la Democracia Cristiana?* (Lima: Ediciones del Sol, 1962), pp. 76–80.

[37] *La Prensa*, June 29, 1963, p. 18. As early as 1961 Manuel Seoane had publicly praised Belaúnde and the Christian Democrats; Martín, *Política Peruana*, p. 113. See also McCoy, "Aprista Party, 1948–63," pp. 91–92, and *idem*, "Aprista Party, 1965," p. 9.

La Tribuna article in July. It cited the large 1963 vote for APRA (exceeding 1962 in absolute and relative terms) and stated that it had been necessary to (1) show who were the real supporters of the party, (2) disprove charges of fraud in the previous election, and (3) test the junta's promise of free elections.[38]

Congressional Supremacy

The circumstances in which APRA had to operate when the new Congress convened evidently had not been foreseen in party calculations, and it had to make the best of the situation at hand. Having made a somewhat imprecise deal with Odría, the party eventually set about sublimating its condition through renewed emphasis on Congress as an independent power factor. Thus the goal of changing the division of powers and the tactic of coalition control were mutually reinforcing. They tended to exclude or set aside the objectives of program application through control of the executive.

In justice to the Apristas, the campaign for congressional supremacy was not pure expediency. They had advocated the parliamentary system not only in 1945–48 and after 1963, when it was to their advantage, but also when they were not dominant in Congress. Moreover, the principle has had a long history in Peru.

As early as the constitution of 1856, and the similar and even shorter-lived document of 1867, Peru made faltering attempts to build up the power of Congress at the expense of the executive. The key feature of ministerial censure was proposed even earlier, enacted into ordinary law in 1856, and considered repeatedly thereafter. It did not attain constitutional status until 1920, but was continued in the constitution of 1933.[39]

In the constitution of 1933, still valid in the sixties, there are at least 30 articles (out of 236) which establish parliamentary independence or deal with the executive or the president personally in order to limit the arbitrary use of power in favor of the cabinet (*Consejo de Ministros*), or Congress, to which the cabinet is formally responsible. The provisions governing censure are re-inforced by those permitting unlimited interpellation, surprise confidence votes, and congressional investigation. On the other hand, the so-called veto power of the president, while not clearly provided in the constitution, has been accepted in practice. The general

[38] *La Tribuna*, July 10, 1963, p. 1; Castro Bastos, *Golpismo*, pp. 62–64.

[39] *La Prensa*, July 26, 1957. Chirinos called this aspect of the Peruvian constitution unique in Latin America, but it is not without historical parallels, as, for example, in the Cuban constitution of 1940; see Stokes, *Latin American Politics*, pp. 437ff.

character of government, however, which could be parliamentary under the constitution, has been entirely presidential in practice.[40]

In addition to those already mentioned, the constitution of 1933 includes several other limitations on the powers of the president.

1. *Congressional action in lieu of presidential:* to convoke by-elections for either or both chambers (article 97); to convoke regular sessions of Congress (Article 107); to begin deliberations even though the president does not attend the installation (Article 110); to promulgate laws passed by both chambers if the president has not done so after ten days (Articles 128–29).

2. *Congressional independence of the executive:* to avoid conflicts of interest between legislative and other (including executive) responsibilities (Articles 99–106); to continue indefinitely in special session (Article 108); to determine its relations with the Executive (Article 116); to exclude armed forces from congressional premises except as Congress requests (Article 118).

3. *Cabinet concurrence required for presidential acts:* to call special sessions of the Congress (Article 108); to deliver messages to Congress (Article 149); to appoint or remove diplomats (Article 154); to act officially, in general (Article 166); to initiate constitutional amendments (Article 236).

4. *Impeachment and trial of the president* (Articles 121–22).

Many of these provisions admittedly are, or have been, neglected in practice. Bustamante failed to appear for the inauguration of the 1948 session of Congress, but it was the lack of a quorum, caused by a conservative boycott of the Senate, which really prevented it from acting.[41] The tactic was repeated in 1967.

All these provisions have received increased attention in the Aprista campaign since 1963 to emphasize parliamentary power. Such real power as is available to Congress, however, resides in the more directly usable provisions relating to the investigation of executive acts, interpellation and censure of ministers, and the vague question of the presidential veto.

The investigative powers of the Peruvian Congress are sweeping, in that committees of inquiry can be appointed by either chamber. Executive as well as judicial authorities at all levels "are obligated to submit . . . the

[40] Castro Bastos, *Golpismo*, p. 65; Chirinos, *El Perú*, p. 64; interview with Enrique Chirinos Soto, March 3, 1966. See also Chirinos' articles in *La Prensa*, January 5, 1957, p. 8, and July 26, 1957. He wrote on this issue well before it became a political issue among the parties active in the sixties.

[41] Sánchez, *Haya de la Torre*, pp. 440–41; *Economist*, September 9, 1967, p. 879.

information and documents which they request." Although this is not interpreted to include the power of subpoena, it is similar in other respects to the powers of the U.S. Congress.[42]

Closely related to congressional investigation, and perhaps more effective, are the powers of interpellation. Very briefly the constitution states that Congress or either chamber may require the cabinet or any individual minister to appear (Article 169), that the written interpellation requires the votes of only one-fifth of "the sitting representatives" (*hábiles*) (Article 170), and that it shall specify the day and hour of the reply (Article 171). These powers in turn lead to those concerning cabinet responsibility and censure.

The general principle of ministerial responsibility to Congress is suggested in the requirements that the president present messages to it at the end of his term and at the inauguration of Congress "in ordinary legislature." These and any special messages must be submitted to the cabinet for approval (Article 149). In addition, upon taking office, the prime minister and cabinet must appear before each chamber separately to explain executive policy (Article 167).

The rules for censure are equally simple. They state that a vote against the cabinet or any minister may be moved by an individual deputy or senator, and that the vote shall be taken during the same session (Article 172); that a censured minister must resign, and that his resignation must be accepted by the president (Article 173); and, finally, that non-approval of a ministerial initiative is not interpreted as censure unless the minister concerned makes it a matter of confidence (Article 174).

These provisions have been interpreted in the abstract as seeking to make the president "politically irresponsible" by requiring cabinet concurrence in all his official acts. The president "is, in a way, placed above the political debate." On the question of censure, the same analyst later wrote, "With a hostile majority in the chambers, the president simply cannot govern except as he adjusts the makeup of the cabinet to the demands of the parliament." The Peruvian constitution lacks even the safeguards of stability of the French Fourth Republic, for Article 172 sanctions the surprise motion of censure, and a simple (rather than absolute) majority of deputies or senators can dismiss a cabinet.[43]

[42] Article 119 of the constitution of 1933. All references and quotations are from the English translation published by the Pan American Union, checked against *Constitución Política del Perú* (Lima: Cámara de Diputados, 1950). Interview with Chirinos, March 3, 1966.

[43] *La Prensa*, January 5, 1957, p. 8, and July 26, 1957. Article 134 of the constitution states that "the president of the republic is the head of the state, and personifies the nation."

The question of presidential veto power is more complex. Before 1933 the presidential power of "observing" a law passed by Congress had been recognized, but it was not made explicit in the constitution adopted that year. The defect was remedied in 1939 by President Benavides, who ordered a referendum to amend the constitution. The effects of this *plebiscito* and other "laws of repression" were repealed in one stroke as one of the first acts of the Aprista-led Congress in 1945. Even this act was promulgated by Congress over the objection of President Bustamante.[44]

In the same year, Congress passed a press law which the president returned with an objection. Anti-Apristas argued that the traditional power of observation had not been expressly repealed. The repeal was established, in effect, when Congress amended the law to satisfy the ostensible flaw and returned it to the president. Thus both a limited veto (or power to observe) and the right to override presidential objections were accepted.[45]

The veto controversy did not end there, however, for the Apristas maintain that Congress is supreme. Haya restated the principle forcefully and without qualification in one of his *coloquios* of the mid-sixties. In practice, successful presidential exercise of the power to observe congressional acts probably depends on the balance of executive-legislative power when the question arises.[46]

As late as 1967 the problem arose over tax reform. Unable to get his bill through the Congress, Belaúnde increased customs duties by executive action. Congress annulled the increases, but Belaúnde vetoed the law. Because this happened during the conservatives' boycott of the Senate, Congress was unable to respond, and the higher duties continued in effect.[47]

Uses of Congressional Power

Since 1963 the APRA/UNO coalition has made the greatest use of constitutional provisions relating to investigation, interpellation, and censure. The first two often have been the prelude to the third, and all have been directed mainly at the question of subversive activities, either in the government or in organizations engaged in guerrilla-type insurgency.

[44] Law no. 10,334, cited in *Constitución Política*, pp. 72–74; Washington Durán Abarca, *Plebiscito* (Lima: Editorial "Thesis," 1964), pp. 92–94.

[45] Sánchez, *Haya de la Torre*, pp. 346, 408–10.

[46] Campos, *Coloquios*, 2: 195–96. This question is discussed in Chirinos, *El Perú*, pp. 65–67, no. 1. He had written his thesis for the LLB degree on the subject, and proposed amending the constitution to include a specific veto, although presumably not to require, as had the 1939 plebiscitary modification, a three-fifths vote to override presidential objections (*ibid.*, pp. 64–65).

[47] *Los Angeles Times*, August 23, 1967.

Congressional powers thus have served to re-inforce the explicit Aprista effort, first to achieve ". . . the categorical rejection and condemnation of the so-called unconventional warfare type of infiltration and its maneuvers to annul Peruvian sovereignty and the institutions of representative democracy in which it manifests itself; second, to express our solidarity with the armed forces which have valiantly taken command of the defense of our sovereignty and of our democracy. . . ."[48] A listing of the first four censure votes illustrates how the APRA/UNO coalition used congressional powers against the executive:

1. Labor Minister Miguel Cussianovich in October, 1963, was censured for failure to deal decisively with the Communist-backed slowdown by the Union of Bank Clerks. The wage increase decreed by the government was seen as a measure supporting the Communist effort to gain control of CTP.[49]

2. Interior and Prime Minister Oscar Trelles in December, 1963, was censured for failure to cope with clashes between police and *campesinos* in the southern sierra, which resulted in several deaths. He was replaced by Schwalb as premier and Languasco as interior minister; the latter took strong action against the land invasions on grounds that they were inspired by Cuban-directed Communist organizers. An investigating committee of deputies, headed by a UNO member, concurred.[50]

3. Minister of Development and Public Works Carlos Pestana Zevallos in April, 1964, was censured for declining to discipline the head of *Cooperación Popular*, who advocated a plebiscite on the question of dissolving Congress. Funds for the program later were cut sharply by Congress.[51]

4. Minister of Education Francisco Miró Quesada in September, 1964, was censured for failure to respond to the interpellation concerning Communist influence in the school system. APRA denied personal animus against this member of the *El Comercio* family, but the case had been building up by way of an interpellation in June. It concerned charges of politically motivated personnel changes and teaching about communism in the secondary schools.[52]

[48] Townsend's Chamber of Deputies speech was quoted in *Presente*, September–October, 1965, pp. 58–66. In the same issue an editorial denied the charge that congressional investigation of Communists in the government amounted to a witch hunt. In translation the title read, "Neither McCarthyites Nor Cat's Paws" (*ibid.*, pp. 26–27).

[49] *HAR* 16, no. 10 (1963) : 991–92; Delmas, "Peru's New Politics," p. 38.

[50] *HAR* 16, no. 12 (1963) : 1178–79, and 17, no. 3 (1964) : 249.

[51] *Ibid.* 17, no. 4 (1964) : 347; McCoy, "Aprista Party, 1965," p. 27.

[52] *HAR* 17, no. 4 (1964): 348; McCoy, "Aprista Party, 1965," p. 27; Andrés Townsend Ezcurra, *Interpelación y Fuga: Por Qué Huyó Miró Quesada* (Lima: Ediciones Pueblo, 1964).

The congressional pressure continued, with at least one cabinet or minister resigning each year after being censured or threatened with it, until by mid-1967 a total of ten such incidents had occurred during Belaúnde's term. By 1966, however, the guerrilla bands had been wiped out and the subversive theme began to lose its force as a weapon against the Belaúnde administration. Attention shifted to economic problems. Together with related issues of corruption and smuggling, or foreign investment and nationalization, inflation and economic controls dominated executive-congressional relations from 1966 to 1968. Between September 1, 1967, when he devalued the sol, and October 3, 1968, when he was overthrown, Belaúnde appointed five different cabinets.

The economic theme was signaled by Haya in February, 1966, when he opened the campaign for the municipal elections of November by attacking the Belaúnde administration over the rising cost of living. Both the 1965 and 1966 budgets had been cut by the APRA/UNO coalition, but the Christian Democratic agriculture minister resisted the 1966 reduction so strongly that he threatened the stability of the governing alliance.[53]

Inflation reached 15.0 percent in 1965, dropped back to 8.5 percent in 1966 with the help of tightened internal credit, but worsened again in 1967. Continued budget deficits were blamed, but foreign economic relations also were troubled. The drop in world sugar, cotton, and fishmeal prices in 1966–67 cut deeply into Peruvian export proceeds, and Belaúnde had difficulty negotiating foreign loans and credits. Devaluation in September, 1967, bought only a temporary solution.[54]

Part of the economic problem was attributed to Belaúnde's imperfect grasp of the financial side of development. He was blamed for unduly depending on foreign aid as the key to development, his approach to which was considered "uniquely technocratic and visionary."[55] Others criticized the fiscal orthodoxy of "neoliberals" such as Pedro Beltrán, former prime minister and publisher of *La Prensa*, which supposedly worked to the advantage of export-oriented interests.[56]

Belaúnde had considerable trouble obtaining legislative authority to combat economic ills. Early in 1967 he began trying to win passage of a tax reform measure, having already restricted credit lines to foreign firms. Import duties were raised on consumer goods over the objections of

[53] *La Prensa*, February 27, 1966; March 3, 1966, p. 14; and March 9, 1966, p. 2. See also *HAR* 17, no. 8 (1964): 733–35, and 18, no. 9 (1965): 827–28; *Expreso*, March 11, 1966, pp. 2 and 10. Vice-President Seoane was quoted as favoring an austere budget, but he was generally on the opposite side from *La Prensa*, critics of which say that it prescribes "fiscal orthodoxy" as the cure for both economic and social ills.

[54] *Los Angeles Times*, August 23, 1967; *New York Times*, October 25, 1967, p. 14.

[55] *Oiga* (Lima), November 15, 1968; *Washington Post*, December 29, 1967.

[56] Bourricaud, *Poder y Sociedad*, p. 208.

Congress. It was not until 1968, however, that he began to get further powers. Intensified import controls were applied on March 1. Special economic authority was granted by Congress in June and again in August, each time for only sixty days. The coup came before the latter period expired.[57]

The five years of Belaúnde's presidency showed a progression, by no means uninterrupted, from hostility to something resembling rapprochement between the executive and Congress. From the beginning in 1963, the APRA/UNO coalition was accused of pursuing an obstructionist policy in Congress. This led some members of the AP/DC alliance to propose the dissolution of Congress and the holding of a special plebiscite to elect members more favorable to the president's program.

The plebiscite idea was favored by Vice-President Seoane just after the December, 1963, municipal elections, which seemed to show AP/DC stronger than it had been in preceding presidential elections. Belaúnde finally declared himself against the proposal, after it had been severely attacked by the Apristas as "gambling with the stability of the legitimately constituted system." When the plebiscite theme was revived in 1966, Haya himself spoke against the thought that the forthcoming municipal elections could be regarded as a national plebiscite.[58]

Although the totals for the whole country in those elections showed little change from three years before, there were signs of shifts in voter preferences. The AP/DC candidate made certain gains in the normally Aprista North, while the APRA/UNO coalition and third parties made inroads in the southern sierra. In 1967, by-elections brought victory to APRA/UNO in the Lima contest for a seat in the Chamber of Deputies and the withdrawal from the cabinet of the already divided Christian Democrats.

Meanwhile, the minority boycott of the Senate in August, 1967, had immobilized Congress for more than a month. Begun as a dispute over technicalities, it became a test of obstinacy which finally was settled only by the resignation of the UNO Senate president and the AP/DC cabinet after the pressures for devaluation became unbearable.

In 1968 AP and UNO also splintered, the former over policy differences and the latter supposedly because former President Odría planned to run again for the presidency in 1969. APRA's competitive position as the only

[57] *Journal of Commerce*, September 19, 1968; *New York Times*, August 30, 1968; *International Commerce* (U.S. Department of Commerce, Washington, D.C.), July 15, 1968.

[58] Quotation from *Presente*, March, 1965, pp. 48–49. See also McCoy, "Aprista Party, 1965," pp. 28–29; Duran, *Plebiscito*, esp. pp. 48–53 and 69–70; and *La Tribuna*, February 27, 1966, p. 2.

major party left intact was thereby distinctly improved. Belaúnde already had made the conciliatory move of personally consulting with Haya and Odría in October, 1967, when they agreed to give first priority to reducing the current budget deficit and balancing the 1968 budget.[59]

By some accounts, Belaúnde obtained cooperation in 1967 by pointing to the threat of intervention by the armed forces. The purchase of sophisticated weapons for the air force, with corresponding claims by the other services, helped to increase budget deficits. By mid-1968, however, the president was less able to bargain than ever. Following the division and purge in AP, a new cabinet of technicians was installed in June. This was alleged to be payment to APRA, for its agreeing to grant emergency powers to Belaúnde.[60]

The Apristas had meanwhile been talking confidently of the prospects for the 1969 presidential election, without at first naming their candidate. At a press conference in May, the army minister replied to a question on another subject (paradoxically, the charge that officers were involved in smuggling) with the statement, "The word veto has been erased from the military dictionary in Peru." This was interpreted as a lifting of the disqualification of Haya, and there was jubilation at Aprista headquarters. In July it was announced that Haya would run and that Belaúnde had given assurances that whoever won the election would be president.[61]

Evidently the time was already too late, however, to reconcile APRA and AP in mid-1968. APRA had little to show, in a positive sense, for its five years of dominance in Congress. The supremacy of Congress had not been established, the political party system (except for APRA and the extreme Left) had once more disintegrated, and no broad-gauged Aprista program had been enacted or applied.

[59] *New York Times*, October 26, 1967, p. 14.

[60] Astiz, *Pressure Groups*, p. 265. Astiz says that, "since 1967, Belaúnde Terry appeared to have been only trying to survive and complete his term of office" (*ibid.*, p. 122).

[61] *Los Angeles Times*, May 3, 1968; see also *Washington Post*, May 3, 1968, and *Miami Herald*, July 14, 1968.

VII

THE AGRARIAN REFORM ISSUE

THERE WAS AT LEAST ONE FLAW in the temptation of Apristas to think that a milestone had passed with the return of free government in 1956. The willingness to work within the system was a choice particularly attractive to the regional and particularistic elements in APRA, and these were the party's most influential elements.

The Solid North and organized labor, particularly the urbanized and middle-class elements, had the greatest voice and the most to gain by protecting what had already been won. The choice of reform ran the risk, however, of overlooking the interests of those who were inarticulate and non-participant in the country generally, but particularly the Indian *campesinos* and *comuneros* of the southern and south-central highlands. The problem of these people has come to be epitomized by the issue of land reform. If industrialization would directly benefit the coastal and urban sectors, land reform was, and is, of primary importance to the welfare of the rural Indians. It has long been a major policy question for any Peruvian government.

The land reform issue is a convenient one for in-depth study because it culminated in the first comprehensive law on the subject (no. 15,037), enacted after exhaustive debate and considerable compromise in Congress, on May 21, 1964. The circumstances in which the law was considered were fully as important as its specific content. It was the first major legislation submitted in 1963 by the new, Belaúnde administration. The debate reached its climax at about the same time that land invasions and quasi-guerrilla activities in two parts of the country were building up to new intensities. This in turn was the issue when the first censure vote of many was directed at, and succeeded in unseating, Belaúnde's first prime minister. All of these conditions were highlighted by the division in control of the executive and Congress between the AP/DC alliance and the APRA/UNO coalition.

APRA's Dilemmas

The opportunity for passage of the agrarian reform law should have been the occasion for rejoicing and self-congratulation in APRA. The fact that it was not was attributed to a series of dilemmas that confronted the party. The first two of these were purely political. Aprista championship of agrarian reform was clearly on record; the only fault that might have been found with its previous handling of the issue was an apparent tendency to let it be studied to death, first within the party in the 1945–48 period and then by the Commission on Agrarian Reform and Housing (CRAV) from 1956 to 1960.

In the 1963 presidential campaign, however, "practically all the political parties included in their action platforms the need for agrarian reform and the promise to carry it out."[1] APRA thus was no longer alone in the field. Its first problem was made apparent when Belaúnde, using the talents of his first vice-president, Edgardo Seoane, gained the psychological advantage by getting the administration bill submitted immediately after his inauguration. There were no radical differences between this and the Aprista bill submitted about two months later, but there was a great temptation (on both sides) to make them seem different in order to avoid the "me too" position. There could be no question of APRA opposing the AP bill, or even seriously obstructing it, but ways were sought to avoid letting the president's party take all the credit.

The second dilemma of APRA also was political, but even more acutely tactical. The party had only just made its pact with the party of Odría, the external vagueness of which probably betrayed a considerable indecision within the party as to how it would work in terms of substantive compromises. The formal position was that the two parties had agreed only to organize Congress, that is, to cooperate in electing their respective candidates to presiding positions.

The first big issue to be faced, however, would clearly divide them and run the risk of making the coalition a farce. The general tendency seemed to be to go as far as possible to give the appearance of cohesion, in order to preserve the advantage of majority control. This also met the need for a

[1] CIDA, *Tierra y Desarrollo*, p. 401. Agrarian reform headed the list of subjects on which the party announced in July that it was considering submitting bills; *La Tribuna*, July 11, 1963, p. 1.

certain show of obstruction of the AP bill, but it laid the Apristas open to the serious charge of opposing reform at the behest of UNO—the party most closely identified with the forces of reaction.[2]

Not only was the initial situation uncomfortable for APRA, but its coalition partner compounded the difficulty by submitting its own agrarian reform bill some weeks after that of the government. Not many weeks later APRA came in with its own. The manner in which this legislative glut developed is not clear to the outsider, but what happened can safely be inferred.

APRA obviously was taken by surprise by the speed with which the executive acted, possibly having thought it would have time to continue studying the problem. In these early days of Belaúnde's administration the door was not closed to some kind of cooperation between his AP/DC alliance and one or both of the opposition parties.

APRA and UNO did not formalize their coalition until late in July, when Belaúnde was inaugurated. Talks had meanwhile been directed toward possible four-party participation in the cabinet and/or in the organization of Congress. The cabinet idea was rejected early in July, and the congressional negotiations failed just before inauguration of the new Congress on July 28.

After the government reform bill appeared in mid-August, the Odriístas evidently decided that they could not fail to present a substitute. Once they had done so, APRA faced its basic dilemma in still sharper terms—it ran the risk of being identified, in tangible form, either with the satisfactory bill of AP, its principal competitor, or with the unsatisfactory bill of UNO, its partner in Congress. Neither position was tenable. When AP forced the play, the UNO joined in, the Apristas apparently concluded that they had no choice but to present a third alternative.

The Insurgency Dilemma

The third respect in which APRA's problems were intensified was in the coincidence of land invasions and the agrarian reform debates. Land invasions had been mounting since about 1960, were concentrated increasingly in particular regions (such as the departments of Junín and Cuzco), and represented the results of organizational work by *campesino* syndicates.

Around mid-1963 a difference appeared, however, in that large numbers of *campesinos* became involved (300,000 is the estimate of an outside source), the invasions often preceded rather than followed the resort to

[2] Terry L. McCoy, "The Politics of Agrarian Reform in Peru," mimeographed (Madison: University of Wisconsin, Land Tenure Center, 1965), pp. 23–24.

legal argumentation, and they were directed at cultivated lands as well as at open pastures.[3] The part played in this by extremists was fully evident, and a danger existed that leadership of the *campesinos* would go to them by default.

An article on agrarian reform in the Aprista party paper in July had already accused the Communists of trying to create chaos by inciting *campesinos* to attack haciendas and police outposts. In that same month, FENCAP sponsored in Huancayo, capital of Junín, the First Regional Congress of Central Communities, which concluded that there would be no economic development "without first resolving the problem of the land from a social revolutionary standpoint." Nevertheless, the Indians were counseled to try to regain their lands by legal means.

Still prior to submission of the government's bill, an editorial in *La Tribuna* again condemned Communist activities but said that land invasions would accelerate enactment of a law. Meanwhile, at the end of July, a community (San Pedro de Cajas) in the Huancayo area had moved about 2,500 *campesinos* onto 8,000 acres of disputed land. *La Tribuna* favored their demands to the extent of giving the episode and a similar one (at Yantac) prominent display for several days, while FENCAP asked the government to avoid using force, except to maintain order among the invaders.[4]

APRA finally sought to manage this dilemma by renouncing illegal action, but it used carefully controlled political tactics. Apparently the party concluded that it could not compete with the Communists in encouraging land invasions. Late in August, CTP ordered a twenty-four-hour strike in protest over an incident at Yantac in which the Civil Guard wounded seven *campesinos*. When the strike did not become "general," *La Tribuna* blamed the Communists in the trade unions. The paper already had urged the government to proceed with certain expropriations to relieve the most urgent *campesino* demands.

As the number of invasions and disorders continued to rise, Belaúnde announced that, in return for the agreement of *campesinos* in Junín and Pasco to cease invasions, he would order the purchase and distribution of 215,000 hectares of land in those departments as another pilot project (comparable to the earlier one ordered by the junta in Cuzco). The Chamber of Deputies nevertheless called upon Prime (and Interior) Minister Trelles to investigate the disorders and finally, on December 31, censured him for failing to cope with them.[5]

[3] CIDA, *Tierra y Desarrollo*, pp. 395–98.

[4] *La Tribuna*, July 15, 20, and August 1, 2, 4, 8, and 25–27, 1963.

[5] *Ibid.*, August 25–27, 29, and September 3, 1963; *HAR* 16, no. 10 (1963) : 991, and no. 12 (1963) : 1178.

Thus APRA gradually (but over a short span of six months) dissociated itself from sponsorship of direct action by the Indians and thereby gave up some influence in the control and direction of land invasions. Townsend, in presenting the Aprista agrarian reform bill on October 15, 1963, explained: "Our agrarian reform is a constitutional and democratic reform. It is not the occasion or the moment, nor is it the historical era, to initiate . . . agrarian reform by violent means. And more: we do not advocate that method. We are . . . advocates of the right of rebellion against tyranny. We are not advocates of violent methods. . . ."[6] Instead, the APRA/UNO coalition turned to the twin levers of (1) urging resolute action by police and armed forces against "foreign-directed guerrilla" activities, and (2) interpellation and censure of cabinets failing to take such action. On these points they could agree.

By mid-1965 the ambush of a Civil Guard patrol in central Peru provided the spark which forced the government to engage the armed forces rather than continue to leave the problem to the police. Another cabinet was censured a few months later, and by the end of the year most observers, and President Belaúnde as well, agreed that the guerrillas had been defeated. APRA had sacrificed a chance to champion a *campesino* cause and, by some estimates, had gone too far in playing up the guerrilla threat. On the other hand, it had distracted attention from its own predicament by pressing the government and, it was claimed, had succeeded in improving in some degree its relations with the armed forces.[7]

The Substantive Dilemma

The merits of the several agrarian reform bills also posed problems for the Apristas. Although by 1963 there was general acceptance of the need for agrarian reform, there was little or no consensus on how it should be carried out. The subject of agrarian reform has been termed "complex in the extreme, as complex as the rural structure of the country."[8] Agreement on the general principles was not impossible, as we have seen in the issuance of the decree-law on agrarian reform (no. 14,238) by the military junta in 1962. But few could agree on the resolution of conflicting approaches, their application to specific cases, and the precise lengths to which social aims should be pushed at the expense of economic goals.

[6] Townsend, *Reform Agraria*, p. 20.

[7] *Presente*, no. 102 (September–October, 1965), pp. 16–51; *Christian Science Monitor*, December 27, 1965; John M. Goshko, "Peru Chief Belittles Disorders," *Washington Post*, September 4, 1965, p. A7, and March 4, 1966, p. A14; McCoy, "Agrarian Reform," p. 28, and "Aprista Party, 1965," p. 31; interview with Haya de la Torre, March, 1966.

[8] CIDA, *Tierra y Desarrollo*, p. 401.

It could almost be said that it was impossible to write a law which would be fair when applied to specific cases yet detailed enough to provide sufficient guidance for working officials. The variations in conditions among and within the different regions of Peru are too great, the detailed knowledge about them too rudimentary, and the capacities of interested parties and officials too varied, to foresee all contingencies.

Despite the technical complexity of the subject, some aspects of it have been made extremely simple politically. The political touchstone of agrarian reform is the expropriation of land and its redistribution in small individual, or larger collective, parcels. Once this is said, the problem becomes complicated again, for the experts insist that land division by itself merely sacrifices productive capacity until either it is recombined in efficient sizes or the new occupants gain the technical know-how needed to use it productively.[9]

The questions of the taking of land, of which land, and of how, remain the politically sensitive points on which the widest variations of view are seen. For example, the bill presented by the deputy of the Communist-dominated FLN (*Frente de Liberación Nacional*) simply demanded the outright confiscation of all holdings over a stated size. At the other extreme, the UNO proposal provided only for partial and proportional expropriation of very large estates, as long as they were efficiently cultivated, against payment at prices averaging capitalized rental value and sales of similar properties.[10]

The political "magic" of expropriation emerges in various ways. Seldom if ever are specific acreage figures mentioned in partisan speeches and literature. The intent is conveyed by the use of phrases such as eliminating "feudalism" or the *latifundio*, which often amounts to mere sloganeering. More frequent is the emphasis on the supportive and preparatory activities of providing credit, technical assistance, training, agricultural experimentation, meteorological stations, etc., as a way of skirting the sensitive issue.

Still more remote from expropriation and redistribution is the emphasis which deals mainly with projects for irrigation, reclamation, and colonization. This approach means that division of existing estates, if not completely avoided, can be subordinated to expansion of the total area under cultivation. Technically sound, these angles of attack supply politicians with plausible grounds for delaying or defeating land redistribution as a step toward structural change. They seize upon the technical excuse for

[9] T. Lynn Smith, ed., *Agrarian Reform in Latin America* (New York: Alfred A. Knopf, 1965), pp. 8–11. With respect to Peru this was noted as long ago as 1938 by Moíses Poblete Troncoso; see Ford, *Man and Land in Peru*, p. 127.

[10] *HAR* 16, no. 11 (1963) : 1082.

evading the politically sensitive issue, even with respect to lands that, by subsistence standards, are underexploited.

The difficulty in Peru is that no single approach by itself would be adequate. The redistribution of some lands, insufficient in isolation to satisfy the need, and damaging to production if carried too far, would be necessary—even a prerequisite to other solutions—if only because "the large estate brings into existence and perpetuates a large number of other highly important features of the social system in the area it dominates...."[11]

An initial point of general agreement on expropriation has been that it should apply first to lands not under cultivation. Article 47 of the constitution of 1933 incorporated this qualification, although not to the exclusion of other types of land. In its 1931 plan, APRA broadened the definition to include "such farms as the state judges appropriate," mentioning as criteria "excessive size, absenteeism, irredeemable mortgages, location adjacent to cities, etc."

Although the party always has adopted the comprehensive approach, supplementing expropriation with measures for intensifying and extending cultivation, the emphasis since 1945 has shifted away from expropriation—without ever actually abandoning the device. This is seen most clearly in the 1946 discussion by Alfredo Saco. He emphasized that APRA "recognizes and respects private property and, in the event its agrarian program is applied, it will be guided strictly" by the constitution.[12]

The next party congress, in May and June, 1948, was less cautious, but also less explicit. In the approved agrarian program running to more than fifty action points, two were devoted to expropriation:

I—Agrarian Legislation

1st—Redistribute the *latifundio*, creating cooperative concentrations of parcels, after study by the National Economic Congress. To this end, a National Agrarian Council will be created to coordinate, as quickly as possible, the bases of such a congress with our agrarian conditions of the coast, sierra, and jungle.

III—Agricultural Development

11th—Expropriation and distribution of estates, the cultivation of which by small farmers organized into cooperatives would ensure the development of food production.[13]

[11] Smith, *Agrarian Reform*, p. 16.

[12] Saco, *Programa Agrario*, pp. 21–22.

[13] PAP, *Plan Agrario*, pp. 21, 29–30. When this plan was approved, the conservative members of the Senate had already been boycotting sessions for more than a year, a state of siege had been used the previous year to break an Aprista-sponsored general strike, and an all-military cabinet had been in office for three months. The month following the Aprista congress, the cabinet resigned in protest against the president's refusal to outlaw the party, and in July constitutional guarantees were again suspended. See Kantor, *Peruvian Aprista Movement*, pp. 18–20.

With the Odría coup occurring only a few months after the adoption of these proposals, Aprista plans for agrarian reform became mere historic documents.

After the return of political freedom in 1956 and the possibility that APRA might exercise some influence on the Prado government, the agrarian theme was revived, but with new assurances concerning expropriation. Speaking to the Third Party Congress, Manuel Soeane said: ". . . the position of the party regarding . . . agrarian reform implies the desire to improve the condition of the farmer. It is not the crude and simple statement of saying: 'We're dividing this estate, we're taking such-and-such lands.' This is not our aim. It would resolve the problem only in part."[14]

Also in 1956 the party publication setting forth "philosophy, doctrine, [and] program" summarized its agrarian reform proposals by listing property, tenancy, and profit systems as the first of a series of factors to be "taken into account."[15]

Having said that APRA became more cautious in describing its program, one must also recognize that it did not disguise it. On the contrary, it continued to be more specific in its proposals than were its main competitors. This is seen most clearly in interviews with presidential and congressional candidates of several parties by a single journalist, just before the 1962 and 1963 elections.

Each candidate was asked in 1963 what his party could offer to the departments of the Peruvian interior, mentioning Arequipa, Cuzco and Junín (the latter two being centers of land invasions). The Apristas all gave strong replies. Seoane said that solutions were interdependent but that agrarian reform should be "authentic . . . immediate, [and] audacious," leading to the reforms of industrialization, decentralization, and education. In brief, he thought that Cuzco required the "destruction of *latifundismo*" and industrial pro-promotion, and that Junín needed agrarian reform, tourism, industrialization, and a road network.[16]

[14] Seoane, *Obras Apristas*, p. 54. Seoane went on to portray the rural area as "the natural market of consumers" for Peru's growing industry and to stress technical aid and the extension of cultivated areas.

[15] Véliz Lizarraca, *Principios*, p. 89.

[16] Martín, *Política Peruana*, p. 118. This, and Martin's comments in notes 17–20, are offered only to show that the Apristas spoke no less forcefully and specifically than the AP and DC party candidates on expropriation. McCoy ("Agrarian Reform," p. 19) pointed out that Belaúnde tended to emphasize measures other than the redistribution of land. This is apparent from Belaúnde's inaugural speech, in which he spoke of *Cooperación Popular*, civic action tasks for the military, and construction of the Andean highway, but not of agrarian reform or expropriation; see Martín, *Política Peruana*, pp. 137 51). Cornejo Chávez had been more specific in his 1962 campaign as DC's presidential candidate, even warning of the tendency to confuse colonization and irrigation measures with agrarian reform (*Qué se Propone*, pp. 41–44, 55, 118–23).

Prialé replied (to the same question) that the country needed "an accelerated evolution based on transformation of the economy and reforms that could not be postponed," first among which he mentioned agrarian reform. Among the examples he cited were the elimination of feudalism and making the *campesinos* masters of the land and of the fruits of their labor.[17] Luís Alberto Sánchez put special emphasis on doing something for regions "where a feudal and extremely underdeveloped situation is most acutely maintained."[18]

Although some of the Aprista statements qualify as political slogans, they stand in sharp contrast to those of competing candidates. Belaúnde viewed all three departments in terms of their capitals, which he said should be regional centers. Cuzco "offers a broader agricultural prospect than Arequipa, but its industrialization also should be sought." Tourism and crafts should be promoted. Huancayo (capital of Junín), like Cuzco, should balance its economy with the support of tropical production from the nearby selva. Of national dimensions, Belaúnde concluded, were his plans for the highway along the eastern slopes of the Andes, and for *Cooperación Popular*, which would be built on the ancient Inca self-help institutions of *ayni* and *minka*.[19]

The third main contender for the presidency, Odría, had outlined his views on agriculture to the same reporter in 1958. For the coast he stressed increasing the area under cultivation through irrigation and for the sierra the modernizing of techniques and the use of idle land. A few months before the 1963 election Odría responded to the standard question by saying that Cuzco should benefit from public health, industrialization, and agrarian reform programs, and should take part in those for housing, labor, and education. His chief lieutenant in UNO, Julio de la Piedra, prescribed a number of steps that were planned for the interior departments, but without going beyond irrigation in the agricultural field.[20]

The Aprista difficulty of trying to be both radical and reasonable was apparent in the presentation to Congress of the party's agrarian reform bill. Andrés Townsend explained:

> . . . The goal of our reform is revolutionary because we need a complete transformation of the system of property, tenancy, and labor on the land, but the methods that we propose are the methods of a peaceful revolution, of a democratic revolution, of a revolution within the limits of the law. . . .
>
> The agrarian reform which we foresee . . . consequently faces the contradiction which, in our judgment, seems often exaggerated, between the

[17] Martín, *Política Peruana*, p. 122.
[18] *Ibid.*, p. 126.
[19] *Ibid.*, pp. 67–71.
[20] *Ibid.*, pp. 89, 93, and 99.

urgency of redistribution or distribution and the urgency or need of producing or maintaining and improving productivity.

Positions in this respect become, at times, extreme and irreconcilable. Some believe that the most important of all is justice and that justice is distribution, to give land to the *campesino*; and some believe that the most important of all is to produce. We believe that this contradiction, more apparent than real, must be resolved in a constructive way. . . . We aspire to a synthesis to assure production within a just system of democratic cooperativism.[21]

Dilemmas of the Press

This same conflict, between the sociopolitical goal of justice through expropriation and the economic need to maintain productivity, figured prominently in the press of Lima beginning about 1956. A general survey of press content on agrarian reform during this period shows some of the same political orientations and how they affected editorial statements and the slant of feature articles.

Heavy emphasis was given to agrarian problems throughout this period by *La Prensa* (and the associated afternoon *Ultima Hora*), the paper of Pedro Beltrán, initial chairman of CRAV and later prime minister from 1959 to 1961. Beltrán is credited by some, in fact, with bringing discussion of agrarian reform out into the open, beginning about 1954, because of a personal belief that it was becoming inevitable. Others condemn his fiscal orthodoxy and neoliberal economics.[22]

In the early years of the Prado presidency, *La Prensa* printed many discussions of the problems of agrarian reform, most of which sought to be "educational" in tone and moderately pessimistic about what could be accomplished in a short time. Expropriation was discussed, but mainly in terms of "purchase and distribution of unproductive lands . . . in regions of strong demographic pressure and concentration of rural population."[23]

As CRAV studies continued, *La Prensa* became more partisan in defending it against the criticism of delays resulting from investigations of reform in Peru and other countries. By 1959, opposition pressure and a consciousness of the technical difficulties of maintaining production while

[21] Townsend, *Reforma Agraria*, pp. 20–22.

[22] Although Beltrán is often attacked as an upper-class landowner, his press interests probably outweigh what has been called his "part interest in family property of some hundred hectares" (interview K, March, 1966). A tacit alliance is observed to have existed in recent times between APRA and *La Prensa* in contrast to differences in the remote past. The understanding is evident in the friendly neutrality with which news of the party is handled (interview with Alan Sloan, March, 1966). This is undoubtedly in part a reflection of the differences which both have with *El Comercio*. See Astiz, *Pressure Groups*, and Bourricaud, *Poder y Sociedad*, for contrary views.

[23] *La Prensa*, August 26, 1956, p. 10. The quotation is from the CRAV preliminary report.

redistributing large amounts of land, seemed to force *La Prensa* toward an emphasis on the "mistakes" of land division without education, technical assistance, etc. Finally, after CRAV's report and legislation were submitted at the end of September, 1960, *La Prensa* displayed an excessive enthusiasm for the consequences by headlining such slogans as "*Techo y Tierra* [house and land] *en 1961*."[24]

The other leading daily in Lima, *El Comercio*, was initially more cautious than its rival in discussing anything having to do with expropriation or land distribution. Its whole emphasis in the early years of Prado's second term was on the means of expanding cultivable land and preparing the *campesinos* for more intensive tilling of the limited area available. For example, after citing the benefits of education, an *El Comercio* article concluded that other courses would be counterproductive ". . . for a population that is not mentally prepared for the initiation of reform. . . ."[25]

Prior to the 1956 election, the statement had appeared that "the idea of dividing rural property for the purpose of making it available to all, overlooking the difficulties of an economic and technical nature, was not only impossible but absurd and, in essence, ingenuous." Later, the paper printed a series based on studies by the Food and Agriculture Organization (FAO) to support its point, saying, "The realistic course . . . is to limit the scope of reform to the changes absolutely necessary and seek the possible solution within the existing system."[26]

In the latter part of 1962, when *La Prensa* ran repeated editorials urging preventive reform in La Convención Valley of Cuzco, where land invasions were intensifying, *El Comercio* objected to the terms of the junta's expropriation decree (no. 14,197). Its efforts were frustrated by the landowners, but the following March, after a change in its composition, the junta issued a special decree (no. 14,444) on agrarian reform in Cuzco.[27]

Similarly, in August and September, 1963, when *El Comercio* supported the president's call for urgent passage of his bill, *La Prensa* carried almost

[24] *Ibid.*, January 9, 1959, p. 10, February 10, 1959, p. 10, and April 23, 1961, p. 14. The commission had just overcome an opposition (AP/DC) effort to deny it funds in the new budget. Another slogan was "Victory over the Enemies of the Transformation"; *ibid.*, May 1, 1961, p. 8.

[25] *El Comercio*, August 30, 1956.

[26] *Ibid.*, September 29, 1957, p. 19, and January 1, 1959, p. 9. See also the issue of July 6, 1957, p. 4; the series of July 13, 20, 30, and 31, 1958, in the first of which the writer opposed placing size limitations on estates; and the October 13, 1958, issue, p. 14.

[27] CIDA, *Tierra y Desarrollo*, p. 398; *La Prensa*, August 31, November 2, 16, 21, 23, and 26, December 2, 1962, and January 27, 1963; *El Comercio*, October 20, 1962. In this last, the paper was supported by the National Agrarian Society, which the following year led the fight against Belaúnde's reform bill; see McCoy, "Agrarian Reform," p. 26.

daily editorials counseling further study and planning.[28]

These statements indicate that in the fifties, before partisan considerations became paramount (during and after the 1962 and 1963 elections), there was not much over-all difference between the two papers on the subject of agrarian reform. The fact that *La Prensa* likened both the military junta's *Ley de Bases* (1962) and the APRA agrarian reform bill (1963) to the one earlier submitted by CRAV should be read as part of its publisher's role in that commission. The support by *El Comercio* for the administration bill of 1963 cannot be assessed apart from its endorsement of Belaúnde's presidential candidacy against Haya de la Torre.[29] One may infer from these comparisons that neither side in the debate was in the possession of eternal verities; rather, both were in the clutches of the stubborn complexities of partisan and substantive issues which could be neither ignored nor resolved by law alone.

Main Legislative Issues

Because APRA was the third major party to submit a reform bill, it had the advantage of being able to draft a bill which took into account some of the valid objections to the others which had been brought out in the weeks of preliminary discussion. The major issues were: (1) the extent of expropriation; (2) the valuation of, and compensation for, land taken; (3) the procedure for distributing land by zones; (4) the autonomy of executive implementation; (5) exceptions for sugar plantations; and (6) special measures for certain recipients of land.

Expropriation

The key feature of the extent of expropriation was not one that was easily dramatized in the debates, for any formula had to be complicated if it was to take into account differences in land productivity and manner of use, to mention only the major criteria.

The UNO bill avoided the issue by not specifying any limits on size. The other important bills (AP/DC and APRA), and the final act, specified in

[28] *El Comercio*, September 6, 1963, p. 2. It also had charged that a campaign was being carried on by the opposition to alarm the public about land invasions in order to produce a climate adverse to agrarian reform; *ibid.*, August 10, 1963, p. 2. *La Prensa* had urged the expropriation of thirteen estates in Junín, Pasco, and Puno, the first two departments being scenes of invasion; see its issues of August 11, 1963, p. 14, and August 23, 24, and 25, 1963.

[29] *La Prensa*, November 24, 1962, and *Ultima Hora*, October 17, 1963, p. 10; Ramírez, *Elecciones*, pp. 25–27. This frankly pro-Belaúnde publication states that *El Comercio* also supported Odría in 1962 but, by implication, not in 1963.

different ways a basic level to which the least efficient, absentee-operated, anachronistic estates would be reduced, while allowing exceptions, according to certain broad standards, for those rising above this level. The basic and exceptional levels of expropriation provided in the three bills for the best category of owner-operated lands in the country are charted in Figure VII–1.

The AP/DC bill stipulated a modest level of expropriation which had the effect of allowing retention of one half or more of the estates of up to almost 3,000 hectares (about 7,500 acres). Above this level all would be taken unless a high degree of efficiency and the absence of nearby demographic pressure could be shown. Curves *A* and *B* in Figure VII–1 show the exceptional and basic levels of land retention, respectively, contemplated in the administration bill.[30]

In contrast to this progressive scheme, the Aprista bill proposed a basically extreme course of permitting expropriation of all land above a minimum level (curve *D*), regardless of the original size of an estate. On the other hand, its exceptional treatment would have allowed the retention of entire estates shown to be exemplary in terms of efficiency of operation and other criteria of a social nature, as shown by curve *C*.[31] The APRA bill, therefore, interestingly contemplated giving more discretion to the administration than did the AP/DC bill.

The final act (no. 15,037 of May 21, 1964) contained a scheme that was more or less a combination of the two party bills. It used the progressive method of the administration, including the point system by which individual areas and farms would be rated, but it lowered the basic retention level (curve *F*) by increasing the percentages and by reducing to 2,000 hectares (5,000 acres) the "leveling-off" point above which all land could be taken. The limit of exceptions (curve *E*) was reduced from both bills.[32]

This result was considered by the experts to be "rather conservative" and to leave "in large part without adequate solution the dramatic problem of land in Peru." Contrary to some of the charges against APRA, the effect of interparty debate on this point was not to water down the administration bill, but rather to strengthen this key feature.[33] It was calculated,

[30] Articles 10 and 11 of the text as printed in *La Prensa*, August 14, 1963, p. 3.

[31] Articles 14, 57, and 60 of the text as printed in *La Crónica*, October 16, 1963, pp. 8–9.

[32] Articles 30–36 of the translated text as transmitted by the American Embassy, Lima (Airgram TOAID A–106, July 21, 1964), to the Agency for International Development. Parenthetical references below are to articles in this act, unless otherwise noted. See also CIDA, *Tierra y Desarrollo*, pp. 401–64; and Richard W. Patch, "The Peruvian Agrarian Reform Bill," *AUFS*, RWP–2–'64, March, 1964.

[33] CIDA, *Tierra y Desarrollo*, p. 405; McCoy, "Agrarian Reform," esp. pp. 18–25, which cites mainly such anti-Aprista sources as *El Comercio*.

however, that the areas subject to expropriation under the final act would meet only about 10 percent of the need for land in the whole of Peru, or about 4 percent in the sierra.

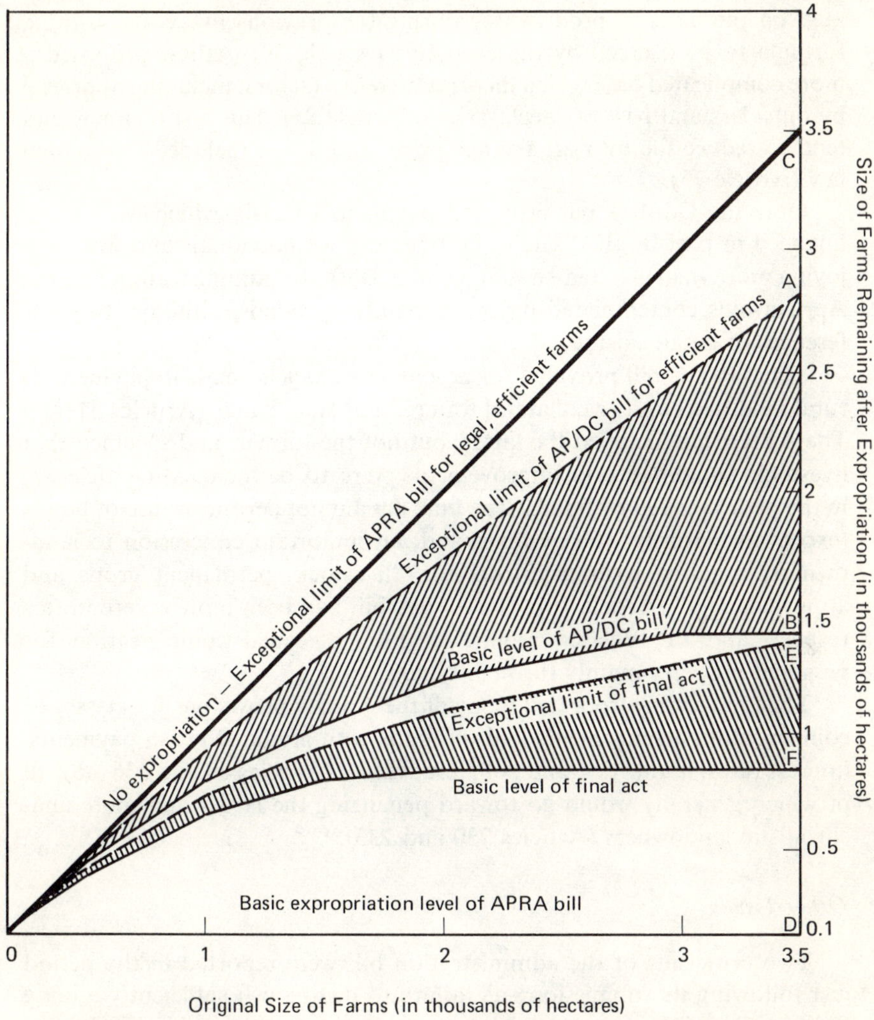

FIGURE VII–1. EXPROPRIATION LEVELS OF AGRARIAN REFORM BILLS

Farm sizes are those of permanently irrigated land in the coastal zone. Sizes elsewhere generally are multiples of these and therefore are proportional. The basic level of the APRA bill is fifteen times the "family unit," for which we have used the maximum value from CIDA, *Tierra y Desarrolla*, p. 63, or ten hectares. Values for the final act are from *ibid.*, pp. 491–92. The remaining values were calculated from published texts of the bills.

Compensation

The question of evaluating and paying for expropriated land also was a subject for heated debate. In the administration bill land was to be evaluated on the basis of productivity during the previous five years, using a formula to be decreed by the executive (Article 39). APRA proposed a more complicated base which incorporated five factors, including appraisal by outsiders and past tax declarations (Article 85). This last factor would tend to reduce the over-all average price, and it was included in the final law (Article 75).

Only the Odriísta bill proposed payments in cash, which were to be financed in part by the "sale of certificates" to individuals and firms enjoying more than a stated annual income. Both the administration and the Aprista bills contemplated payment mainly by bonds, although two differences of detail existed.

The AP/DC bill provided for acceptance of such bonds in payment of rural land taxes and as collateral for credit at state banks (Articles 41–43). The APRA bill included the latter, but not the former, and specified that livestock, buildings, and improvements were to be included (Article 87) in the price covered by bonds. The final act did not permit the use of bonds (except at maturity) to pay taxes and, an important concession to landowners, required cash payments for "livestock, permanent crops and appurtenances" (Article 76). The APRA bill had been more severe in this respect, and the Velasco regime in 1969 provided compensation for personal property mainly through bonds.

The final act incorporated many of the Aprista provisions for classes of compensation arrangements and of bonds with graduated cash payments, interest rates, maturities, and collateral values (Articles 89 and 236–46), all of which generally would go toward penalizing the larger and more anachronistic landowners (Articles 230 and 233).[34]

Other Issues

Two criticisms of the administration bill were reported in the period just following its submission: its failure to distinguish sufficiently among the sections of the country, which would require different kinds of treatment, and its tendency to leave certain important matters to the discretion of the executive and the cabinet.

[34] The constitutionality of using bonds in payment for expropriated lands was settled by constitutional amendments (Articles 29, 47, 211) duly adopted in the 1963 and 1964 sessions of Congress. See CIDA, *Tierra y Desarrollo*, pp. 505–6, for texts. This could not have been done without splitting the majority APRA/UNO coalition.

In both instances the Apristas certainly had an interest, but the bill that they submitted did not contain the remedies. The final law did provide, however, that the designation of zones of agrarian reform should proceed sequentially in accordance with stated priorities (Article 50), although all actions need not await such designations (Article 52 and Title XV). The procedure for distinguishing zones was one of the features which made the final law much longer and more complex than the bill first submitted.

Another cause of lengthening was the spelling out of procedures, such as land valuation, which the administration bill would have left for later elaboration by decree. In other respects, and particularly in the key area of expropriation, the APRA and UNO bills would have seemed to leave to the executive more discretion than did either its own bill or the final act. The effect would depend, of course, upon how free the executive would be to act independently.

The main respect in which the discretion of the executive might be limited was in the establishment of the National Agrarian Council and the Technical Council of Agrarian Reform and Promotion. The concept of the former was found in the APRA bill (Article 210), but its membership was reduced in the final act (Article 195). It was described as the governing body of the Institute of Agrarian Reform and Promotion. Although the National Agrarian Council included members from CTP and FENCAP, who surely would be Apristas, and one each from the agricultural societies and the livestock associations, who might be Odriístas, it was chaired by the minister of agriculture and had a majority of official members. The Technical Council, similar to one proposed in the UNO bill, was larger and clearly enjoyed only an advisory position (Articles 206–11).

The issue on which APRA was most vulnerable to criticism was the inclusion of a sweeping exemption of the coastal sugar plantations from expropriation (Articles 38–43). Although commercialized and efficient, most of the largest of these operations were of foreign origin and had grown at the expense of surrounding peasants and communities.[35] Support of the exemption by the APRA/UNO coalition inevitably drew attacks from opponents who, regardless of substantive views, gained political capital in certain sectors by voting against the provisions.[36]

APRA was influenced not only by its coalition partner but also by the fact that the sugar workers, Aprista-led and well organized, did not care to

[35] CIDA, *Tierra y Desarrollo*, pp. 19–23, 44–45.

[36] *La Prensa*, January 15, 1964, p. 2, and editorial. Arguments that the sugar plantations are really factories, not farms, and that even Castro's land reform in Cuba had exempted such operations apparently had little effect (interview with Alejandro Arias, secretary of Chamber of Deputies, March 18, 1966). Vice-President Seoane differed on the latter point, saying that in Cuba, Mexico, and Venezuela, small and medium producers supply the sugar mills; quoted in CIDA, *Tierra y Desarrollo*, p. 499, n. 22.

have anything upset their source of livelihood and hard-won worker benefits. Although some public emphasis was laid on the provisions permitting the workers to vote to transform the sugar mills into cooperative enterprises, this possibility was practically eliminated in the final version because of a Senate amendment requiring concurrence of the owners. The issue was revived when the Velasco regime seized the sugar plantations and mills in 1969.[37]

As if seeking to recoup the political damage done in the sugar debate, APRA presented an amendment to effect "the surrender of the land to those who work it." It was attacked by the government parties as demagoguery and "typically diversionist and fallacious." The Apristas replied that the final act, although called "reactionary, conservative, and anti-revolutionary, has opened the doors of social justice for 120,000 peasant families."[38]

Technically, the provision (Title XV) was not quite so simple. It cut through some of the procedures of expropriation by zones, promising *feudatorios* occupying less than fifteen hectares on the coast, or thirty in the sierra or selva, that they would be issued provisional titles to the land they had been working. Some critics noted that this would tend to perpetuate small uneconomical plots and that the "absolute preferences" established for different groups of peasants in different parts of the act were likely to raise conflicts. Nevertheless, the "automatic" feature of the amendment may have added a needed psychological element to an otherwise moderate measure.[39]

Despite the emphasis it had laid on the resolution of the conflict between the goals of distribution and production in agrarian reform, APRA failed to incorporate into the final law provisions strongly promoting cooperative enterprises. The APRA bill had contained numerous statements on the subject and would have given cooperatives preference in access to technical assistance, credit, land, irrigation, and colonization (Articles 98, 108,113, 167, 199, and 200). Most of these were watered down in the final act, however, as they probably had to be if there was to be any meaning in the terms "priority" and "preference." Apparently in their place the final act elaborated on the theme of the inalienability of community lands and gave the Indian communities and cooperatives the "same priorities" to lands as the landless peasants (Articles 92, 128–39, 181–84). Most significant from a legal standpoint, perhaps, was the provision nullifying

[37] CIDA, *Tierra y Desarrollo*, pp. 411–14; *New York Times*, June 26, 1969, p. 4; *Washington Post*, December 16, 1969, p. 13.

[38] *Presente* no. 101 (May–June, 1965), suppl. 5, quoting Senator Prialé, who presented the amendment on March 31, 1964.

[39] CIDA, *Tierra y Desarrollo*, pp. 415ff.

transfers of land out of the communities, or to individual members, subsequent to the constitution of 1920, which first sought to prevent such divisions.[40]

The Results

This broad review allows some general inferences about APRA's role in the enactment of the 1964 Agrarian Reform Law, particularly in terms of the relationship between that experience and general questions of party strategy and tactics. Such considerations, plus party membership interests, played a more important part in Aprista behavior on the agrarian reform question than did the substance of the problem.

The whole problem of land and the Indian masses had changed its character since 1956. Those who favored preservation of the status quo gradually had been forced to recognize that the problem existed and that something had to be done about it. The delay tactics of the fifties became the dilution efforts of the sixties. Reform parties were highly conscious of the need to avoid forcing the pace, but they suffered from internal dissidence concerning what pace was tolerable.

Out of the confusion over ways and means, technical versus social guidelines, and cautious as opposed to radical solutions, the matter was inevitably transformed into a political question. Bargaining, in which the nuisance value of contemporary land invasions and guerrilla activities was one of the counters, largely replaced rational calculations. Or, more accurately, out of the technical options and instruments available to them, the politicians assembled an agreement which was generally acceptable to them in accordance with their power positions. The anachronistic landowners of the sierra, for example, would bear the brunt of expropriation.

For APRA the process put major emphasis on preservation of the party position, primarily as a conventional party in the system of conventional political parties. Competition with AP, coalition with UNO, and maintenance of its own support—for example, among the sugar workers—seemed to be the principal ingredients of APRA's decision. The last of these, involving Aprista relations with the community, reflected a narrow view of the party's constituency as a consequence of its reliance on tactical maneuver, sometimes at the cost of long-range strategy.

In relation to the state, APRA's experience in the adoption of an agrarian reform law may have represented a basic misjudgment of the situation. While the party was concentrating (among other objectives) on the need to defeat guerrillas protesting land problems in the sierra, certain

[40] *Ibid.*, pp. 403–4, 459.

members of the army were formulating the views which led them, when they intervened in 1968, to make radicalization of agrarian reform one of the first actions to be taken.

In broader terms, the 1964 act was not a solution to the land problem, if indeed any total solution was possible, but it was significant in two other ways. First, it formally legitimized the principles of land redistribution, which had been increasingly accepted tacitly during the preceding decade. Second, it accurately reflected contemporary capacities for consensual innovation among the political parties and leaders of Peru. It was this pair of circumstances—the recognition of need and the inability to meet it—which led logically to the military coup of 1968, bringing a new pause in the Peruvian development of a more open political system.[41]

[41] Arthur J. Coutu and Richard A. King, *The Agricultural Development of Peru* (New York: Frederick A. Praeger, 1969), pp. 6–7, 12, 51, 140–44, and esp. p. 84; Bourricaud, *Poder y Sociedad*, pp. 331–49; Astiz, *Pressure Groups*, pp. 200–203.

VIII

OTHER REFORM PARTIES OF LATIN AMERICA

THE EXPERIENCES OF APRA were paralleled by those of several other Latin American mass reform parties. Not only were the parties similar in form and outlook, but the events and problems they encountered were much like those in Peru, and often were roughly contemporaneous with them. It is illuminating to study closely the two parties that seem most to resemble the Aprista case. They are the now defunct National Revolutionary Movement, or MNR (Movimiento Nacional Revolucionario), of Bolivia, and Democratic Action, or AD (Acción Democrática), of Venezuela. The Institutional Revolutionary Party, or PRI (Partido Revolucionario Institucional), of Mexico, is a supplementary source of comparative experiences.

These mass reform parties differed from APRA in that they succeeded in achieving higher degrees of power and in holding it for longer periods than did APRA. The fact that they did so with different characteristic features—different from APRA and from one another—helps to indicate some of the attributes of the mass reform party that may be significant for particular purposes. These features have functioned differently, for example, in separate phases of each party's existence and in its relationships with the state, community, and other parties.

BOLIVIA AND MNR

Bolivia is probably the best available standard of comparison with Peru. Although smaller, less developed, and much more isolated than Peru, prior to 1952 the country showed the features which also have distinguished

Peru—a large, unassimilated, and agricultural Indian population, living mainly within a feudal system of traditional haciendas; an industrial sector dominated by extractive, foreign-oriented enterprises mainly engaged in export; a military officer corps serving landowner and entrepreneurial interests; and an incipient intellectual and middle group open to reformist ideas. The differences, particularly those of phase and degree, also are important and will be taken up after the parties have been examined individually.

Ideology and Program

Among mass reform parties MNR stands at almost the opposite extreme from APRA in terms of the clarity of its doctrine. Ideology and program must to a large extent be inferred from MNR actions and associations and composed out of a web of conflicting forces and tendencies. Once completed, the process of inference and composition leaves no doubt as to what the party stood for in the final analysis. But the fact that its stand on substantive issues was either unclear or in actual dispute among its contemporaries must have had important effects on the way the party developed.

In several ways MNR can be seen as the *product*, rather than the *producer*, of the reformist spirit that animated parts of Bolivia in the 1930s. Defeat in the War of the Chaco with Paraguay (1932–35) raised questions that focused resentment on the performance of the army. It was not so much "Why did we fight a useless war?" as "Why did we lose?" In this atmosphere, fascist influences were strong in the group of young officers whose insurgency set off a series of five military presidents, both reformist and reactionary, from 1936 to 1946. Future MNR leaders were among the civilian participants, but were by no means the major leaders, in the reform movement. The establishment of MNR occurred so informally that its exact date, probably sometime in 1941, has been disputed even among its founders.

Into the new party came some elements which had supported the first two of the reformist presidents (Toro and Busch, 1936–39) and would provide a third (Villarroel, 1943–46). None of these regimes were MNR-dominated, but the last, especially, gave the party leaders a taste of power, perhaps prematurely, and identified them with both the accomplishments and the excesses of early attempts at reform. Nazi-fascist influences may have persisted in some of the party attitudes and techniques, but as ideology they were combatted from the first by certain civilian leaders and were publicly repudiated as early as 1944.[1]

[1] Alexander, *Bolivian National Revolution*, p. 31, as well as his historical résumé, pp. 22–45; Richard W. Patch, "The Last of Bolivia's MNR?" *AUFS*, RWP–2–'64, June, 1964, pp. 1–11.

Another strong external ideological influence on MNR was Marxism. Leading MNR both in sequence of organization and in clarity of doctrine were two competing parties of Marxist orientation. The independent Partido de la Izquierda Revolucionaria (PIR) and the Trotskyite Partido Obrero Revolucionario (POR) were established in 1940 and retained their potency for at least ten years.[2] Disagreement within MNR over doctrine during this period is illustrated by the arguments of Wálter Guevara Arze in his 1946 "Manifesto to the Citizens of Ayopaya." He rejected socialism as a system, saying it was not wholly applicable to the conditions and stage of development of Bolivia. In terms reminiscent of Haya de la Torre, Guevara denied the utility of class warfare or proletarian revolution in the Bolivian situation, which, he said, called for a nationalism bridging the artificial and restrictive lines of class.[3]

MNR was strongly nationalist in that it was more certain of what it opposed than of what it advocated. In 1944 Víctor Paz Estenssoro expressed party goals summarily in the phrase "economic liberation and reform of the agrarian system." In place of explicit ideology or a specific program, MNR had two implicit aims: to broaden political participation for purposes of modernization, and to promote rapid economic development, including agrarian reform.[4] These combine with the theme of nationalism to form the three program elements on which MNR acted after 1952—nationalization of tin mines, destruction of the *latifundios*, and extension of universal suffrage to the illiterate. But before 1946, and perhaps even until 1952, these aims had mainly to be inferred.[5]

The best empirical indications of what MNR stood for before it came to power are provided by the actions of the Villarroel regime, in which MNR ministers were an influential minority. Its modernizing bent was shown, perhaps most importantly, in the sponsorship of a strong trade-

[2] Alexander, *Bolivian National Revolution*, pp. 28–30; Wálter Guevara Arze, *P.M.N.R.A.: Exposición de Motivos y Declaración de Principios* (n.p.: Partido del Movimiento Nacionalista Revolucionario Auténtico, 1960), pp. 112–13; Richard W. Patch, "Bolivia Today," *AUFS*, RWP–4–'61, March 17, 1961, p. 9.

[3] Wálter Guevara Arze, *Teoría, Medios y Fines de la Revolución Nacional*, pt. 1: *Manifiesto a los Ciudadanos de Ayopaya* (Cochabamba, Bolivia, 1946), pp. 19–21. This "manifesto" is also quoted extensively in Guevara's "exposition" of 1960, issued after he defected from MNR and formed the "authentic" MNR.

[4] Quoted in Alexander, *Bolivian National Revolution*, p. 31; interview with James M. Malloy, March 7, 1966.

[5] Interview with Víctor Andrade, March 7, 1966. Guevara (*Exposición*, pp. 61–70) cites these three elements as "results" of the revolution. Although logical consequences of prior attacks on the system, there is little evidence that they were planned in advance; there are abundant indications that the need for immediate agrarian reform, in particular, took the party by surprise. Guevara explains the lack of clear party doctrine "as much by the incapacity of the party leaders as by the fact that the satisfaction of their personal ambitions and interests" did not demand it (*ibid.*, p. 10; interview with Wálter Guevara Arze, March 8, 1966). See also Richard W. Patch, "A Note on Peru and Bolivia," *AUFS*, RWP–6–'59, July, 1959, p. 23.

union movement in the mines, which became a major element in MNR power. It also called a national Indian congress, which was the first sign of official interest in peasant grievances in many decades. It proposed to abolish compulsory personal service by Indian tenants and to give the vote to members of Indian communities, but neither measure was applied.

More characteristic of the 1943–46 period, however, was chaos, which included military uprising, political murder, official corruption, and strikes by teachers and students. It is not surprising that, according to a member of APRA, MNR in neighboring Bolivia was not recognized by the Apristas as a fraternal party until after the overthrow of Villarroel's regime in 1946 by a mob aided by studied army inaction. Nor is it strange that the Bolivian and Mexican revolutions are considered to be movements "... onto which reality has ingrafted social content even when they *had none* originally. . . ."[6]

Organization and Methods

If MNR was deficient in doctrine, it was still more seriously handicapped in other respects, particularly in its relations with mass elements and in Paz Estenssoro's style of leadership. There is no doubt, though, that it qualified, both in its impulses and its performance, as a mass party. Its strength during the 1946–52 gestation period was largely limited to the trade unions, and of these particularly the miners.

A broadening influence was present in the party, however. In his 1946 manifesto Guevara Arze spoke repeatedly of the workers, peasants, and white-collar employees as the base of the nationalist revolution, as distinguished from narrow Marxism and what he later called the "verbal revolutionaryism" in miners' boss Juan Lechín's contemporaneous "Thesis of Pulacayo." The broad and general support the miners and *campesinos* ultimately gave to MNR (reflected in elections held before and after the adoption of universal suffrage) illustrates mass endorsement of the party as the symbol of the revolution.[7]

[6] Alba, *Alliance Without Allies*, p. 87, italics added; interview D, February, 1966. Richard W. Patch says that, while MNR leaders "left their stamp on the changes, they have also been borne along" by them ("Bolivia: The Restrained Revolution," *The Annals* 334 [March, 1961]: 125). In another article he wrote that Bolivian nationalism succeeded not because MNR had invented it, "but because it seized on the themes of. nationalism and revolution which had been imbedded in the public mind . . ." since the 1920s and 1930s; see Richard W. Patch, "Peasantry and National Revolution: Bolivia,' in *Expectant Peoples: Nationalism and Development*, ed. K. H. Silvert (New York: Random House, 1963), p. 112.

[7] Guevara, *Manifesto*, p. 5, and *Exposición*, pp. 24–27; SORO, *U.S. Army Area Handbook for Bolivia* (Washington, D.C.: American University, 1963), pp. 351–54, 358.

As with its ideology, MNR did not originate the organizational structure which it ultimately acquired. Unionization, especially among the miners, was in progress during the thirties and forties. It was the Marxists of various affiliations, particularly PIR and to some extent POR, who dominated the early trade unions. MNR led the political protest in the National Assembly against the "Catavi massacre" of 1943, but it was not until that year that the rising labor leader, Juan Lechín, joined the party. Although influenced by POR, he lent his strength to MNR as its organizing effort intensified, especially among the miners, under Villarroel. As a result, and because of its cooperation with the succeeding government, the rival PIR lost its advantage and ran last in the election of 1951.

After the revolution in 1952, Lechín consolidated his trade-union following by forming the Central Obrero Boliviana (COB), which absorbed or isolated most of the unions previously under other political control. Already a hero among the miners, by 1945 Lechín had become executive secretary of their federation. In 1952 he also became executive secretary of the new COB and minister of mines and petroleum. He was soon to be a senator, then president of the Senate, and, in 1960, vice-president in the second term of Paz.[8] Lechín's name was almost synonymous with trade-union—or at least miner—support for MNR.

Among the Indians, the other mass sector which MNR ultimately captured, the picture was less simple. Writers have put great stress on the influence of the Chaco War in the "awakening" of the rural Indians, which culminated in the semi-spontaneous land divisions of 1952 and later. It is difficult to determine, however, precisely how the organizational activities of the Chaco veterans developed and finally came to serve political purposes.

Few specific cases of early organizing are cited in studies of Bolivia. At least one such group in the Cliza area, "which was to be the prototype of the *sindicatos campesinos*," in 1936 tried unsuccessfully to rent the *latifundio* on which their village was located. This was followed (at least by 1947) by an organizational effort in the vicinity of Ucureña after the *campesino* congress in which the Villarroel regime advised the *campesinos* to build *sindicatos* in anticipation of future land expropriation. Beginning in 1949, MNR students from Cochabamba were politically active among the neighboring *campesinos*.[9]

[8] SORO, *Handbook for Bolivia*, pp. 540–43; Richard W. Patch, "The Last of Bolivia's MNR?" *AUFS*, RWP–4–'64, p. 20; Alexander, *Bolivian National Revolution*, pp. 123 and 126.

[9] Eduardo Arze-Loureiro, "The Process of Agrarian Reform in Bolivia," in *Agrarian Reform*, ed. Smith, pp. 132–33; SORO, *Handbook for Bolivia*, pp. 128 and 465–66; Guevara, *Exposición*, p. 43; Patch, "Peru and Bolivia," p. 22.

The extent of pre-revolutionary organization of the *campesinos* can be exaggerated, however. It probably all took place within the vicinity of Cochabamba. The "model" peasant unions, partly controlled by POR, helped to precipitate land seizures mainly *after* MNR had taken power in La Paz. One of the "most important tasks" of the new Ministry of Indian and Peasant Affairs in 1952 was to organize "a network of peasant unions."[10] In fact, as it took power, MNR probably was faced with a combination of conflicting factors. A few militant *sindicatos campesinos* around Cochabamba were acting on their own. They were independent of MNR or were controlled by competing politicians, and thus threatened to take the initiative away from the new regime.

A study of agrarian reform was launched and MNR embarked on its own organizing drive among the *campesinos.* This activity was strictly "from the top downward," for political purposes. A participant recalled later that events of this period "were accompanied by an intense agitation, *directed systematically from the cities*, for the purpose of securing a massive intervention of the *campesinos.*"[11]

The resulting network of *sindicatos*, built up by the end of 1952, "owed nothing to the government and could act independently of it." The government soon resorted to the arrest of rival organizers and leaders in order to get control of the regional labor federation. Unable to displace one leader, MNR had to woo him and then expend considerable effort trying to bring into its orbit the *campesinos* that he had organized, men whose personal loyalties were to him and who thus had "only an indirect allegiance to the MNR."[12]

By 1961 the party's problems with the *campesinos* intensified. "The wielding of the great power . . . has turned out to be no simple problem. At present the Government can command this power only in bloc voting in national elections, which are events of no great moment to most *campesinos*, and through the still great influence and popularity of President Víctor Paz. But MNR has never been able to command the movement, nor fully absorb it into a loyal organ of the party."[13]

[10] Alexander, *Bolivian National Revolution*, pp. 60–61. Patch states that "they took no direct part in the 1952 revolution"; see his "Peasantry and National Revolution," p. 111.

[11] Patch, "Peru and Bolivia," p. 23; SORO, *Handbook for Bolivia*, p. 466; Alexander, *Bolivian National Revolution*, p. 61; interview with Wálter Guevara Arze, March 8, 1966; Smith, *Agrarian Reform*, p. 135, italics added. Malloy supports this thesis, saying that MNR's connections with the *campesinos* began in 1952 or later, while those with trade unions went back to 1944. He quoted a Bolivian who said that the *campesinos* were mobilized ideologically by POR and politically by MNR (interview with James M. Malloy, March 7, 1966).

[12] Patch, "The Restrained Revolution," p. 129, and "Peru and Bolivia," p. 22.

[13] Patch, "Bolivia Today," p. 14.

Thus, in both the labor and *campesino* sectors after 1952, MNR faced the basic problems of assimilating the masses of supporters who had benefitted from the revolution. Factions within the top leadership developed almost at once. Lechín and what came to be known as the "left sector" of the party used COB as an instrument for intimidation of the government itself by making demands on behalf of the miners who were now employees of the state mining corporation, COMIBOL.

> . . . When the revolution triumphed in April, 1952, worker participation in the government became logical and natural. Nevertheless, the standard-bearers of this participation, which no one opposed, were not clearly aware of the aims of their action and their future directions. Instead, they rapidly bureaucratized and enriched themselves, and in the name of the workers began organizing more or less autonomous groups within the government and in the party fold, which served them above all as instruments to assure their personal predominance. . . .[14]

The *campesinos* also shared in the factionalism among the leaders. Evidently to mollify the left wing, the vice-presidency was given to the first minister of *campesino* affairs, Nuflo Chávez. Soon afterward he tried to block moderate President Siles' stabilization program with a general strike call; when it failed he was forced out, and factional lines hardened. The left wing (this time Lechín) again was given the vice-presidency in 1960, when Paz returned for a second term, and as a result Guevara Arze of the "right wing" defected from the party. Four years later Lechín did the same when Paz himself stood for a third term.[15]

The *campesino* leadership problem became more and more one of "outsiders who knew nothing about agrarian development," but only "how to use the peasants for political purposes."[16] By 1964 it was necessary and feasible to use the reconstituted army to "challenge the miners . . . and control the *campesinos.*" In turn, it was possible for Army General Ovando and Air Force General Barrientos to challenge Paz and later that same year to unseat him.[17]

MNR thus suffered from defects of ideology, program, and organization. None of these need necessarily have been fatal had they not been reinforced by a personal kind of MNR leadership. The problem of factionalism was due not only to substantive differences but much more to the ambitions of subordinates, the latter being consciously cultivated by Paz

[14] Guevara, *Exposicion*, pp. 25 and 44–48; see also SORO, *Handbook for Bolivia*, pp. 343–45.

[15] SORO, *Handbook for Bolivia*, pp. 365–66; Patch, "Bolivia Today," pp. 9–10, and "The Last of Bolivia's MNR?" p. 18.

[16] Interview with Wálter Guevara Arze, March 8, 1966.

[17] Patch, "The Last of Bolivia's MNR?" pp. 3 and 22–23.

Estenssoro until finally the movement had six or seven splinters. (Paz saw himself as the only unifying element.)

Víctor Paz Estenssoro has been contrasted with Haya de la Torre. Haya, it is said, was always the romantic intellectual more than the practical organizer, and APRA has been a "revolution on paper," full of speculation. Paz is described as exactly the opposite, posing as an intellectual but "actually not even an economist." Instead, he is very realistic, practical, and hungry for power. Exaggerated greed for power carried MNR "beyond its proper limits," and, after twelve years of this, Paz convinced himself that he was the source of the power.[18]

The picture of Paz as an opportunist goes back to the thirties, when he was a lawyer for the Patiño tin mines, and the forties, when he is said to have joined the Peñaranda government solely to discredit it by resigning eight days later.[19] He did not emerge as the real leader of MNR until after the fall of Villarroel (1946), and the circumstances of the 1951 election (when he got at least a plurality) and the 1952 revolution suggest that he was surprised by both. He was in many respects unprepared to take full advantage of success. "His genius was to capitalize on the work of others for political purposes."[20]

The circumstances of twelve years of MNR rule in Bolivia support the charge that Paz tried to perpetuate his rule indefinitely and that, sincerely or cynically, he let the revolution go off the rails. The presence of an unusual number of capable leaders in MNR by 1964 and the stubborn retention of power by Paz led to the shattering of unity after "conversion of the party from a movement to a personal vehicle dependent on outside help. . . ."[21] Perhaps it never was a party, or even a cohesive movement; as a kind of coalition, or holding company, it joined the constituent interest groups but never rose from its own power base.

In MNR there was little room for groups outside the lower classes. The party received some degree of sympathy or, at least, tolerance from the middle sectors. It lacked support among the organized students. The upper

[18] Interview C, March, 1966. The same source agreed that this power complex tended to put Paz into the Peronista category and added that, out of power, Paz was acting still more like an exiled Perón. Betancourt of Venezuela was described as "more practical than Haya and less greedy than Paz." Lipset ("Political Cleavages," p. 42) puts MNR in the Peronista category.

[19] Patch, "The Last of Bolivia's MNR?" pp. 6, 7, and 9; Guevara (*Exposición*, pp. 57–58) elaborates on the story and suggests that Paz was built up by a press campaign and by ghost-written articles and speeches.

[20] Interview C, March, 1966. Although the three main points of the revolutionary program were set forth in the 1951 campaign, a close associate says that Paz never felt strongly on land reform until he saw how the *campesinos* were being organized by others.

[21] Patch, "The Last of Bolivia's MNR?" p. 24; interview I, June, 1966.

class was the obstacle and the target, and it was destroyed by the revolution.[22]

Strategy and Tactics

Of greater interest are MNR's relationships with the state and with other parties. In Bolivia the party situation has differed from that of Peru, in that competing reform parties which were not subservient to Moscow communism pre-dated and for a time coexisted with MNR. This fact saved MNR—at least until after 1946—from being the main target of repression that APRA was for many years in Peru. The function of officially sponsored rival of the principal reform party, which in Peru often belonged to the Communists, in Bolivia fell—at least for a time—to PIR.

Perhaps the decisive strategic step by MNR was its insistence in 1951 on nominating Paz for the presidency, instead of supporting some other party's candidate. Thereupon, the Trotskyite POR and the newly formed (Moscow) Communist party supported Paz. He won a plurality which, although vetoed by a reluctant military junta, gave the color of legality to the 1952 revolution. MNR thus seemed to succeed with the tactics of dealing with other parties pragmatically while in opposition, and fairly ruthlessly—for purposes of eliminating or absorbing them—once it came to power.

More significant was the behavior of the military. Reformist elements within it dated from the mid-thirties and Bolivia's defeat in the Chaco War. Earlier Bolivian militarism had been somewhat parallel to that of Peru, but lacked Peruvian professionalism. The conservative Bolivian military element seems to have been permanently weakened by reformist officers. From the mid-thirties, military control alternated between the irreconcilables and the reformists. Just before the 1952 revolt the army general in charge of the national police defected to MNR and provided this degree of military support for the effort.[23]

MNR thus had experienced both military veto and cooperation after the early "trial" period under Villarroel (1943–46). Each MNR period in power, including that of 1952–64, began and ended with military (or police) intervention or acquiescence. On the other hand, it is possible that the party stayed in power as long as it did only because it had destroyed the army in 1952.[24]

[22] Guevara, *Exposición*, p. 110; Enrique Chirinos Soto, *Drama, Riesgo y Futuro de Bolivia* (Lima: Ediciones Peru, 1965), p. 28.
[23] Alexander, *Bolivian National Revolution*, pp. 40–41, 143–45; SORO, *Handbook for Bolivia*, pp. 40–41.
[24] Patch, "The Last of Bolivia's MNR?" pp. 8–11; Chirinos, *Bolivia*, p. 21.

Much has been said about the use of armed workers and peasants in revolts such as that in Bolivia in 1952. The difficulty lies in establishing the degree to which paramilitary groups were formed, or even armed, prior to the revolution. *Campesinos* were not organized in large enough numbers to have greatly aided in the seizure of power, although they helped to consolidate it by moving against landholders. Unorganized violence came easily to the miners, who later won special privileges in return for serving as shock troops against the armed forces. Arms had been seized from police and soldiers in unsuccessful uprisings during the preceding decade, and workers in La Paz during the 1952 revolt received arms from the police. The support of such units was considered decisive to the MNR victory in 1952.[25]

The lesson of armed power had not been lost on the party in any event, and after the revolution MNR tried to regularize the militia units. Most of the armed peasant units, formed after 1952, were never as well controlled from the capital as were those of industrial workers. By the end of Paz's first four-year term, militiamen were estimated to number 50,000 or more, compared with 18,000 in the pre-revolutionary army.

In 1953 the decision was made to re-establish the regular army under the name "Army of the National Revolution." Meanwhile, the militia units, formed more out of personal than party loyalties, were unstable and easily manipulated, and came to pose a subversive threat to the party itself. By early 1963, the units had deteriorated to 16,000 men or less. MNR found that it needed the army to protect itself against the militia, particularly that of the miners. Thereafter it erred in thinking that the army could be "nothing but an instrument of the party."[26]

Little or no use seemed to be made of the Bolivian Congress as a means of bringing MNR to power, although in the early forties it was at least a forum for agitation by a few reform-minded members, notably Paz Estenssoro. After the 1952 revolution, sessions were not even held until 1956. The practice, as incorporated in the 1961 constitution, was authoritarian and highly centralized rule.[27]

VENEZUELA AND AD

The problems of reform which have existed in Venezuela are different from those of Peru, Bolivia, and Mexico. Two basic differences are the higher degree of cultural homogeneity (at least in the lack of a large,

[25] Alba, *Alliances Without Allies*, p. 180; Alexander, *Bolivian National Revolution*, p. 147.

[26] SORO, *Handbook for Bolivia*, pp. 660–62; Alexander, *Bolivian National Revolution*, pp. 145–52; Chirinos, *Bolivia*, p. 21.

[27] SORO, *Handbook for Bolivia*, pp. 313, 661, and 666.

unassimilated Indian population) and the availability of readily marketable economic resources (crude oil and iron ore), which help finance reform in Venezuela. In other respects there were until recently similarities in the dominance of latifundism as a land system, of an extractive industrial sector, and of a military officer corps in the government.

Since the 1930s, however, the middle sectors of the Venezuelan population have grown more rapidly than those in perhaps any other Latin American country. Stimulated mainly by oil development, and complemented after World War II by European immigration, developments that were semi-independent of government policy in less than a generation produced sharp contrasts between a traditional past and a future open to the ideas of reform.[28]

Ideology and Program

The party which became Acción Democratica (AD) arose in the late thirties in circumstances much like those of APRA in the twenties, yet without the early enunciation of an elaborate ideology and program like *Aprismo*. In 1935 the death of dictator Gómez released tensions comparable to those that had appeared at the ouster of Leguía in Peru. Reform leaders were the students who, like Rómulo Betancourt, had earlier revolted to become the outlawed "generation of '28." They returned from exile in 1935 only to find that Gómez' successor, López Contreras, was wary of mass movements, much as Leguía had been in Peru. The proto-Adecos were driven underground again from 1937 to 1941.[29]

Two factors influenced the content of AD doctrine when the party was first organized under that name in 1941. First, in an effort to win legal recognition from the new Medina government, an overly concrete or detailed statement was avoided. Second, the long struggle against Gómez had given the opposition groups (AD among them) a preoccupation with political liberties as the first step toward a social revolution.

Broader elements of thought were present, but they were vaguely phrased or conditioned upon further study. Marxism was a primary influence (Betancourt had been a Communist while exiled in Costa Rica); the Mexican Revolution and the Peruvian Aprista movement were secondary. Betancourt later said that the proto-Adecos of the thirties were attached to the principles of economic nationalism, agrarian democracy, and social justice.

[28] Edwin Lieuwen, *Venezuela*, 2d ed. (London: Oxford University Press, 1965), pp. 12–13, 106, 153. Gino Germani, however, questions the degree of middle-class self-identification in Venezuela, noting marked differences in the degree of participation in the national society (*Política y Sociedad*, p. 169).

[29] Lieuwen, *Venezuela*, pp. 50–51; John D. Martz, *Acción Democrática: Evolution of a Modern Political Party in Venezuela* (Princeton: Princeton University Press, 1966), p.121.

Busy with organizational efforts, clandestinely and later legally, the Adecos found themselves participants in the 1945–48 regime before they had issued more comprehensive statements of ideology or program. By then, practices were more important than statements. The coup of 1948 again gave them respite in which to study doctrine, but the results are not apparent until 1958, when, once more legalized, they published a series of "theses."[30] As in the case of MNR, the party's early doctrine must be studied against its actions when it had power, temporarily, in the trial period of 1945–48.

AD probably accomplished more in its trial period than did either APRA in the same period or MNR from 1943 to 1946. This was due in part to the fact that it held power more independently and directly controlled the executive. The period "marked a structural transformation that has provided the basis for future national development" and taught AD "lessons which are still being applied."[31]

One of the first acts of the party was to broaden electoral participation, initially by decree and later by law. This fact gives to initial AD actions a political character. The expanded electorate voted first, for the Constituent Assembly (October, 1946), which framed the constitution of 1947; second, for the president and congressional representatives (December, 1947), who formerly had been elected indirectly; and third, for municipal offices throughout the country. Betancourt and the junta ruled by decree for more than two years, however, before popularly elected representatives could attack the problem of substantive reforms.[32] The delay was apparently justified by the basic significance of political liberties established in this period, which later served as an opposition rallying point during the 1948–58 decade under Pérez Jiménez.

Meanwhile, without waiting for legislative action, Betancourt had moved to the areas of economic and social reform, particularly that of sharing in the profits of the oil industry. In negotiations with foreign-owned oil companies, he achieved the 50–50 formula which set a precedent for other oil-producing countries, but he avoided outright nationalization of the kind that had interrupted Mexican access to international markets in the thirties. Increased oil royalties in turn facilitated the tasks of reform in the fields of wages, health, education, and industrial and agricultural development and diversification. Thus the AD regime acted with a certain logic to establish democracy, obtain the resources it needed, and apply them to areas in need of reform.

[30] Martz, *Acción Democrática*, pp. 35, 46, 123, 125, 224–27, and 234.
[31] Alexander, *Prophets*, pp. 119–20.
[32] Martz, *Acción Democrática*, p. 377; Lieuwen, *Venezuela*, pp. 71–76.

One reform task remained, however, agrarian reform, which Betancourt believed would detract from achievements in agricultural production as long as it went unsolved.[33] It would appear that this had not been a part of the explicit AD program and that only during the 1945–48 period had the party definitely decided that a drastic redistribution of land was required. Nevertheless, reform "moved slowly and cautiously," beginning with public lands, excluding efficiently operated private estates, and promising fair compensation for all lands expropriated.[34]

Unlike the earlier decree actions, the agrarian reform law was adopted by Congress, but only in time to be set aside by the 1948 coup. The principles it contained continued to represent party doctrine after a decade in exile, however, and were reproduced in the law of 1960. Even then the course of moderate, peaceful, and legal land reform was to serve as one of the pretexts for a major split in the party and its *campesino* counterpart in 1961–62.

Other elements of doctrine also emerged more clearly in practice than in pronouncements, either because they were organizational principles taken as articles of faith or because they had to be learned from experience. Although some of the clichés of class warfare have been retained, both predecessor parties of AD in the late thirties stressed unification rather than division of the classes, and it was over this issue that the Communists left PDN (Partido Democrático Nacional) in 1938.

AD's stand on the Church was not highlighted. The history of mid-nineteenth-century anticlericalism in Venezuela made the issue less significant than it had been in Peru. It first emerged, therefore, after 1958, when AD educational policies began to encroach on that aspect of religious interests and through AD differences with the Christian Socialist party (COPEI).[35] This example illustrates AD's tendency to be more pragmatic than ideological.

Organization and Methods

The element of organization—that which clearly makes it a mass party—is the most strikingly successful feature of AD. Although the party has had its "personalist phase" (after 1945), and before that its

[33] Quoted in Alexander, *Prophets*, p. 124 (see also pp. 117, 120–28); Lieuwen, *Venezuela*, pp. 76–83.

[34] Lieuwen says that "AD was thus *forced to the hard conclusion* that without land redistribution its whole programme for agricultural development must fail" (*Venezuela*, p. 38, italics added). Martz says that the junta "*soon realized* that basic reform was necessary rather than gradual or partial alterations" (*Acción Democrática*, p. 276, italics added).

[35] Martz, *Acción Democrática*, pp. 30, 35, 83–84, 127–28, 188–89, and 247–50; Lieuwen, *Venezuela*, pp. 87 and 188.

"theological" period, the most recent stage, since 1958, has been called "organizational." The current emphasis goes back to Betancourt's insistence that the "party rather than the person" be placed first, and to his attachment to the principle of a multiclass, rather than a proletarian, party. Although the personal popularity of Betancourt has been indispensable in elections and during certain factional disputes, these organizational features have demonstrated the strength of the party and its associated interest groups as a cohesive institution.[36]

Employee groups had some share in the proto-Adeco activities of the late 1930s, but the leaders were mainly students of the "generation of '28." The exile period of 1937–41 and the succeeding four years of legality were largely devoted to grass-roots organization, especially with regard to labor (both urban and rural), which was then only beginning to organize.[37] AD leaders followed the principle that no corner of the country should go unvisited. Spadework of the underground period made possible a rapid expansion after 1941, and by 1945 AD had defeated the Communists to become dominant in the labor movement. By the mid-sixties, organized labor (urban and rural) had a membership of 1,300,000 (from an electorate of 3,000,000), and AD was the dominant party. The last AD president, Raúl Leoni, owed his prominence partly to his service as labor minister in 1945–48.[38]

Organized labor, and particularly the Venezuelan Confederation of Workers (CTV), represents the main strength of AD, even though it is more than a mere labor party. In turn, CTV is said to be "intimately linked with, though not subservient to," AD.[39] Both Venezuelan labor law and AD party doctrine prohibit political affiliation by organized labor. As in Peru, however, the AD/CTV linkage functions effectively because "nearly all major labor leaders are national figures in their political parties"; that is particularly true of AD.

CTV differs from its Peruvian counterpart by including COPEI leaders but not Communists, for extremists have been expelled from the con-

[36] Martz, *Acción Democrática*, pp. 30, 147, 284–86, and 377–81. Martz notes that AD's "machinery" has been the single most important factor in its election successes, but qualifies this statement with regard to *campesino* organization. Powell differs, stating that, although Betancourt was predominant in the organizing period of the late 1930s, and Quijada was the first *campesino* leader to emerge, no single leader can be identified in the combined task of organizing peasant *sindicatos* and forming a "massive popular-based political movement" (John D. Powell, "Preliminary Report on the Federación Campesina de Venezuela," mimeographed [Madison: University of Wisconsin, Land Tenure Center, 1964], p. 2).

[37] Lieuwen, *Venezuela*, p. 162.

[38] Martz, *Acción Democrática*, pp. 29–30, 49–50, 54, 119, 126, and 132; see also pp. 235, 255, 259, 264–67, and 368.

[39] Schmitt and Burks, *Evolution or Chaos*, p. 140.

federation. The AD doctrine of 1958 insists on labor independence and the pursuit of its own interests, but it states that labor can be an important party ally, keeping the party in line and preserving its unity. In practice the distinction probably is made only when it suits AD and CTV purposes.

The picture of rural labor is comparable, considering the differences in conditions. AD began its organizing effort very early. The first peasant *sindicato* was organized in February, 1936. Major *campesino* leaders have since been AD leaders. Many *sindicatos* that had existed illegally came forward to register under the AD junta in 1945, bringing the number from 53 to 515 and membership from 3,959 to 43,302 (from 16 percent to 32 percent of all union members) in the three-year period. After 1948 they were vulnerable as legal unions but difficult to suppress as clandestine units of political resistance. By 1963 there were almost 3,000 rural unions with an estimated membership of 457,000.[40]

The otherwise favorable picture of AD rural strength was marred by the 1961–62 defection of Quijada, the oldest of the party's *campesino* leaders, ostensibly in protest over agrarian reform policy but actually as part of a broader, personalist dispute within the party. The 1963 presidential election gave AD a plurality, however, which, as in 1958, was based largely on rural rather than urban votes.[41]

Quite aside from the delivery of votes, a mutually beneficial relationship between party and *campesino* federation seems to have been built. "The Venezuelan case is a spectacularly successful example of the incorporation of the *campesino* masses . . . into a modern-type interest-group relationship within a democratic political system." The dissenting view is that AD strength "has been largely that of *party* organization and mostly that of its candidates' popularity" rather than a result of "politicizing the peasantry."[42]

The actual process of organizing was thorough. "Through the late 1930s and early 1940s . . . Acción Democrática extended its partisan organization into the rural, pre-modern sector of the society, tapping the virtually unexploited reservoir of consent that lay outside the major cities. Through alliances with and encouragement of labor unions and peasant leagues it created a substantial power base. . . ."[43]

In the middle sectors AD has been relatively successful in the past, even though its recent experience somewhat resembles that of APRA. As already noted, the major Adeco leaders were, and still are, the rebellious

[40] Powell, "Federación Campesina," pp. vi, 6–7, 10–13.

[41] Lieuwen, *Venezuela*, p. 199.

[42] Powell, "Federación Campesina," p. 80; Martz, *Acción Democrática*, pp. 284–86, italics added. Martz concedes, however, that "the fact of a growing organization" is not in doubt.

[43] Anderson, " 'Reformongering,' " p. 33.

student leaders of 1928. They have included prominent literary figures such as novelist Rómulo Gallegos, elected president by AD in 1948, and poet Andrés Eloy Blanco, who helped give the party standing among the intellectuals. The 1948–58 decade of illegality probably weakened AD among such groups, as it did in organized labor. Upon its return to legality, however, AD elected party men as heads of the principal professional organizations. As a result, in 1958 the party leadership was believed to be for the first time truly multiregional and multiclass.

Difficulty soon developed, however, over the ideological differences between generations. The younger generation of Adecos had borne the heaviest load of underground activity under Pérez Jiménez. They were impatient with the moderation of the older leaders not only in Venezuela but elsewhere within the democratic Left of Latin America, and they focused on Castroism and cooperation with the Communists as their main issue. Disagreement in the party came to a head in April and May, 1960, and the dissidents resigned before they could be disciplined, taking with them an estimated 80 percent of the youth movement. They eventually formed the Movimiento de la Izquierda Revolucionaria (MIR), building close ties with communism and a commitment to radical reform and violence.[44]

The more serious internal splits that followed were personalist rather than ideological in nature. The first also had generational characteristics. As early as 1945–48 a group of young Adecos, which came to be called the Grupo ARS (after the advertising agency slogan "let us think for you"), had criticized the party leadership for moving too slowly. Late in 1961 they accused the older generation of loss of revolutionary doctrine in such areas as agrarian reform (where they had the support of *campesino* leader Quijada), cooperation with other parties, and restoration of constitutional guarantees. The basic aim of ARS, however, was to seize control of the party. Its expulsion in January, 1962, deprived the governing coalition of its independent majority in the Chamber of Deputies.[45]

Neither of these splits of 1961–62 proved fatal to the party, mainly because student-MIR support was strongest in Caracas and because ARS—after a sharp struggle for control of the *campesino* organizations—

[44] Robert J. Alexander, *The Venezuelan Democratic Revolution* (New Brunswick, N.J.: Rutgers University Press, 1964), pp. 76–80; Martz, *Acción Democrática*, pp. 176–180, 182–83, 211. In a speech at about this time, Rafael Caldera, head of COPEI, identified four "generations"—'28, '36, '46, and '58—each with different experiences and outlooks. See the Inter-American Association for Democracy and Freedom's *Report of the Second Inter-American Conference for Democracy and Freedom, Maracay, Venezuela, April 22–26, 1960* (New York, 1961), pp. 25–26.

[45] Martz, *Acción Democrática*, pp. 187–92.

also limited its efforts to the federal district. A more fundamental test came in 1968.

AD support among nonpartisan groups was for many years outstanding in three areas: teachers, students, and women. Much like the workers and *campesinos*, teachers began to organize in the thirties. Luís Beltrán Prieto became the first president of the Federación Venezolana de Maestros (FVM) and later was secretary general and vice-president of AD. When he failed to get the AD presidential nomination in 1968, he decided to run on a separate ticket. He placed fourth, but drew almost 20 percent of the vote, allowing Rafael Caldera of COPEI a slight plurality over Gonzalo Barrios, the AD majority candidate.

During the decade of its legal existence, AD declined from a command of 49 percent of the presidential vote, when Betancourt ran in 1958, to slightly more than 28 percent for Barrios in 1968. In 1963 Raúl Leoni polled only about 33 percent of the vote, but nevertheless won by a plurality. Betancourt told the press just after the 1968 election that AD's loss was the result of party factionalism, but he called for better organizing activity to attract independents.[46]

Communists and Castroites also made inroads into AD student strength during and after the 1948–58 decade, but the party has maintained and perhaps increased its strength in the provincial universities. Women were attracted to AD by the adoption of universal suffrage in 1945, and subsequent competition by other parties has not been serious. The party's statutes, however, forbid the formation of a separate women's organization, on grounds of equality of the sexes.[47]

Strategy and Tactics

AD has been remarkably adept in most of its dealings with the military and with other parties. The military element is particularly prominent in Venezuela because Bolívar's description of the country as a "barracks" remained accurate for more than a century. "Particularly in the latter half of the nineteenth century . . . the armed forces became an essentially predatory institution."[48]

The modern pattern was set by Juan Vincente Gómez, who ruled Venezuela, in and out of the presidency, from 1908 until his death in 1935. Like his predecessor, Cipriano Castro, and all of his successors, Gómez was an *andino* from Táchira near the far western border with Colombia. Although he modernized the army, making it a more efficient instrument

[46] *Washington Post*, December 8, 1968, p. A29.

[47] Alexander, *Venezuelan Revolution*, pp. 80–84; Martz, *Acción Democrática*, pp. 191–92, 202, 278–98.

[48] Lieuwen, *Venezuela*, pp. 156–57.

of oppression, he also established the Táchira tradition of involvement in politics.[49]

It was this kind of military meddling which gave AD its first chance at power in 1945. Military dissatisfaction had already taken the form of a 1944 conspiracy against Medina. When he failed to find a logical successor, the officer group asked AD in June, 1945, to join in a coup to install Betancourt as head of the government. The party agreed to the plan only after it concluded that constitutional avenues had failed and that the conspiracy would go forward with or without it.

Although the coup had to be triggered prematurely, it succeeded after a few hours of street fighting in Caracas. A junta with an AD majority was established in accordance with advance conditions laid down by the party. The military apparently was sincere in its agreement to an AD government without military interference. "The Junta as such existed only in name. After a few weeks . . . the individual cabinet members reported to Betancourt as if he were president of the republic."[50]

Undue dependence of the regime on the military officers who brought it into power, however, was to defeat it in time. This was a recognized hazard which AD had sought to eliminate:

> . . . From the very beginning AD stuck to an exclusively civilian political thesis. It believed that the armed forces should be non-political, that their function should be a professional and technical one only, and that they ought to be completely subordinate to the civilian executive power. AD accordingly endeavored to convert the military to this viewpoint. . . . However, the political habits of the military, the result of over a century of tradition, were not something that could be broken in a few years. Despite AD's repeated assurances to the contrary, the army increasingly suspected that AD meant to destroy its status. . . .[51]

From this situation of mutual distrust, which was re-inforced by the alienation of certain elements of the population by AD reforms and authoritarian behavior, Pérez Jiménez led a conspiracy to overthrow President Gallegos, elected to succeed the junta in 1948. On the AD side, efforts were made to block the overthrow by transferring unfriendly officers and by creating a party militia as a counterweight to the army, but neither succeeded.

After AD's return to power in 1959, Betancourt and then Leoni followed a different course in dealing with the military. Recognizing that it

[49] *Ibid.*, pp. 43 and 45–50; Martz, *Acción Democrática*, pp. 299ff. Military dictators or presidents from Táchira have been Cipriano Castro (1899–1908), Gómez (1910–35), López Contreras (1935–41), Medina Angarita (1941–45), and Pérez Jiménez (1950–58).

[50] Alexander, *Prophets*, pp. 115–16; see also Martz, *Acción Democrática*, pp. 300–302, and Lieuwen, *Venezuela*, pp. 62–63, 68–70.

[51] Lieuwen, *Venezuela*, pp. 87–88.

would be impossible to neutralize it completely as a political force, the party sought to re-establish and maintain the best possible ties with this crucial factor in government stability and survival. Military loyalty and nonpartisanship were stressed in official speeches, and personal friendships were encouraged even between military officers and trade unionists.[52]

A special effort was needed to overcome the image of AD which had been cultivated in the military services during the Pérez Jiménez dictatorship. Betancourt began by rejecting the idea that the military would seek to prevent his taking office. After becoming president he visited military posts of all three services extensively and held a weekly open house for officers at the presidential palace. He took a personal interest in seeing that the armed forces received fringe benefits and adequate appropriations for professional improvements. Although several coups were attempted during his term, none succeeded.

Other parties played a significant rôle in AD's rise to power, just as they did in Bolivia with MNR. Although AD seemed to have the field of reform as much to itself in its early days as did APRA in Peru, its competitors were already active in the thirties.

COPEI was not formed until 1946, but its founder, Rafael Caldera, had been in politics before World War II. The other nearest AD competitor, Unión Republicana Democrática (URD), also was formed in 1946, by Jóvito Villalba, a member of the '28 generation who soon left the party to become an independent. The Communists had begun organizing in Venezuela in the twenties and posed the strongest threat to AD in the trade unions, although between World War II and 1958 they split into opposing "Red" and "Black" parties. Thus, by 1948, "all organized political groups tended to accept the general outlines of *adeco*-inspired reforms."[53]

AD had early experience with the strategy of indirect control of the executive. In 1945 it had actually decided to support a candidate of national unity nominated by the party of President Medina. First, however, it tried unsuccessfully to change the constitution to permit the election of the president directly, rather than by Congress. It abandoned its alliance with Medina's party when the nominee turned out to be a nonentity.[54]

In the process of establishing constitutional government in the 1945–48 period, AD tried another device. In 1948 it decided that its candidate in

[52] Tad Szulc, *Twilight of the Tyrants* (New York: Henry Holt & Co., 1959), pp. 275–76; Martz, *Acción Demacrática*, pp. 310–14.

[53] Martz, *Acción Democrática*, pp. 377–78 (see also pp. 66–67); Lieuwen, *Venezuela*, pp. 71–73.

[54] Alexander, *Prophets*, p. 114. AD also had sought promises of reform in exchange for its support; see Martz, *Acción Democrática*, pp. 58–59.

the first popular election of the president would be the novelist Gallegos, who had strongly influenced Betancourt as a student. This apparent effort at national unity has been called "perhaps the greatest error" of the party in this period. Gallegos was indecisive; he failed to move against the military conspiracy building up against him, became "unexpectedly authoritarian," and lost "no opportunity to antagonize the military."[55] Thus AD had no better results in this experiment than did APRA in its concurrent experiment in national unity.

In the 1952 elections held by Pérez Jiménez before he dropped all pretense of democratic rule, AD made another attempt to gain indirect control of the executive by quietly supporting the candidacy of Villalba. He appeared to be winning when the results were revised; Villalba's candidacy was annulled and Pérez Jiménez was elected. Once again, in 1963, AD considered supporting Rafael Caldera, the COPEI candidate for president, but decided that it needed to demonstrate AD strength and unity in another election following the 1961–62 defections.[56]

Between the forties and the sixties a transition had taken place in AD tactics of interparty cooperation. In his long exile of 1948–58, Betancourt concluded that the party had erred in its former hostility toward competing parties. Thereafter he tried to reach agreement with COPEI and URD on a pact of mutual renunciation of the resort to the military as a means of upsetting a legally constituted regime.[57] His effort marked a third stage in the AD attitude, which had developed through (1) stubborn opposition to rival parties (before 1948), (2) the beginning of informal exchanges (from 1952), and (3) three-party coalition governments (from 1959).[58]

The process by which interparty cooperation led to the overthrow of Pérez Jiménez should be a case study in popular insurgency, but in fact the published accounts present a picture of a three-way division of effort without close coordination. The military dissidents, the underground within Venezuela, and the exiles abroad each seemed to be working in semi-isolation. Actually, there probably was more coordination than appearances indicate. The students inside the country mounted the first organized opposition to the regime, following earlier clashes with the regime, by forming the University Front as a clandestine group late in 1955.

Pamphleteering was carried on individually by the parties, however, beginning late in 1952 when COPEI and URD followed AD into pro-

[55] Alexander, *Prophets*, p. 131.

[56] Martz, *Acción Democrática*, pp. 213 and 326–27; Szulc, *Tyrants*, p. 288; Lieuwen, *Venezuela*, p. 99.

[57] Alexander, *Prophets*, p. 139.

[58] Martz, *Acción Democrática*, pp. 315ff.

scription. The Church joined openly with the pastoral letter of May, 1957. Only in that year did the three parties, plus the Communists, openly form the Junta Patriótica, which is said to have smuggled arms into Venezuela. It received basic instructions from its exiled leaders but enjoyed tactical independence within the country.[59]

Meanwhile, conspiratorial groups had been formed independently in each of the armed services, and they precipitated the struggle against the regime on New Year's Day, 1958. The first effort was abortive but it was reinforced by street demonstrations in reaction to the arrest of five priests. Finally, a general strike on January 21 and a naval revolt the next day forced Pérez Jiménez to resign on January 23.

Collaboration among the exiles in this period did not figure prominently in the conspiracy. It was only in January, 1958, that the principal leaders of AD, COPEI, and URD met in New York and agreed "to work together for the reestablishment of democratic constitutional government and . . . to cooperate to preserve it at all costs once it was achieved." The uncertainty of the transitional situation in Venezuela is indicated by the fact that Betancourt did not return there until about a month after the overthrow of the old regime.[60]

The three-party Venezuelan Civilian Front continued to seek a unity presidential candidate while a caretaker junta governed. The Civilian Front succeeded only in agreeing on a common minimum program, the principle of coalition government, and a commitment to honor the results of the election, in which each would run its own candidate. Upon his election on December 7, 1958, Betancourt formed a cabinet which included COPEI and URD members and set about, more moderately than in 1945, to apply the AD program.

Although the composition of later coalitions was varied, the basic AD tactic continued unchanged, despite internal dissension, until the change of government in 1969. By 1964 it could be said that the party system was "distinguished by a spirit of conciliation and of coexistence that was new in Venezuela." Both AD and the opposition parties were satisfied to operate within the competitive system.[61]

Comparisons

The degrees of similarity of the three mass parties in Peru, Bolivia, and Venezuela are now more apparent. In the twenties and thirties they had their amorphous beginnings, although APRA took form earlier than the

[59] Lieuwen, *Venezuela*, pp. 99–101; Szulc, *Tyrants*, p. 299.

[60] Alexander, *Prophets*, pp. 139–40; see also Lieuwen, *Venezuela*, pp. 101–2, and Martz, *Acción Democrática*, p. 146.

[61] Martz, *Acción Democrática*, p. 337; see also Lieuwen, *Venezuela*, pp. 103–4, 186.

others. In the forties each had its trial period and enjoyed a taste of national power.

From that point on, however, their strategies diverged. During the fifties MNR and AD came to power, but in radically different ways, while APRA devised the *convivencia* as a way of improving its long-range prospects. Each of the three parties in its own way saw success and failure in the sixties. APRA dominated the congressional majority but was prevented by another coup from capturing the presidency. MNR re-elected Paz, only to have him overturned by the military forces he had re-made; it then disappeared as a separate entity. AD carried out Venezuela's first peaceful elective transfer of power when it elected Leoni in 1963, but it had to repeat the transfer to its chief competitor after the election of 1968.

Table VIII–1 presents the chronology of principal events for the three parties during almost four decades and indicates the degrees of influence each had in the executive administrations listed.

TABLE VIII–1: CHRONOLOGY OF ATTEMPTS BY CERTAIN MASS REFORM PARTIES TO GAIN POWER

Year	APRA in Peru	MNR in Bolivia	AD in Venezuela
1931	Party organized: lost election to Sánchez Cerro; APRA outlawed (1932)		Betancourt exiled, 1930–36
1933	Benavides named president by Congress; APRA outlawed	Chaco War, 1932–35	
1936	Election annulled; Congress extended Benavides term	Toro coup	Death of Gómez
1937		Busch coup	Proto-Adecos outlawed
1939	Prado elected; APRA boycott	Busch elected, dies; generals take power	
1941		MNR organized	AD organized
1943		Villarroel coup	
1945	Bustamante elected; APRA legalized, dominates Congress		Betancourt brought to power by military coup
1946		La Paz revolt; MNR outlawed	

Year	APRA in Peru	MNR in Bolivia	AD in Venezuela
1948	Odría coup; APRA outlawed		Gallegos elected; military coup leading to Pérez Jiménez regime; AD outlawed
1950	Odría elected		
1952		MNR Revolution; Paz president	AD supported Villalba election; election annulled
1956	Prado elected; APRA legalized	Siles elected	
1958			Military coup; Betancourt elected
1960		Paz elected	
1962	Election annulled by military junta		
1963	Belaúnde elected; APRA dominates Congress		Leoni elected
1964		Paz re-elected; Barrientos coup	
1968	Velasco coup		Caldera elected

Key: Single underscore, regime influenced by reform party or allies; double underscore, regime dominated by reform party listed.

Differences in the degree of formalization of doctrine among the three parties have been noted. The contrasts were not so much in the formulation as in the degree of public articulation which the parties gave to their ideologies and programs. The Mexican and the Peruvian examples mark the extremes in this regard.

Ideology can hardly exist for a mass party if it is not publicized. It is the basis for the consensus which holds the membership together. Ideology which does not reach the level of political enunciation is probably characteristic of movements or other inchoate groupings rather than of parties. Especially is this true in a revolutionary situation, "since a revolution by its very nature rejects the customary social order and its traditional implicit norms to put different explicit, consciously stated norms in their stead."[62]

[62] F. S. C. Northrop, *Philosophical Anthropology and Practical Politics* (New York: Macmillan Co., 1960), p. 123; see also p. 129.

In Mexico after 1910, ideology was explicit only for a very few and implicit for the great majority of effective participants. Or, I should say, it was explicit for the many at a very low level of elaboration. One of the major philosophers of the Mexican Revolution took the position, for example, that "rebellion even *for the sake of one knows not what*, is better [than] supine acceptance of an imperfect reality."[63] Even after fifty years, "with the possible exception of this very general idea of progress and change, there is no integrated and official ideology of the Mexican Revolution. . . ." And even that developed only in the process of evolving "an ideology of pragmatic experience."[64]

This is not to suggest that between 1910 and 1920 the Mexicans had any doubt about what they were fighting *against*, but only—as the personalist and factional fighting showed—that they were very uncertain of what they were bringing into being. Both points, the negativism and the low level of elaboration of ideology, were evident in the slogans of the Mexican Revolution. It represented a revolution of protest, which was more effective as a way of seizing power than as a plan for holding it.

It is paradoxical that the elaborate doctrine of *Aprismo* was inspired in large part by the Mexican Revolution. This was hardly accidental, for Haya de la Torre sought deliberately to avoid the chaos that he saw there:

> In this country [Mexico] we find a spontaneous revolution, without program, almost a revolution of instinct, without science. Mexico could have succeeded in fulfilling a mission for Latin America, perhaps as great as that of Russia for the world, if its revolution had followed a program. But the Mexican Revolution has had neither theoreticians nor leaders. Nothing is organized scientifically. It is a marvelous series of improvisations, trials, stumblings, rescued by the force of the people. . . .[65]

The doctrinal developments in MNR and AD fall somewhere between the extremes of Mexico and Peru. Both parties had the benefit of deeper involvement during trial periods in power than did the reformers of APRA and PRI. MNR and AD thus had opportunities to decide what they thought and would do about the problems of their countries and to demonstrate these decisions to their supporters in the form of actions. This can best be seen in terms of the content of their programs.

In Bolivia, MNR was more creature than creator of its revolutionary movement. Opportunism, some dissension within the movement, and a

[63] William Rex Crawford, *A Century of Latin-American Thought*, rev. ed. (Cambridge, Mass.: Harvard University Press, 1961), p. 277, italics added.

[64] Robert E. Scott, *Mexican Government in Transition* (Urbana: University of Illinois Press, 1959), p. 100. Scott also cites ideologists of disparate views to show the lack of a single spokesman for the revolution (*ibid.*, p. 99).

[65] Quoted in Cossío del Pomar, *Víctor Raúl*, p. 224.

great deal of neglect contributed to the tardiness of formalization of the party's program. On the other hand, the need was not as great as it was in a more developed country such as Peru. The Bolivian Revolution was initially a nationalist phenomenon, in that it focused the grievances of the miners against the foreign or expatriate "tin barons."[66] It is doubtful that, without this key attack on the country's major export resource, the secondary elements of *campesino* demands for developmental (land reform) and political (universal suffrage) changes would have become operative.

The Venezuelan situation was quite different. When it was first organized in the forties, AD deliberately avoided making its doctrine explicit, in order not to excite reactions that it would have been unable to withstand. This does not mean that plans did not exist, at least in the minds of Betancourt and other old-line leaders. They adopted the strategy, however, of concentrating first on political liberties. "Opposition groups agreed that a social revolution would be impossible in Venezuela without universal suffrage, which would lead to a re-allocation of resources into the long-neglected sectors of agriculture, education, and health."[67]

Political doctrine thus was seen by AD as the party's primary goal; it was also considered instrumental to the attainment of more basic objectives. In this respect, Venezuela followed the Mexican pattern. Betancourt moved quickly in the 1945–48 period to put into effect the nationalist (oil revenues) and developmental (agrarian reform) aspects of AD programs. The result was that all parties (including PRI in Mexico) converged with programs of general similarity in their political, nationalist, and developmental elements; only the priorities and tactical sequences varied from one country to another.

How each party marshaled the resources of the community had direct effects on its success. The organization of support groups probably could be regarded as the *sine qua non* of revolution or reform by a mass party, but the methods vary widely. In Mexico, the forces at hand were the *campesinos* and a few fiery leaders who aroused them to redress old grievances. In the process of destroying the old society, many fell prey to personal ambitions and factionalism, and from their bad examples new institutions and methods ultimately evolved:

> . . . Mexico has forgotten, and the rest of the world has never known, to what extent the country was laid waste by the revolution. It wiped out the governing echelons and the official bureaucracy . . . it did away with

[66] Patch says that nationalism was a primary factor in the MNR revolution, although his definition of the term may be broader than mine; see his "Peasantry and National Revolution," p. 105.

[67] Letter from a former labor attaché in Caracas.

the army and the federal police . . . the old landholding class and especially the *latifundista*, the nucleus of its political and economic power. . . .
As it destroyed the old society, the Mexican Revolution was creating a new one. . . . Besides entirely new political groups, the revolution fashioned a popular army. . . . The peasant and the worker, political forces undreamed of in the *ancien regime*, were exalted by the revolution, and their welfare was declared to be the principal and sole purpose of the whole movement.[68]

Mexico could not pretend to have consolidated its revolution, however, until the mid-thirties, when Cárdenas perfected the institutionalized party. Earlier, under Calles, "the party was little more than a coalition of semi-independent local organizations dominated by individual military or civilian bosses." Yet even then the process of strengthening the party was beginning, "often at the expense of the heads of local political machines and the leadership of functional interest organizations which were its principal components."[69]

Ultimately, the corporate structure of the party integrated the functionally based sectors of agriculture, labor, popular (or political) interest, and armed forces. In all but the last, the basic unit was the local organization—the peasant league, labor union, or political association—and these in turn were pyramided through state and national federations.

The MNR experience was similar to the early stages of the Mexican Revolution, but briefer and much less bloody. The critical difference was that in Bolivia the personalism and factionalism intensified and became regenerative, until the process of governing the revolution deteriorated and it became unmanageable. When the leaders of miner and *campesino* factions clashed, each sought support from the military, which again became the arbiter and exacted a price. Bolivia did not have the luxury of time which in Mexico allowed the chaos slowly to take form and stabilize.

In Venezuela a larger part of the organizing process occurred under party sponsorship and before AD came to power. The result was nevertheless somewhat similar to the integration of support groups that emerged painfully out of the destruction and disorder in Mexico. Betancourt succeeded in not threatening the "clans and institutions inherited from the past," but he insisted that they not play leading roles in the government.

[68] Daniel Cosío Villegas, "The Mexican Left," in *Politics of Change*, ed. Maier and Weatherhead, p. 127. The revolution had its factions, and the internal struggle within the revolution is regarded by this authority as "the initial instrument of a savage renovation that prevented the new ruling class from perpetuating itself in its entirety." The effort of Obregón to legalize his re-election is believed to have fostered his assassination. See *ibid.*, pp. 128–29.

[69] Scott (*Mexican Government in Transition*, pp. 116–32) notes that this process of institutionalization was gradual and cannot be equated with changes in the party name in 1929, 1937, and 1945 (when it became PRI).

He kept the trade unions, peasants, and cooperative movement dependent upon the state by way of the political parties.

AD has not been spared personalism and factionalism, however; rather, it has tried to resolve them, when other means fail, through the generally accepted process of electoral politics. In Mexico they are resolved within the party and are largely concealed from the public. Both countries are examples of the exercise of power amid a diversity of forces, all of which are tolerated and listened to as long as they do not threaten the system.[70] By contrast, Bolivia has had neither the self-denying process of the Venezuelan elections nor the discipline of the Mexican revolutionary institution to provide ways of avoiding disintegration.

APRA follows the Venezuelan example, but with the decisive difference that it has neither come to terms with institutional groups nor maximized its organizational and popular support. Its regional base in the Solid North and its lack of a disciplined organizational base outside the trade unions imposed limitations on the exercise of party power (in agrarian reform legislation, for example) and on the expansion of party influence (in the dynamic middle class or among the Indians of the southern sierra).

Circumstances in which parties have acquired influence or power also have varied. It may be significant that in Bolivia and Venezuela all changes of regime giving important benefits to the reform parties were brought about by force.[71] In Peru, on the other hand, APRA was able to improve its position only by means of the electoral process (1945, 1956, and in Congress, 1963). Each of these instances terminated a period of dictatorial rule. Resorting to force has invariably been damaging to APRA.

None of these parties followed a uniform strategy in its relations with the state and other parties. Some experience in the exercise of power was offered to each during the trial periods of the 1940s. For MNR and APRA this was hardly productive or conclusive, while for AD it may have been crucial to that party's later success in returning to power. Nowhere has the control of the legislature been effective in winning access to executive power. Of greater significance was the way in which each party related to the military.

Both MNR and AD enjoyed cordial relations with some part of the armed forces at critical moments in their attempts to gain power. Thereafter their tactics diverged. Paz deliberately destroyed the armed forces after taking power, only to find that he had to revive them later. They then destroyed him. Betancourt courted the military assiduously and appeased them even after he was solidly in power and might have tried to

[70] Luis Mercier Vega, *Roads to Power in Latin America*, trans. Robert Rowland (New York: Frederick A. Praeger, 1969), pp. 163–83.

[71] Martz, *Acción Democrática*, p. 337.

adopt a different approach. APRA may have been in communication with substantial factions of the military from time to time, but the relationship was never effectively turned to the advantage of the party. Nor did efforts in the sixties to appease the armed forces produce enough trust on the military side to permit APRA to compete for the presidency by election in 1969.

Cooperation with other parties was proportionate to reliance upon legislative power. MNR was in competition with other reform parties from its very beginnings. Some of its success probably was due to the ability of Paz to outmaneuver other parties. He never consented, for example, to support another party's candidate for president, but instead obtained their support for his candidacy. Once he took power, he moved aggressively to absorb or isolate his competitors. He created an effective one-party regime and wasted little effort on legislative actions.

AD began with a policy of exclusiveness but changed to cooperation before it came to power in 1958. Without attempting any shift in executive-legislative relationships, Betancourt and Leoni tried to ensure that the governing coalitions which they led reflected clear majorities in Congress. The only time AD supported another candidate for president was while it was outlawed, although it considered doing so at other times. AD endorsement of the candidate led to his proscription and thereby to the strengthening of the underground against Pérez Jiménez.

APRA went further than either of the other parties in interparty collaboration and emphasis on legislative power. Neither it nor AD (after 1958) accepted the cooperation of Communist parties. On the other hand, neither declined the support of conservative parties. In general, however, AD pursued a strong and direct approach to the presidency, as did MNR, while APRA vacillated between this and the weak, or indirect, strategy. The salient attributes of the three parties are condensed in Table VIII–2.

In summary, none of the other parties considered here was as ideological as APRA. Instead of being doctrinaire, MNR in Bolivia was personalist and AD in Venezuela is pragmatic. PRI has evolved from a personalist movement into a pragmatic institution. All four parties have been plagued by factionalism, but the pragmatic parties—AD and PRI—have the broadest and best integrated bases in support organizations. An ideological party like APRA may be particularly prone to a clientelistic narrowing of the support base, which both reduces the risks of splintering and limits the potential for expansion.

The four parties divide into pairs in terms of their predominant attitudes toward other parties. PRI and MNR fall into the monopolistic class as parties of solidarity, which seek to eliminate or absorb competition. AD and APRA adjusted more readily to the open political systems that developed in Venezuela and Peru, even to competition from other non-Communist reform parties. As the experience of AD shows, however, a conciliatory attitude toward other parties does not rule out a successful, direct approach to executive power.

TABLE VIII–2: SUMMARY OF PARTY CHARACTERISTICS AND ATTITUDES ON SELECTED QUESTIONS

	APRA	MNR	AD
IDEOLOGY AND PROGRAM			
Main emphasis	developmental	nationalist	political
Degree of specificity	high	low	moderate
ORGANIZATION AND METHODS			
Nature of mass support	narrow	fractured	broad
To power by	elections, 1945	coup, 1943; election and revolt, 1951–52	coup, 1945; revolt and election, 1958
STRATEGY AND TACTICS			
Influence on executive in "trial periods"	weak (1945–48)	weak (1943–46)	direct (1945–48)
Approach to military:			
before 1948	antagonistic	conciliatory	pragmatic
1948–63	cautious	antagonistic	conciliatory
after 1963	conciliatory	conciliatory	conciliatory
Use of legislature	maximal	minimal	moderate
Competing non-Communist reform parties?			
before 1956	no	yes	yes
after 1956	yes	no	yes
Approach to competing reform parties:			
before 1956	pragmatic	pragmatic	antagonistic
after 1956	conciliatory	absorptive	conciliatory
Supported other party's presidential candidate	1945 (won) 1956 (won)	——	1952 (annulled)
Supported by other party	——	1951 (annulled)	——

Note: Dates used in the far left-hand column were chosen primarily for the Peruvian case. They are approximate for Bolivia and Venezuela.

IX

THE POLITICS OF REFORM

THE COURSE OF POLITICAL EVENTS in Peru, Bolivia, and Venezuela since the 1950s casts considerable doubt upon the efficacy of mass reform parties as instruments of change. From the high expectations of the early sixties, the parties in each country have fallen victim to varying kinds and degrees of frustration, defeat, and decline.

The causes of these conditions need not be sought in the nature of the parties alone. Other factors were important, perhaps decisive, in the developments which positively or negatively influenced the different outcomes in each country. Nor can anyone say with assurance that increments of development occurring in one or all of these countries were not the result of the activities of the mass reform parties.

The lesson to be learned from these cases, and particularly from that of APRA in Peru, is that there is no such thing as an automatically good or bad reform party. Some features of APRA, MNR, or AD were functional for certain purposes in given situations. In other circumstances, their characteristics or conduct may have been counterproductive or self-defeating. Changes in the party system, or in the character of interest groups, could make reform parties more or less effective in other contexts. Evolution of the patterns of society and of the institutions of state also could alter the suitability of settings for party activity.

The task of analysis, therefore, is to find insight in those occurrences which seemed to produce results, and warnings in those which brought forth retrogression. It is not to seek infallible rules or recipes for success which would be expected to apply under all conditions.

Democracy in a Context of Development

It is the habit of twentieth-century liberals, of whom I am one, to applaud the observance of the *forms* of constitutionalism in Latin America and to deplore the resort to any kind of violation of the democratic norm. This is fine, and it should be no other way, all things being equal. The trouble is that things are less and less equal, and customary standards and judgments are increasingly difficult to apply.

When military regimes almost invariably were led by ambitious, power-seeking *caudillos* or acted as cynical instruments of vested interests, no great intellectual effort was required to condemn the use of arbitrary force and the denial of civil liberties. If the alternative often was not the ideal of popular rule desired for North America, at least it was placid, stable, and dignified.

In times of accelerated change, society produces contradictions. Reluctant regimes are not the only, or even the most obstinate, barriers to reform. The real obstacles may lie in the slowness of processes of integration, which allow an unsettled, transitional condition of society to become a workable and responsible political system. Integration is not a simple task, but it is one in which political parties have been known to assist.

One of the efforts that must be made by the political party, however, is that of identifying the precise environment in which it will operate. The conditions that prevailed in Mexico in 1910, or in Bolivia in 1952, produce the stereotypes that occupy most minds. Intolerable and inflexible authoritarian rule may be sufficient provocation to produce a revolution of protest, essentially destructive in its effect and unguided as to its positive aims.

A particular kind of mass reform party, such as MNR for example, may be extremely efficient in these circumstances, but only as a means of winning power. As the Bolivian case showed, it is far from being necessarily the kind of party which is capable of retaining power and carrying out a constructive program of reform. Seizure of power in conditions of extreme provocation may require only the minimal level of ideology needed to bring together a movement, and the weight of sufficient numbers or violence to overcome resistance.

Quite different conditions prevailed in Peru and Venezuela in the fifties and sixties. The dictatorial regime of Pérez Jiménez in Venezuela was repressive, but superficial. Because he was not supported by a system in depth, it was only necessary to unite the reform parties, the Church, and certain military dissidents to overturn him. AD conducted itself in such a way as to take advantage of this situation. It would appear that Betancourt appreciated the fact that what followed the taking of power would be more significant than the act itself.

In Peru the obstacles to change were more deep-seated, but they were also more flexible. With the differentiation of economic interests came shifts in the role of the armed forces in politics, followed by the retirement of wholly conservative forces from overt party politics. Concurrently, the elites continued to accept and absorb some of the socially mobile elements that demanded status at least, if not other forms of change as well. Finally, the military and the Church began to endorse the cause of reform.

Whether change comes by sudden revolution or gradual reform, however, the heart of the matter is how it affects the political system. In Mexico and Bolivia, visible obstacles to reform were quickly swept away, but thereafter a long process was required to begin the realization of the tangible goals of the two revolutions. Great immediate gains were made in the sudden transformation of the way many common people perceived themselves. They had a long way to go, however, and still others had not begun to assume the attitudes of modernity which are needed to take full advantage of the benefits of modernization.[1]

The choice between the good and the bad in Latin America, therefore, is no longer one between brutality and decorum. The authoritarian regime, constituted outside the formal rules of government, usually is the more orderly alternative. Its opposite may be a government which, while duly elected, is ruled through whim and rhetoric by political chiefs who manipulate emotion-ridden masses. Neither regime deserves censure any more than it does unqualified endorsement. Neither type is ideal. The authoritarian regime should be expected to press strongly for social reform; if it does not, there is no excuse for its denial of liberties except the maintenance of a sterile and anachronistic stability. The populist regime should be congratulated for the degree of excitement it can awaken in otherwise apathetic people; motivation is what development is all about. But the populist regime also must show that it can unite the people behind a purpose that is higher than the enrichment or ego satisfaction of individual leaders.

The Party as a Bureaucracy

To consider the role of a mass reform party, such as APRA, in the ambiguities that characterize Latin American political development is therefore to look beyond the goal of seizing power. It is to regard the people as a resource—the only dependable resource available to the mass party—and to determine the nature of the party in correlation with the

[1] Scott, *Mexican Government in Transition*, pp. 5–6, 10.

stage and sequence of development of the community. The question may arise after the party has come to power, as it did for MNR and AD, or it may present itself, as in Peru, when changing social and political conditions shift the emphasis from revolution to reform.

When the reluctant regime has been overcome, or when its former supporters have adopted the tactic of parrying blows, the reform party faces the hard problems of development. These cannot be left entirely to the technocrats, as repeated cases of dichotomous development have shown. Mexico, despite its spectacular destruction of the structures of traditional privilege, is an impressive example. The growing middle class is estimated at more than one-quarter of the population. Yet the 50 percent still living off agriculture produce only about 20 percent of the national product.[2]

More than one million Indians in Mexico speak only their native tongue, and almost twice that many bilinguals, or a total of between 7 and 8 percent of the population, "live remote from national life."[3] "The Mexican Revolution . . . has sacrificed agriculture to industry, and the countryside to the city." At the same time, the appearance of a growing *Lumpenproletariat* in the cities "has in certain respects nullified much of the social legislation passed."[4]

Methods which can be used convincingly to advance reform are limited, even though the worker on a cooperative farm, or *ejido*, sees the gap between his well-being and that of the rest of the population widening. "The objective of decisively raising his standard of living has been accomplished only in those regions of the country where soil and climate make agriculture profitable, as is true in parts of the south and especially in the northwest. In the two great high plateaus, the central and the northern, the economic condition of the *ejidatario* has scarcely changed."[5]

The temptation is almost irresistible in these circumstances for the party to withdraw behind its historical lines, to settle for the extent of support it already enjoys, in short to become a bureaucracy. In this posture the party concentrates on maintaining its interests within the political system, just as individual politicians focus on preserving their positions within the party. And so it may have happened to APRA in the late fifties, if not earlier, when the party could have reached outward to become more of a mass party.

[2] James Nelson Goodsell, "Revolution Revitalizes Mexico," *Christian Science Monitor*, January 14, 1966.

[3] *Excelsior*, March 22, 1966, p. 6A.

[4] Moisés González Navarro, "Mexico: The Lop-Sided Revolution," in *Obstacles to Change*, ed. Véliz, pp. 206 and 225; Stanley Robert Ross, "Mexico: The Preferred Revolution," in *Politics of Change*, ed. Maier and Weatherhead, p. 145.

[5] Cosío Villegas, "The Mexican Left," pp. 131–32; Lucian W. Pye, "The Concept of Political Development," *The Annals* 358 (March, 1965): 11.

To adopt the policy of broadening its base or opening its ranks, a party such as APRA would have to abandon some of the exclusiveness that was carefully guarded during the years of its clandestine existence. Its doctrine might have to be generalized, or popularized, to become a uniting rather than a divisive force. The party would have to become meaningful and attractive to the many without affiliations, rather than to the few already well-disposed toward it. It would have to go to the people, whether in the *barriadas* of Lima or in the inaccessible sierra. The former would present the relatively simple problem of people already mobilized and available for integration. The latter present different problems.

The Indians of Peru offer a challenge more like that of the isolated areas of Mexico, which were long unaffected by cultural change.

> . . . Ideally, in the transformation of our semi-feudal and semi-capitalistic structures, the *external* and the *internal* processes of revolution should balance, illuminate, reinforce and even contradict each other. In Mexico, for example, the external revolution was not followed by an internal equivalent until very recently. Only when the objectives of the Revolution were, more or less, accomplished, between 1917 and 1940, did Mexico's cultural mutation start to affect the mores, sensibility and the intelligence of the country.[6]

Mexico is one of the few countries of Latin America which has a consistent pattern of popular attitudes, based on widely shared values, toward the political structures of the state. Nevertheless, "the integration process is by no means complete" in Mexico, because of the lag that "exists between the appearance of quantifiable indicators of nationalism and change . . . and evolution of more congruous political structures. . . . The real problem of congruity lies in producing participants. The task of converting traditionals into subjects has been accomplished fairly easily [but] the greatest part of the populace remains subjects. . . ."[7] The mass reform party can play a strategic part in this process of social conversion.

[6] Carlos Fuentes, "A Changing Church in Latin America," *Washington Post, Book Week*, April 24, 1966, p. 14, italics added. The book reviewed was William V. D'Antonio and Frederick B. Pike, eds., *Religion, Revolution and Reform* (New York: Frederick A. Praeger, 1964). See also K. H. Silvert, "Some Psychocultural Factors in the Politics of Conflict and Conciliation: Setting up the Problem" (Paper delivered at the 1965 Annual Meeting of the American Political Science Association, Washington, D.C.), p. 5. Fuentes' distinction is more clearly outlined in Julian H. Steward, *Area Research: Theory and Practice* (New York: Social Science Research Council, 1950), pp. 98ff., if "structural" is read to mean "social": "Society and culture are different though complementary concepts. . . . Social change and cultural change . . . must also be distinguished. Societies may experience rather drastic changes of certain kinds without any important alteration of their culture" (*ibid.*, p. 99).

[7] Robert E. Scott, "Nation-Building in Latin America," in *Nation-Building*, ed. Karl W. Deutsch and William J. Folz (New York: Atherton Press, 1963), pp. 75–82. Scott uses "external" in the foreign relations sense, but his distinction between personal and national identity makes his comments parallel those of Fuentes.

Comparable problems exist even in the United States. A municipal reform movement can win victories which, for a time, provide their own justification. Ideology tends to become theology, and positions are preserved on issues that have been overtaken by events until the break with popular demands becomes apparent. Sometimes only defeat will dramatize the true situation. To avoid a progressive narrowing of allegiances around a few restrictive or particularistic appeals is the most difficult task of a successful political organization. Perhaps unquestioning interest-group politics is no longer functional even in highly developed societies.

The Transitional Party

Instead of emerging as an all-purpose instrument of reform, therefore, the mass reform party appears to take a very special place in reform politics. It is particularly well-suited to the needs of the community in certain periods of social and political development. At other times it may suffer the strain of incongruity and have to adjust or transform itself to meet different needs.

This predicament is most evident when the party finds itself surrounded by like-minded competitors. The Peruvian and Venezuelan cases are illustrative. APRA recognized early in its development the need for accommodation with other parties. It may have been distracted from fully appreciating the problem, however, by prolonged periods of illegality. Moreover, APRA had so completely monopolized the field that reform parties other than those of the extreme Left were slow in appearing in Peru.

When they did appear in strength, between 1956 and 1962, the Apristas were already accustomed to dealing with old-line parties and were so confident of their own strength that they thought cooperation was unnecessary. In a situation of maneuver, APRA lost sight of ultimate values because of its preoccupation with the instrumental goal of winning power. As a result, the party which should have been the bulwark of the party system in Peru helped to contribute to the disintegration of that system.

Some parties seem to perform best in opposition. APRA certainly had had opposition experience, but it was of a peculiar kind. It easily assumed that the other parties, and particularly the governing party, would not bring about worthwhile reforms, or, if they did, that they should not get credit for them. Once APRA lost its monopoly on reform, and its pretension to majority status, this attitude became obsolete and the old APRA became somewhat irrelevant.

Although the Apristas never won executive power or made a revolution, they have long served the important purpose of articulating the basic needs of the community in a political system which might otherwise have continued to view them with complacency. With that degree of success, including a considerable measure of legislative reform, APRA should have recognized that it had entered a new phase of politics.

After the revolution is won, or once the ideology of development has been generally accepted, the rules of the game change. Politics enters the continuation phase. It calls for no less vigor, but it may demand a different kind of activity. There is less need for tutelage of the political community, and more need for finding practical ways of creatively putting together its disparate parts. A strategy of sequentially applying reform programs is needed, just as earlier a strategy for gaining power was paramount.

The uneven development of society still may demand a dual approach to party activity. Conventional politics in the cities can seek to profit from social change while taking account of alterations in the aims of the military, the Church, and other political parties. Unconventional politics in the less-developed areas of the country can supply non-political services which, given the limitations of official bureaucracies, perhaps only the mass reform party can adequately provide.

Acquisitiveness is said to be the salient characteristic of industrial society, and this, as well as some of its other features, has been transferred imperfectly to the less-developed world. In a surfeit of industrial goods, the so-called advanced countries are learning the veils of irresponsible over-development pressed to unreasonable lengths at the expense of the quality of life.

The direct approach to the acquisition of power in certain political situations can be equally irrational. Perhaps this is a lesson which can be taught to the post-industrial world by the world that is still mainly pre-industrial, a world in which the virtues of consensus are still strong, in which the artist who synthesizes predominates over the scientists and technicians, who take things apart.

APPENDICES

Appendix A: APRA'S Historical Choices and Decisions*

1, 2, and 3. See text, especially Chapter IV.

4. *Compromise in Congress*

Tried briefly in 1931–32, before APRA was outlawed by Sánchez Cerro, and, necessarily, in the Prado period of 1956–62, when APRA had no formal representation and very few friends in Congress.

5. *Control of Congress*

Tried in 1945–48 and 1963–68. The alliance which elected Bustamante did not hold together, a fact attributable in part to excessive Aprista aggressiveness in trying to enact its program.

In the Belaúnde period of 1963–68 the Aprista plurality, in combination with UNO (Odría's party), controlled Congress but did not try as aggressively as it had in 1945–48 to apply its full program.

6. *Support Non-Aprista President*

Tried in 1936, 1939 (support withdrawn), 1945, and 1956.

1936: Incumbent President Benavides (a military officer) annulled the election which Eguiguren was winning with Aprista support.

1939: Aprista support for Prado was withdrawn in protest over Benavides' action against the opposition press.

1945: Bustamante was elected with Aprista support but served only until the Odría coup of 1948.

1956: Prado was elected with Aprista support and held the elections of 1962, which were annulled by the armed forces.

* See Figure III–1.

7. *Discredit Incumbent President*

APRA had the advantage of "opposition" position in 1931, 1936, 1945, 1956, and 1963, but not in 1962. The 1963–68 period was its only extended opportunity to play a legal opposition role, but the anticipated election of 1969 was canceled by the Velasco coup.

8. *Appease Military Opposition*

In addition to making reassuring statements (to balance the party image), APRA tried after about 1960 to cultivate personal friendships with officers and to build a strong anti-Communist position, partly for its effect on the military.

9. *Neutralize Military Opposition*

1948: APRA negotiated with military officers to overturn Bustamante, but the premature Callao mutiny opened the way for the Odría coup. This and other uprisings showed evidence of Aprista recruitment in the armed forces, at least among non-commissioned and junior officers.

1962: Information is lacking on specifics, but incumbent President Prado apparently tried, without success, to help APRA by transferring opposing military officers. The last-minute deal in Congress to support Odría's election may have had this aim, but it proved wrong.

10. *Elect Aprista President*

Tried unsuccessfully in 1931, 1962, and 1963.

1931: Failed because of fraud or the lack of an adequate popular base, or a combination of the two.

1962: Failed because of the military coup which took place after the popular vote fell short of the one-third needed for automatic election.

1963: Election lost to Belaúnde by 85,000 votes out of 1,820,000.

Appendix B: Dispersion of Presidential Voting by Department, Elections of 1956, 1962, and 1963

Chapter IV presented summary results of the comparison of votes received by Haya de la Torre in 1962 and 1963 with those of Prado in 1956, and of votes received by Fernando Belaúnde in those years with his own record in 1956. In category I, comprising the five departments of La Libertad, Lambayeque, Cajamarca, Pasco, and Ica, the Aprista vote for Haya in both 1962 and 1963 exceeded that for Prado in 1956, when APRA supported him.

The second category is not uniform, but subdivides into two groups. The Aprista share of the total vote fell somewhat below the 1956 Prado share, but in II–A it amounted to more than 40 percent of the total, and in II–B it amounted to 25 percent or less.

With minor exceptions, the departments in categories I and II–A are the same as those in which APRA received pluralities or better in the 1962 and 1963 elections, as shown on Figure IV–1. Thus, much the same areas are indicated whether the magnitude or the continuity of Aprista popular support is measured.

The same was not true of Belaúnde's support, which offers indications of the nature of the support the Apristas received or failed to get in the 1962 and 1963 elections. In every one of the category I departments, Belaúnde's strength against Prado in 1956 was reduced in 1962, when he opposed Haya. In the core of the "Solid North" (Cajamarca, La Libertad, and Lambayeque) the drop was between 4 and 9 percent of the departmental votes. In the other two departments showing this characteristic (Pasco and Ica), Belaúnde's losses were much greater than Haya's gains, and the surplus went to Odría or the minor candidates. With these two geographically isolated exceptions, the salient feature of this category is nevertheless Aprista dominance.

In the departments in which Haya fell slightly below Prado's share of the 1956 vote (category II), divergent movements occurred in Belaúnde's votes. Where APRA was dominant, at least through 1962 (II–A: San Martín, Amazonas, Ancash, and Apurímac), Belaúnde gained between 1956 and 1962. Where APRA was weaker (II–B: Cuzco, Piura, and Tacna), Belaúnde lost ground in 1962 but regained it in a smaller field of candidates in 1963. This subcategory exhibits a stable, but low and inelastic Aprista strength through three elections.

In the remaining nine departments of some significance (category III) Haya's votes of 1962 and 1963 fell markedly (ten percentage points or more) below those of Prado in 1956. They can be subdivided according to the behavior of Belaúnde's support:

III–A. Belaúnde did not pick up in 1962 the 1956 Prado votes which Haya lost.
1. Belaúnde failed to maintain his own 1956 share of the vote.
2. Belaúnde maintained his 1956 share of the vote.

III–B. Belaúnde gained substantially in 1962 from the Prado votes which Haya lost.

Belaúnde's record in 1962 for the first subgroup (III–A–1: Departments of Lima and Arequipa) is evidently the direct result of strong competition, particularly by Odría and, in Arequipa, by Cornejo Chávez (Christian Democrat). In 1963 Belaúnde more than regained his 1956 share of the total vote in both places, not only through shifts of support by

Cornejo and others, but to an even greater extent by monopolizing increases in the electorate.

In three other departments (III–A–2: Callao, Junín, and Loreto), Belaúnde suffered no losses between 1956 and 1962. Both he and, to a lesser extent, Haya increased their shares of the total in 1963 through the withdrawal of minor candidates. In the other four (mainly highland and rural) departments (III–B: Huánuco, Ayacucho, Huancavelica, and Puno), Belaúnde gained tremendously with the shift of APRA support from Prado in 1956 to Haya in 1962, although both Haya and Belaúnde generally improved their positions in 1963.

The significance of category III for APRA is dual. First, the drop in Haya's votes compared to Prado's votes in 1956 showed that this many votes had never been Aprista. Second, the Aprista vote could not compare with that of Belaúnde in strategic centers such as Lima, Callao, and Arequipa. In 1963 APRA improved somewhat (despite the support of AP by other parties) in the sierra of central and south-central Peru and in the jungle departments, but not in the far-southern sierra.

INDEX

AD (Acción Democrática), 166–77; and the Church, 169, 177, 187; doctrine, 167–69, 180–81; factions in, 60, 170–73; mass reform character of, 11–15, 177–85, 186–92 *passim*; middle-class support of, 172–73; organization of, 169–73, 182; relations with Communists, 167, 169–70, 172, 175, 177; strategies, 173–77, 183–85, 187–88; worker and *campesino* support of, 170–71, 183. *See also* Betancourt
Agrarian Reform Act of 1964 (Peru), 120–21, 138, 149–56. *See also* Peru
Alegría, Ciro, 18
Alexander, Robert J., on party types, 12–13
ANSCE (Asociación Nacional de Servidores Civiles del Estado), Peru, 91
AP (Acción Popular), 50–51; agrarian reform bill, 120, 140, 149–52 *passim*, 155; coalition with DC, 67–68, 69–71, 87–88, 127, 134–36, 139–40; geographic strength of, 77–81; reform character of, 45, 62; middle-class support of, 87–88, 90. *See also* Belaúnde, Fernando; *Cooperación Popular*
APRA: and executive power, 22–23, 53–73, 74–75, 114, 155, 178–79, 192–94; *Casas del Pueblo*, 106, 110–11; coalitions in Congress, 54, 68, 111, 126–30, 134–36, 139–40; conventional and unconventional programs of, 111–13, 155, 192; election coalitions, 64, 72, 87–88; foreign inspiration for, 4, 15, 16–18, 21, 180; ideology, 15–16, 18–19, 104, 106–7, 179–81 *passim*; image of violence, 107–9; internal cohesion of, 22–23, 106–7, 189; international activities of, 11–12, 15–16, 160, 167; leadership and control, 16–18, 61, 67, 105–6; legislative power, 114, 126–37, 193; mass reform character of, 12–13, 177–85, 186–92; membership, 109; middle-class support of, 88–94, 190; organization of, 21–23, 55–56, 74–102, 183; origins of, 15–18, 44–45; and popular universities, 17, 110, 113; programs, 16, 19–21, 114–37, 138–56; relations with Indians, 20, 94–102, 190; societal relationships, 53–54, 71–73, 155–56, 186; sources of support, 75–82, 183, 188–90; tactics, 125–26, 155, 189, 191–92; trade unions, 20, 61, 66, 82–85, 90–93, 96. *See also* CTP; FENCAP; Haya de la Torre; *La Tribuna*
APRA Rebelde. *See* MIR
Arciniegas, Germán, 18
Ayopaya, Manifesto of, 159

Bank Clerks, National Union of, 90, 134
Barriadas, 42–43, 52, 86–88
Barrientos, René, 163
Barrios, Gonzalo, 173
Basadre, Jorge, 18
Bedoya Reyes, Luís, 69
Belaúnde, Rafael, 51
Belaúnde, Víctor Andrés, 51, 85
Belaúnde Terry, Fernando, 45, 50–51, 58; on agrarian reform, 138–39, 141–42,

145 n.16, 149; as candidate in 1956, 59 n.7, 60, 75–76, 86; as candidate in 1962–63, 62–65, 67–68, 76–81, 146, 193–96; as president, 68–70, 114, 118, 134–35
Beltrán, Pedro, 135, 147
Beltrán Prieto, Luís, 173
Benavides, Oscar (Peruvian president, 1933–39), 45, 58, 119, 133, 193
Betancourt, Rómulo, 11, 167–70, 173–77, 181–84, 187–88. *See also* AD; Venezuela
Blanco, Andrés Eloy, 172
Blanksten, George I., on party types, 12–13
Bolivia: economy of, 158–59, 161–62, 164, 181; Indians in, 31–32, 158, 160; influence of military in, 158, 165–66, 183; revolution of 1952 in, 13–14, 181, 187–88; social conditions in, 13, 157–66; suffrage in, 159, 181. *See also* MNR
Brazil: *Estado Novo*, 104; social conditions in, 13. *See also* Vargas, Getulio
Busch, Germán (Bolivian president, 1937–39), 158
Bustamante y Rivero, José Luís (Peruvian president, 1945–48), 58–59, 75–76, 116, 120, 123, 133, 193–94

CAEM (Centro de Altos Estudios Militares), Peru, 49
Caldera, Rafael (Venezuelan president, 1969–), 173, 176. *See also* COPEI
Callao, revolt of 1948 in, 49, 107, 194
Calles, Plutarco Elías (Mexican president, 1924–28), 182
Cárdenas, Lázaro (Mexican president, 1934–40), 182
Castro, Cipriano (Venezuelan president, 1899–1908), 173
Castroism. *See* Communism
Catavi massacre (Bolivia), 161
CCP (Confederación de Campesinos del Perú), 100
Chaco, War of, 158, 161, 165
Chamber of Deputies (Venezuela), 172
Change, cultural, 3, 33, 52, 93, 186–92; among cholos, 33–34; criollism, 49, 52; among Indians, 29–30; initiation of, 7, 24–25; among mestizos, 28; relation of to structural change, 25, 52, 94. *See also* Development
Chávez Ortiz, Nuflo (Bolivian vice-president, 1956–57), 163
Chile, social conditions of, 13
Chirinos Soto, Enrique, 76 n
Christian Democratic Party. *See* DC
Civilistas (Peru), 44
Class structure: middle-class, 34–36, 39–43, 85; "oligarchy" in Peru, 37, 68, 116; in Peru, 27, 33–45; Peruvian compared to European, 36; political appeals to, 50
Coalitions, as bases for parties of representation, 10. *See also parties by name*
COB (Central Obrero Boliviana), 161, 163
COMIBOL (Mining Corporation of Bolivia), 163
Communism: as mass movement in Russia, 10–11; in Peru, 60, 88–89, 100–101, 133–34, 141–43
Convivencia. See APRA; Prado
Cooperación Popular (Peru), 54, 112, 125, 134
COPEI (Christian Socialist party, Venezuela), 169–70, 173–74, 176–77. *See also* Caldera
Cornejo Chávez, Héctor, 69, 87, 145 n.16, 195. *See also* DC
CRAV (Comisión para la Reforma Agraria y Vivienda), 121–23, 139, 147–49
CSEPP (Confederación Sindical de Empleados Particulares del Perú), 90
CTP (Confederación de Trabajadores del Perú), 82–84, 90–91, 96, 99, 118–19, 141, 153
CTV (Confederación de Trabajadores de Venezuela), 170–71
Cussianovitch, Miguel, 134

DC (Christian Democratic party), Peru, 50–51, 68, 77, 87–88, 90, 100, 127, 135, 195
Declaration of Lima, 12–13
de la Piedra, Julio, 146
de Lavalle, Hernando, 58, 75–76
Democratic party (Peru), 44
Dependence, 7; of Indians, 28, 34, 52, 95; of middle class, 41
de Piérola, Nicolas (Peruvian president, 1895–99), 17, 44
Development, 1–5, 24–25, 29 n, 33–34, 51–52, 111–13; obstacles to change, 5–7. *See also* Change
Doctrine. *See* Ideology; Programs

Eguiguren, Luís Antonio, 58, 193
El Comercio (Lima), 148–49. *See also* Miró Quesada

FAO (United Nations Food and Agriculture Organization), report on agrarian reform, 148
FCV (Federación Campesina de Venezuela), 170 n.36

FENCAP (Federación Nacional de Campesinos del Perú), 95–99, 141, 153
FENEP (Federación Nacional de Educadores del Perú), 91
Figueres, José, 12
FLN (Frente de Liberación Nacional), Peru, 68, 143
FVM (Federación Venezolana de Maestros), 173

Gallegos, Rómulo (Venezuelan president, 1948), 172, 174, 176
Gómez, Juan Vincente (Venezuelan president, 1908–35), 167, 173
González Prada, Manuel, 17–18, 46, 51
Grupo ARS (Venezuela), 172
Guevara Arze, Wálter, 159–60, 163

Haya de la Torre, Víctor Raúl, 16–18, 21, 85; and founding of APRA, 11, 15, 85; on parliamentary supremacy, 126, 133; on party ideology, 18–19, 159; on party program, 59, 125, 164; *personalismo* of, 103–6; as presidential candidate, 58, 61–62, 67–68, 70, 75–82, 129, 194–96; as teacher, 106, 110; on violence, 108. *See also* APRA
Housing Corporation (Peru), 123

Ideologies of change, 8–9, 11, 179–81
Institute of Agrarian Reform and Promotion (Peru), 153
Interests, system of, 6, 37, 39–41, 45, 51–52, 94
International Petroleum Corporation, 70
IRAC (Agrarian Reform and Colonization Institute), Peru, 121–22

Junta Patriótica (Venezuela), 177

Kantor, Harry, 71, 115

La Prensa (Lima), 135, 147–48
La Tribuna (Lima), 109–10, 141
Lavalle. *See* de Lavalle
Lechín, Juan, 160–61, 163
Leguía, Augusto (Peruvian president, 1919–30), 44, 85, 167
Leoni, Raúl (Venezuelan president, 1964–69), 170, 173–74, 184
Lindley, Nicolas, 67
López Contreras, Eleazar (Venezuelan president, 1935–41), 167
Luna, Juan P., 118

Mariátegui, José Carlos, 18, 36
Mass parties, 9–10, 45; functions of, 7, 10–11, 93–94; in Latin America, 11–15
Medina, Isaías (Venezuelan president, 1941–45), 167, 174–75
Methods, party. *See* APRA: internal cohesion; leadership and control
Mexico: revolution of 1910 in, 14–15, 160, 167–68, 181, 187–88; social conditions in, 13, 189–90. *See also* PRI
MIR (Movimiento de la Izquierda Revolucionaria): in Peru, 88, 100; in Venezuela, 172
Miró Quesada: family of, 45; Antonio, 45; Francisco, 134. See also *El Comercio*
MNR (Movimiento Nacional Revolucionario), Bolivia, 157–66; doctrine, 158–60, 180–81; factions in, 163–64, 182–84; mass reform character of, 12–15, 178–85, 186–92 *passim*; nazi-fascist influence on, 158; organization of, 160–64, 182; relations with Communists, 159–61, 165; strategies, 165–66, 183–85; worker and *campesino* support of, 160–63, 166, 181. *See also* Paz Estenssoro
Movements, as bases for parties of solidarity, 10

National Agrarian Council (Peru), 18–19, 144, 153
National Agrarian Society (Peru), 45
National Assembly (Bolivia), 161, 166
National Economic Congress (Peru), 19, 144
Nationalism, 4, 52, 128, 181
National Office of Cooperative Development (Peru), 123

Odría, Manuel A. (Peruvian president, 1948–56): as candidate, 58, 61, 67–69, 75–81, 146, 193–95; as president, 9, 87, 118–25, 145. *See also* UNO
Odría, Sra., candidacy of, 51, 69
Organization, of mass reform parties, 11. *See also support groups and relations under party names*
Ovando Candia, Alfredo, 163

Pacific, War of the, 44
Palma, Ricardo, 18
PAP. *See* APRA
Pardo, Manuel (Peruvian president, 1872–76), 44
Parliament, Latin American (Parlamento Latinoamericano), 15 n
Participation, in mass parties, 11; by classes in Peru, 32, 34, 45, 95, 123

Partido del Pueblo. *See* APRA
Parties: of change, 7–11; of opposition, 114–16, 191; of representation and solidarity, 10, 22
Paz Estenssoro, Víctor (Bolivian president, 1952–56 and 1960–64), 104, 159–60, 162–63, 164–66, 183–84. *See also* Bolivia; MNR
PDN (Partido Democrático Nacional), Venezuela, 169
Peñaranda, Enrique (Bolivian president, 1940–43), 164
Pérez Godoy, Ricardo, 48, 67
Pérez Jiménez, Marcos, 168, 172, 174–77, 184, 187
Perón, Juan, 9, 12, 104
Peru: agrarian reform in, 120–22, 138–55; agriculture in, 27–28, 35–38, 95–102; armed forces of, 47–50, 61, 125, 184 (*see also* Velasco); the Church in, 44–45, 46–47, 50, 65, 188; congressional powers in, 54, 68, 114, 130–37, 138–39; constitution of, 117, 120, 130–32, 144, 155; cooperatives in, 123, 154; economy of, 27, 36–39, 124, 128, 135–38; education in, 124; elections in, 74–82, 86–88, 136–37, 139, 145–46, 194–96; history of 44–45, 47–71; housing, 123 (see also *barriadas*); and immigrants, 38–39; Indians of, 27–32, 52, 94–95; junta of 1962–63 in, 48, 118, 122, 142; labor legislation in, 117–19; land tenure in, 28–29, 33–35, 119–23; local elections in, 69, 123, 128, 136; local government in, 54, 69, 124–25; middle classes of, 33–36, 39–43; migration within, 27, 30, 33, 41, 43, 81; military coups in, 47–50, 54, 58, 63–64, 66, 70, 136–37, 142, 156, 194; physical features of, 25–26; political parties of, 50–51, 68–69; population of, 26–27; presidential powers in, 53–57, 130–37; public administration in, 124; Senate boycotts in, 136, 144 n.13; social development and change in, 24–25, 28–34, 36–38, 40–43, 48–50, 52; trade unions in, 74, 82–85, 117–19, 129, 141 (*see also* CTP, FENCAP); upper classes of, 36–39, 44–45; violence in, 32, 62, 100–102, 122, 133–35, 140–42, 155. *See also* APRA
Pestama Zevallos, Carlos, 134
Piérola. *See* de Piérola
PIR (Partido de la Izquierda Revolucionaria), Bolivia, 159, 161, 165
PLN (Partido de Liberación Nacional), Costa Rica, 12–13
Pope John XXIII, death of, 68
Popular Parties, League of, 12
POR (Partido Obrero Revolucionario), Bolivia, 159, 161–62, 165
Prado Ugarteche, Manuel (Peruvian president, 1939–45 and 1956–62), 45, 58–65, 72, 74–92 *passim*, 145, 147, 193–96
PRD (Partido Revolucionario Dominicano), Dominican Republic, 12–13
PRI (Partido Revolucionario Institucional), Mexico, 12–15, 157, 177–85 *passim*, 187–88, 190
Prialé, Ramiro, 105–6, 122, 146
Programs, of mass reform parties, 11

Quesada, José, 58
Quijada, Ramón, 171–72

Reform parties, 4–5, 191; Afro-Asian, 10; European and North American, 4, 9, 15, 115; Latin American, 5, 11–15, 104, 157, 179–80; Peruvian, 43–51. *See also* Parties, of change

Saco, Alfredo, 144
Sánchez, Luís Alberto, 146
Sánchez Cerro, Luís (Peruvian president, 1930–33), 58, 193
Schwalb López Aldaña, Fernando, 134
Seoane, Edgardo (Peruvian vice-president, 1963–68), 69–70, 136, 139
Seoane, Manuel: as candidate, 61, 67; on organization, 21; on party program, 59, 124–25, 145; position of in party, 105; on tactics, 127
Siles Suazo, Hernán (Bolivian president, 1956–60), 163
SINPES (Sindicato Peruano de Educadores Secundarios), 91
Social Progressive Movement (Peru), 68
Socialist party (Peru), 68
Strategies, party. *See* APRA: power; societal relationships
Sugar Workers Federation (Peru), 96, 153

"Thesis of Pulacayo," 160
Toro, David (Bolivian president, 1936–37), 158
Townsend Ezcurra, Andrés, 15 n, 105–6, 142, 146
Trelles, Oscar, 134, 141
Trujillo: Aprista revolt of 1932 in, 65, 107; and origins of APRA, 17; student politics of, 88

Union of Trolley Operators (Lima), 90

University Front (Venezuela), 176
UNO (Unión Nacional Odriísta), 50, 77, 90; agrarian reform bill, 140, 143, 149, 153; coalition with APRA, 50–51, 64, 68–70, 87–88, 127–37 *passim*, 139–40. *See also* Odría
URD (Unión Republicana Democrática), Venezuela, 175–77
Ureta, Eloy G., 58, 75–76

Valcárcel, Luís, 18
Vargas, Getulio, 9, 12, 104
Vargas Prada, Pedro, 65
Vasconcelos, José, 18
Velasco Alvarado, Juan (Peruvian president, 1968–), 58, 70, 120, 152, 154, 194
Venezuela, 169, 174, 176–77; economy of, 167–69, 181; elections in, 168, 173–77; influence of military in, 167, 173–75, 183–84, 187; social conditions in, 13–15, 187. *See also* AD
Venezuelan Civilian Front, 177
Villalba, Jóvito, 175–76
Villanueva, Armando, 105
Villarroel, Gualberto (Bolivian president, 1943–46), 158–59, 160–61, 164–65

THE JOHNS HOPKINS PRESS

Composed in Linotype Times Roman with Neuland and Neuland Inline display
by Baltimore Type and Composition Corporation

Printed on 50 lb. Lockhaven
by Universal Lithographers, Inc. and

Bound in Interlaken ARCO Vellum
by Moore and Company, Inc.